THE
FLEXIBLE
FOODIE

For Harriet

A RedDoor Book

Published by Ember 2023

www.emberprojects.co.uk

© 2023 Lynn Davis

The right of Lynn Davis to be identified as author of this Work has been asserted by her in accordance with sections 77 and 78 of the Copyright, Designs and Patents Act 1988

ISBN 978-1-7392844-0-4

A CIP catalogue record for this book is available from the British Library

Cover design: Clare Connie Shepherd

Typesetting: Megan Sheer

Photography by Josh Pulman, Paul Burroughs and Oliver Ford

THE FLEXIBLE FOODIE

DELICIOUS RECIPES FROM THE HEART OF A KENT KITCHEN

LYNN DAVIS

ember

CONTENTS

PART 1: GETTING STARTED

PART 2: THE RECIPES

Give me a lemon, some garlic, olive oil, salt and pepper and I guarantee I could make cardboard taste good.

INTRODUCTION

When I was in the first *Observer* cooking competition in the 1980s, coming a creditable second, I was deeply influenced by the exciting flavours I'd discovered on trips abroad and in all the ethnic restaurants I visited. So, my take on duck was to bone it, French-style, and then crisp it up on the outside, Peking duck-style, with soy sauce and spices. I stuffed the inside with concentric rings of coloured pâtés and stuffings studded with pistachios, so that when you sliced the whole duck it fell into immaculate, intricate slices. I also cooked prawns with ginger and coconut, unheard of in the UK at that time. As usual, my ideas were always a bit too early – a good few years, usually.

I've looked all over the Internet, searching for what was to become known as 'fusion' recipes that existed before mine, and can't find any. But, of course, any immigrant culture will draw partly from tradition and partly from the availability of new ingredients, so fusion cooking is anything but new. As a food term, 'fusion' only came into general use in the 1990s, as the 'Pacific Rim' appeal arrived.

I'm an everyday cook – I work, I love entertaining friends and family and I love cooking. However, being curious, I like to copy those treats we have in restaurants, and after years of putting together my own version of these recipes, I've collected them in this book. It is essentially aimed at the younger generation, like my daughter Harriet, so don't think I'm being patronising or condescending if it all looks a bit simplistic as I want to make the recipes quick and easy for you.

Although dying to emulate restaurant food, try as I may, I just can't help myself. Whether following a recipe I've found, copying a restaurant staple in my style or making up my own, I have a basic inability to stay the same. Uniformity, following the herd and repetitiveness are not my forte, and so I take my hat off to the gallant chefs who produce the same meals day in, day out.

In fact, by restaurant standards I'm a complete imbecile – I can't stand up for long (at least not until recently when I had a remarkable operation on my foot), my knifework is slow, I need oodles of space, I create a messy kitchen and I tend not to clean as I go. Added to that, I own a disadvantaged body type, red-faced and sweaty, which overheats at the touch of any warmth. Recently improved cooking times have helped my poor, booze-laden friends when waiting to be served, but at the beginning of my foodie career, some friends tended to pass out before the starter, such was the length of time waiting. Coupled with all these problems, I'm concerned that the dreaded washing-up is minimised and made as easy as possible, so I employ techniques that may border on the chaotically lazy for some. Wash tomatoes in the paper bag, for instance.

These recipes are only a snapshot of a moment in my culinary history, but you may use them in whatever way you wish. I would commend you to the 'keep tasting' philosophy that has guided me. Cook, add a little, then taste. Keep going. Buy ingredients you don't know. Try them out. What's there to lose?

WE'LL START AT THE BEGINNING AND ASK – WHAT'S COOKING?

To the more prosaically minded, it is the art of controlled burning – burn too much and it's charcoal; just right and it's a golden brown; sometimes it's nicely gooey and sticky and caramelised; sometimes just set, like a fried egg; sometimes warm and soft. At the very least, cooking may just make the raw food more digestible. At best, it should make the food taste great.

You will want to cook foods long enough that they are not just edible but enhanced in flavour, but not so long that they become tough or start to disintegrate. Generally, a good rule is that the cheaper the ingredient, particularly meat, the more cooking is needed to make it taste good.

Steak (fillet, rump, sirloin, etc) needs a minimum of cooking while stewing or braising steak has to be cooked much longer, slowly perhaps with liquid and vegetables. Younger meat and vegetables are more tender than older ingredients, and so need less cooking: veal needs less cooking than beef, lamb less than mutton (not that we see much of mutton these days), and so on.

Like every other self-taught cook, I believe that apart from freshness, there are qualities in food that we learn and techniques that we read about, inherit or simply feel. The science of cooking becomes an art, and it is this dabbling and imprecision that can result in some of the finest improvised dishes.

In the same way as Stephen Bull, chef-owner of many good restaurants, I learned all my basic skills from that great book of French cooking *Mastering the Art of French Cooking* by Beck, Bertholle and Child, a trio of American cooks who put together the very best, but an exceedingly complicated introduction to French food. It may be out of print now but can be bought from specialist shops such as Books for Cooks.

Another way I've learned is to try to re-create what I've eaten in a restaurant. Again, once you have a few techniques up your sleeve, you can put together your own version of a dish with good effect. It's never quite the same, and I wander off course, substituting this and that, improving it in my way, until it evolves into something quite different, eventually becoming one of my staples.

To tell you the truth, try as I may, I cannot follow a recipe. I get to a certain point and think I can do better, or find that I've run out of some ingredient, or speed is of the essence, or whatever, so I maintain the general gist and then improvise.

SHOPPING

What I would love you to do, and urge you to do, is to keep tasting your food while cooking it, so you know how to alter its taste for the best. But, before you even think about tasting, you ought to start with the shopping. Have an idea of what you might want to cook but try not to be too hidebound. It's always better to see what's available, where you happen to be, what's freshest, which speciality shops you find: see if you stumble on a market in your travels and then buy the ingredients. We don't usually have the luxury of buying daily, in the same way as our idealised images of, say, the French and Italians, but we can manage it in a more haphazard way.

The other great theory of shopping is to spend your way out of trouble. If in any doubt, just buy great ingredients that go together by being laid on the table, or, at the most, assembled together. It may not even be the most expensive way of thinking about food. A few luxuries, or at least more unusual ingredients added to the basics will sometimes make a meal. Think about bowls of soft, wrinkled black olives, layers of fine prosciutto, fresh warm bread, rocket...

BEFORE YOU START

Read through the recipe, buy the ingredients and make sure the basics, such as the oven being hot, are done in advance. Plan ahead. Assemble all the equipment before you launch yourself into cooking; not that I am a very good example.

In trying to be more efficient, it's best to prepare things as you go along. You don't want to waste time preparing everything at the beginning, only to have to wait for each ingredient to cook. However, if you are anxious, then by all means chop everything up at the start. As long as you're not sautéing anything or doing something too delicate, then you can keep an eye on the cooking food, stirring occasionally, while you chop up the next ingredient.

Cooking is easy, but you must concentrate, and you must not be distracted and wander off; don't leave it completely, because that's when it will burn. Some things need constant stirring, some just need a watchful eye and a little tinkering. Some food needs long, slow, gentle cooking, which you can happily leave, but if in doubt, just keep checking and tasting.

THE RECIPES

All the recipes are my approximation of quantities. I rarely measure anything and feel my way through, using my taste and experience to tell me when it's right and when wrong. Don't feel put off if you haven't got all the ingredients, just try to adapt the recipes.

I remember talking to Paul Levy of the *Observer* about this, suggesting that unlike the competition that I was entering – The Observer Cook of the Year – where we concocted what we liked, it would be more of a test of competence if the entrants were given a limited number of ingredients and then asked to produce their best dishes. Some years later, the BBC started *Ready Steady Cook* and more recently, *Masterchef*.

There are so many variables – you and your kitchen, the ingredients, how fresh things are, the size of your utensils, such as measuring spoons, your type of oven or hob, your equipment, such as pans – that it is better to cook to your taste and forget (almost) what I am saying. The only time when this advice does not apply is when baking puddings. Then, you need to be precise and weigh everything. However, I must own up to the fact that I have only recently bought some weighing scales, but I can measure by volume well enough. You may believe that precision might lead to uniform puddings, but you can cook each of the individual parts of a pudding by the book and put them together in your own style. An apple sorbet with Calvados, in a panna cotta mould, topped with damson jelly on a bitter chocolate brandy snap base, for instance. Each comes separately as part of your repertoire, but you can choose the individual tastes and textures and how they interact together.

ENJOY COOKING

Cooking, above all, should be a pleasurable experience: after all, your intent is to make your guests, your friends and your family, happy. Try and cook simple recipes, if you want to avoid stress, something you have tried before, if you're entertaining, because your friends want to see you, happy and unfrazzled. Remember they are just pleased to be with you, joining together in the communal performance of good food and wine.

I often wonder, if money were no object, whether eating out at Michelin-starred restaurants would become commonplace and dull. Presumably it would begin to pall, not really because the food is any worse for the repetition, but because great food is very much of its place. The pomp of a truly fine restaurant would in the end begin to overawe the taste of the eating. Even the Queen, it is said, likes to have a simple meal on her lap watching the TV. Perhaps it is in us, as human beings, to crave for the absent and opposite.

Or, put another way, part of being human is to seek out the extra-ordinary. For instance, when we have a continuously super-rich diet, we yearn for a simple citrus fruit or some vegetables. I, like many others, will crave a curry after a period of enforced abstinence, say after a holiday in France, when I will salivate at the thought of an Indian. A curry would have to feature highly as my luxury item on *Desert Island Discs*, but then, it may be cheating, in that perhaps now it's not really a luxury but has become a necessity.

Hunger is also a strong driving force. My memories of some of the best food I've ever had is so honed on my taste buds that I can feel my mouth watering now at the thought of them. I can still conjure up one spectacular but simple meal, when I was driving back from Greece, as a student, with very few funds to eke out. It was either petrol to get home or food. We hadn't really eaten for the whole length of Yugoslavia, and we arrived, surprisingly alive and exhausted, in Austria. Try driving for two days with every other vehicle seemingly hell-bent on your destruction to give you an appetite.

In celebration and in sheer relief, we splashed out on some fresh Liptauer cheese and warm, white, soft bread, sat on top of a lovely grass meadow high up in the Alps, next to my twin-carb Morris 1000 Convertible, and breathed in the luxury of peace and stillness. Being really hungry must have contributed to the memory, as did surviving the statutory game of chicken on Yugoslav roads, but the taste of the food, its simplicity and freshness and the common experience of sharing it with friends transformed the meal into a lasting memory.

COMPLETE LIST OF RECIPES

THE BASICS

STARTERS AND SIDES

SALADS AND DRESSINGS

VEGETABLES AND SAUCES

QUICK AND EASY MIDWEEK DISHES

WEEKEND AND SPECIAL MEALS

PUDDINGS AND SWEET TREATS

PART 1

GETTING
STARTED

THE FIVE SENSES

LOOK

Recently much more has been made of the presentation of food. Even for amateurs, the emphasis in both restaurant reviews and TV programmes has shifted to making a feast for the eyes, as well as taste and smell. We judge more than we think from the way a dish is presented, as scientists have proved. This is how our brains can be fooled into thinking one way, when the truth is different. White wine coloured with undetectable red dye, for instance, will make tasters absolutely sure that they are tasting red wine.

Ferran Adrià, ex-El Bulli chef, and his supporters and followers like Heston Blumenthal, have had a far-reaching influence on the culinary scene. In their restaurants the elements of a dish may be constructed to appear to be very different from our anticipation, such as soil look-a-like is actually crumbled black pudding. While we, as amateurs, may not want to fool our guests into thinking something is not what it appears to be, we still want our dishes to appear attractive, so we can appropriate parts of modern gastronomy.

Basically, on a fundamental level, we can say that clarity is needed and with that a certain separation of the elements. A brown splodge is no longer acceptable. At the very least, it should be topped with another ingredient with an opposite colour, such as parsley with grated Parmesan cheese over minestrone (page 153), or any plain green herbs over just about anything. There is a tendency today to keep the ingredients separate and bold, so that contrasting colours are emphasised. The popularity of various colours of tomato and beetroot are a case in point. For the home cook, this might just be a step too far, in that time is too tight to separately buy and cook small orange, yellow and red tomatoes, say.

Clarity, in the look of the plate, is a sought-after quality. Foams and sauces may be dribbled over part of the dish at the end, and are often now left to the discretion of the guest, in the form of a jugful of sauce. Flavoured oils, which have the advantage of adding colour to the plate, are also dribbled on to further good looks. Herbs such as dill, basil, tarragon and so on, infused in oil, come out as distinctive, bright greens on a plate.

A chef may use a piping bag to spool out an ingredient into a pretty mound. I would venture a guess that this is past most amateurs, who will carefully spoon out an ingredient, unless absolutely necessary to have to pipe it. Certain desserts with whipped cream or meringue might tempt us into piping bags, but otherwise it's just a step too far. To be honest, the most I've used piping bags for is when I'm painting, where I need a controlled fine line on a canvas.

PRESENTATION AND DESIGN OF THE PLATE

Different colours are useful for presentation, such as tomatoes (which I have previously described), but new varieties of vegetables such as potatoes, which may be blue; beetroot, which may come yellow or bright red; and so on, are useful to differentiate parts of the plate. Modern chefs like to garnish dishes with unusual herbs and leaves, including using micro herbs, which you can often buy in supermarkets. They are basically small versions of just about any plant, such as rocket, basil, sorrel and spinach as well as more increasingly exotic leaves like red chard, amaranth and purslane. Some you can buy, most you can grow yourself, and their charm lies in their discreet flavour and interesting, small shape. However, we can easily use ordinary herbs, chopped up finely, or little fronds of dill, small pieces of rocket and the now ubiquitous pea shoots.

The overall design of a plate can also take on numerous guises. Traditionally, food would be served up as separate piles, bound together with a gravy or sauce. Now, the ingredients may be ranked, in serried rows, in a strictly rectilinear form, showing symmetry, with vegetables such as asparagus tied together with spring onion greens. Or, perhaps, they will take the 'strewn' look, more associated with Jackson Pollock, with a gay, abandoned flourish of contrasting spilled sauces, in curling lines and splatters.

Another modern theme comes in a row – the main ingredients are spread out in a line across the plate, piled up with ascending ambition, often finished off with the most expensive or showy ingredient, such as shaved truffle, exquisitely thin, pale cream in the centre with a frilly, burned sienna circumference.

On round dishes the same is true for a circular presentation, where the ingredients are laid out around a circle, with perhaps three or four clumps of each ingredient. Often the sauce is dribbled around the outside of the circle to distinguish itself from the central ingredients and given more emphasis. In the time-honoured way favoured by landscape architects, ingredients (or plants) are separated into odd numbers, so that on a plate you may have one or three or five mounds of the same food. This leads the eye from one to the other, rather than the bluntness created by the unfulfilled symmetry of even numbers.

A modern trend, which is all encompassing and now rather depressing, is the need to spread out, from a dessertspoonful of a stiffish purée, a smear of the item across the plate. This started out from creative top chefs and has dwindled down to reach just about every restaurant in the land. One useful result of the smear, however, is an adjunct: a small dab of an ingredient can be used to anchor an upper ingredient, to stop it sliding around.

Chefs have now taken to using very thin ingredients to emphasise the colour at the edge and to make an interesting shape. Courgettes are a case in point. If cut thinly, unpeeled, either lengthways or horizontally, the pale green interior is sharply focused by the bright green edge. These can be pickled, cooked briefly or even left raw. They can be rolled up into standing 'cigars' to add further drama or draped across the plate. Cucumber has the same sort of look while carrot swathes in ribbons or 'spaghetti' provide interesting shapes and colour.

Further embellishments for the overall look of a dish can now be bought. Flowers are one such item, rather like micro herbs, which can be purchased through the Internet from specialist food retailers. Again, a little restraint is needed, as a little colour goes a long way. Edible flowers, which are easy to grow and/or buy, include nasturtiums, pansies, violas, cornflowers, marigolds, roses, borage, lavender and courgette flowers, among many others.

Powders, either homemade or bought, are also a useful decoration. You can buy some in purpose-made shakers. Mushroom (although brown) has a good taste and will go with most savoury dishes, similarly cocoa shakers over sweet dishes. Fruits, such as strawberries and raspberries, are freeze-dried and chopped, which can then be pulverised into bright powders. Again, the Internet is a good source, but you can make your own by blitzing the dry ingredient in a grinder. Even icing sugar can sometimes improve the look of a dish. You can make cardboard cut-outs to help the design, such as stars, now made popular in coffee shops.

The china you use to set the food on makes a visual impact – a plain, white, glazed plate or bowl can be shaped, so not only the ordinary circular plates, but rectangles and so on, are popular now. Many dishes suit black or dark base colours, so that white or light items show up more. Personally, I prefer plain base colours, because I find decorated plates confusing, unless the presentation is ultra-simple. Cakes will often prove an exception, but this has more to do with our preoccupation with the past, and our feelings about afternoon tea. Again, the gastro-physicists have tested preferences of coloured plates and found that a square, black plate beats a round, white one.

One more plea on the presentational front concerns lighting. In order to see what is on our plate, and indeed read the menu, if there is one, there needs to be enough lighting to be able to see. There seems no point in going to any presentational lengths if the poor customer/eater can't even see it. Critic Jay Rayner, recently reviewing a restaurant, complained that the only way the restaurant in question could survive was by relying on modern technology, whereby all the punters had to use their mobile phones as torches, so they could order and eat. At least at home, I doubt this could happen, but sometimes a cook will sabotage the food for the sake of overall ambience, thinking that strategically placed candles will do the trick. Again, we need to be able to see the food to appreciate it properly, so spare a thought for your long-suffering guest and ensure that at least the table is well lit, even if your attempt at cosy design, in the form of candles, falls short of the mark.

SMALL, LESS-USUAL ITEMS, FOR ENHANCED DECORATION, INCLUDE:

- *Bright-red pomegranate seeds (rather done to death, but still useful)*

- *Thin, mild, red chilli strands (what I call angel hair)*

- *Star anise (strong flavour, pretty left in, although not to eat)*

- *Finger limes or lime caviar, particularly on fish*

- *Real caviar for fish*

- Radishes, thinly sliced to show red outer and white inner skin

- Black garlic, either made into a sauce or thinly sliced – very soft and sweet

- Biscotti or amaretti biscuits, particularly scrunched up and scattered over the top of desserts

- Almost any nut, usually chopped and perhaps caramelised for use in puddings (pistachio is a useful green colour as well to emphasise and offset other ingredients)

- Some mushrooms, such as chanterelles and girolles, which, when thinly sliced, have an interesting shape, like tiny trees, and texture

- Croûtons to give a light colour and crunchy texture

- Cauliflower and broccoli, when thinly sliced, have a similar visual effect to mushrooms

- Grated lime or lemon zest scattered over the finished dish

- Breadcrumbs, best fried for texture, taste and look

- Samphire, washed thoroughly to remove some of the salt, either cooked or raw, with fish and other dishes

- Saffron in rice or potatoes or mayonnaise to add vibrant colour and taste

- Honeycomb crumbled into pieces and scattered over a dessert

- Crispy onions, ready fried and chopped (available in some supermarkets and Asian shops)

- Japanese seaweed cakes or wafers, especially good chopped into squares with fish

- Balsamic vinegar, especially when thickened, and the similar look of pomegranate molasses cast in lines over a plate, can be a useful foil for the rest of the food on top

- Shavings over the top of a dish, such as Parmesan, truffle or bottarga (salted cured fish roe)

SMELL

Although we are often told that our sense of smell is infinitely inferior to our dogs – this is true – we can still differentiate apparently between 1,000 different scents. With our noses not needing to be so reliable today, we have perhaps lost the focus to perceive all of these scents so keenly, but presumably they can be resurrected sufficiently for scientists to prove the point.

The mechanics of our ability to smell start firstly physiologically in air passing into the nose, with the smells intact, which are processed by olfactory receptors in the olfactory bulb. This starts inside the nose and runs along the bottom of the brain. It therefore has direct connections with two brain areas, the amygdala and the hippocampus, which are strongly associated with emotion and memory. Olfaction is sometimes beyond explanation or description, as it's so deeply rooted in our selfhood and personal history, pinpointing events in our past so accurately, in a way that none of our other senses can match.

I often recall a story of when I was writing as a wine critic in London. We were going to a wine tasting at the Café Royal, featuring a whole cellar full of the most exciting wines for auction – real Napoleonic brandy 1819(!), 1920s champagne, 1853 Bordeaux, etc; you get the point – and we were taking the lift, when the grande dame of the wine world, Pamela Vandyke Price, stepped in. She took a deep breath and, in a Lady Bracknell way, exclaimed, 'Perfume! Who is wearing perfume?' My friend Netty stepped forward. 'This is not the done thing at a tasting. It may mask the aromas in the wine.' Castigated and cowed, we went on to enjoy the very best tasting ever.

TASTE

The separation of smell, in the act of eating, from taste, is reputedly ill-advised: if you hold your nose when eating or drinking, you will find that not only do you lose your sense of smell, but your sense of taste will disappear too. The two are more closely entangled than we could imagine.

There is a constant confusion in the eyes of scientists and philosophers concerning how best to define taste and flavour, not least because of what we have discovered about smell and its links to taste. It is often said that '75 per cent of what we perceive to be taste is actually smell'. They have discovered, for example, that when tasting, some of the air in the mouth is pushed up through the nasal passages and we get a secondary waft of smell. It happens without us thinking about it, and we put it down to smelling through taking air directly into our nose, whereas the mechanics are much more complex. In fact, on the tongue there are only certain receptors that distinguish the five tastes – sweet, salt, bitter, sour and umami – and unless you can swish the food around, moving the tongue up to the top of the palate and letting secondary smells come up through the nose, even they are hard to distinguish sometimes.

This book rests on the basic premise that you need to know how your food tastes. This should become an everyday process, to be used in every recipe, so that you can learn the effect of each added ingredient as the food progresses.

Tasting is king!

LISTEN

'Snap, crackle and pop'...the well-loved advertising slogan, from aeons ago, for Rice Krispies, where every child bent down to the bowl of cereal to listen. Little in this way has been repeated. I suppose it's time for another lease of life: in the marketing world of unending repeats, it's time to ask for another food that makes a sound.

Although we do not attribute very much to listening to our food now, even when cooking it, it's there in the background. There's the pop and spit of the roasting meat, as it has come to the end of cooking in the oven, a sure sign that the meat is done and the fat is giving off liquid squirts that hit the top of the oven, which we can hear. Most of the noise of food cooking is nearing the end of its cycle, and the sounds are disturbing, in that by ignoring them, we are close to ruining the dish. Take, for instance, making caramel: the sugar and water is thickening and browning. The little bubbles become great golloping, fearsome plops as the sounds ascend as warnings to us to remove it from the heat quickly and pour it out before it burns.

All items that are boiled make this sort of sound, as the air expands into the bubbles, which eventually break. This sound, although not a warning as such, gives a cook a certain comfort that the liquid is evaporating and the cooking liquor is doing its job, or is being reduced and concentrated. When you turn the heat down, the sounds become a background sizzle and the soothing sounds of a quiet boil disappear into a simmer.

In extremis, this boiling, plopping sound expands in a cloud of steam, with a great hiss. This usually happens when liquid hits a hot pan or hot fat, such as lowering (relatively wet) chips into a pan of hot fat. Again, it is giving the cook a gentle caution.

Different cooking implements give off different sounds; the choice between a wooden spatula (in a pan) sounding relatively soft, and a fish slice (in a wok) sounding intense and metallic, as we scrape off the food from the sides, subtly colours our response to cooking.

Sounds in the cooking stage are relatively benign, even helpful, if acted upon, but it is the eating of the food that is most affected by sound. As we know, most modern restaurants have done away with the softening effects of materials that muffle sound. The carpets, upholstery, wall hangings, banquettes, ceiling undulations, soft chairs and intimate booths have disappeared and given way to more modern, stark and reflective materials which give the interiors a live acoustic, so user-unfriendly. Not only can we not hear what our friends are saying, but the background noise of clutter, scrape and rattle replaces any pleasant food sounds we may have been able to distinguish.

Exacerbating this, is a commonly held belief that we customers want to be further assaulted by loud music, usually pop music, with a constant beat that urges us to eat and drink and swallow, synchronised to this rhythm, in great haste. To the cynical restaurant owner, it has been proven that the hectic atmosphere creates a panic to finish the meal as quickly as possible, thus allowing more sittings and more profit. People apparently drink more too, if loud music is playing, presumably because there is little else to do. This noise also impairs our ability to smell and taste and enjoy the flavour of the food. If all the restaurateur wants is increased profit, then the loud music may do its job, but with some sacrifice. What they might forget, however, is that the customers may never return. In fast-food joints that may not be altogether ruinous, in that there are loads more customers to fill the void, but in good restaurants, it may ruin a meal. And a reputation.

It all comes back to the senses again. At times, we need to be able to concentrate on one thing (if we lump smell and taste together), or two, and enjoy the food, for the sake of the food and the people who have cooked for us. This requires a slow and gentle, unsullied ambience, where conversation is easy and relaxed and where we can taste what we eat and can distinguish one thing from another.

Regardless of following the latest fashion, in design terms, a new restaurant ought to take account of the customers and create an interior sufficiently soundproofed and welcoming to make it attractive in its own right. This is not beyond the craft of designers, but it just needs to be prioritised by the owner. Please put the customer first. Don't follow the herd. Stop hacking off plaster to reveal less than attractive brickwork. And for that matter, don't think that an 'industrial chic' take on design is necessarily state of the art, attractive, useful, interesting or functional. We did it thirty years ago! Unless restaurateurs want to be consigned to the post-apocalyptic, *Blade Runner* kitsch of 2005–2020, then please use designers to promote a different positive creativity in your interiors.

FEEL

So, we come to the fifth of our senses – the sense of touch – so subtle, difficult to focus on and difficult to analyse. While all the other senses are, to a large extent, measurable, touch is infinite, wayward and ethereal. After all the preparation to eat, when we pick up the food, feel it on our cutlery, feel it on our tongue and feel it slip down our throats, we may barely notice. But texture, for this is what we feel, is more than self-defining now, as restaurants realise the power of different textures on the plate.

As important as their contribution to the overall look of a dish is the textural quality of different ingredients. I've mentioned dressing a dish earlier, with added crispness in, say, honeycomb or tuiles or crumbled amaretti. These interesting tastes combine with their texture to contrast with other, softer textures. A good plate of food will use many of these textures, but without seeming to overcrowd, or overload.

What I think you need to avoid is a plate with an unpleasant texture itself – the unglazed quarry tile, the rough piece of wood, the stone-glazed pottery, the ridges of the rustic thrown pot. These can be just off-putting for the guest, but can produce reactions, like scratchy chalk on a board, of intense recoil – not exactly welcoming. We once stopped in the middle of France (as you do, driving from Calais south) at a cheap hotel with an outstanding restaurant. The food, as usual, was splendid but this unfortunate presentational fashion had taken over since the last time we visited, and one course was presented on an unglazed tile. The texture of the food seeped into the absorbent clay, so much so that the blob of food was impossible to get onto the fork as it had almost disappeared. The ensuing scraping and swearing at the unpleasant Sisyphean struggle didn't help.

Your choice of cutlery and glass is also important. Clean, shiny, thin and elegant items will lend sophistication to your food, as your lips and mouth feel the difference. It slows you down; you are forced to pay attention and eat more delicately. Think about the difference between a thick pewter goblet and a clear, ringing glass; a chunky mug, out of the Troika school, and a thin china cup; bendy, plastic picnic cutlery and solid, stainless-steel utensils. Even here, there can be surprise interventions, such as eating off silver and other metals. Once the impression of affluence has worn off, you may become aware of a slight softness in the texture of the cutlery, and with that comes a surprising, unpleasant metallic taste, as if some of the metal has become attached to the food.

Recent studies on the effects of cutlery choices on the perceived enjoyment of food show a marked preference for heavier, quality utensils over canteen-quality cutlery. There is a definite rise in the enjoyment of the meal, and even the rating of its monetary value, when using heavier cutlery. So, we can deduce that somatosensory cues (how the cutlery feels in your hands or mouth) all influence the resulting perception of taste.

When cooking, I doubt that we'll ever really remark on the texture of the food, but it plays an important part, nonetheless. Each of the cooking processes will mark a change in texture: you cannot only see it, but you can feel it through your cooking implements. If you concentrate, you can feel a sauce when it is thickening. You can feel the air in a whisked egg, you know when a food is catching on the bottom, you can tell when to turn a fish, you can feel the crispness and the lack of resistance as the food skids round the pan.

What we have gained in the analysis of the senses is that all the senses play an important role in the enjoyment of food, far more than when we simply say, 'It tastes good'. This understanding, of how our senses interact, makes us aware of how we can be manipulated into thinking we appreciate a food experience, but at the same time, we can, as givers of food to others, try to woo our guests into pleasure and happiness.

TEXTURES YOU CAN ADD

- *Purées and mashed items, such as potato, carrots, broccoli, peas, beans enhanced by added butter, cream, wine, stock and so on*

- *Crunchy textured vegetables, thinly cut, either raw or pickled or cooked, such as radishes, courgettes, onions and carrots*

- *Jelly or gel using any number of base ingredients such as passion fruit, blackberries, rhubarb, basil, mint, stock, shellfish, chillies. These can be used quite small in cubes or small mounds, as they often intensify the flavour, and their texture is very different.*

- *Sweet things can be used on savoury plates*

- *Individual leaves of herbs or flowers*

- *Sauces and creams and mayonnaise and butters*

- *Chutneys, pickles and condiments*

- *Individual berries or slices of fruit*

- *Crusty bread, toast or croûtons: friable biscuits, rice crackers*

- *Foams*

- *Mousses*

EQUIPMENT

A SHARP KNIFE

I use my 20 cm long, carbon-steel knife for almost everything from cutting bread to chopping herbs, so it never needs any special attention, except for sharpening, which I sharpen with a steel. I do this by holding the knife still and moving the steel up in one direction, alternating on each side of the knife. This is possibly the safest way, since the only movement in the knife is to turn it at a small angle away from the steel, on the back and then on the front. The only problem with my method is that no one else does it this way. It seems to work for me though. A carbon-steel knife, rather than a stainless-steel one, will get a better edge, but it does leave a slight metallic taste on some foods, such as citrus fruit and cheese, so you do need a smaller, stainless-steel knife for these things. Carbon steel also gets rusty if it's left with water on it, so you can't put it in the dishwasher; it needs to be washed and dried separately. If you then leave it for a long time before reusing, rub in a little oil on some kitchen paper. A good test of a sharp knife is to slice a tomato; they have relatively tough skins for something so soft and only a really sharp knife will cut one easily.

GOOD PAN(S) IN A VARIETY OF SIZES

Buy pans as heavy as you can afford. This means that the pan will conduct heat better, things will not burn as easily and, most importantly of all, they will be incredibly **EASY TO CLEAN**. I find heavy stainless steel, with or without a copper base to conduct the heat well, the best. Aluminium may taint some food, particularly if it's acidic like citrus fruit, but the small omelette pans recommended by Delia Smith (a cook from the extreme opposite end of the culinary rainbow to me), work a treat. They are called Lune omelette pans (see suppliers on page 237) and, as Delia says, they are 'utterly reliable British-made heavy-duty pans'. In fact, they are not heavy duty at all, but lightweight aluminium. Keep them for just eggs and they work a dream.

Chefs seem to like the modern, heavy non-stick pans, as they don't need much oil to cook with, and they're easy to wash up since nothing should stick to them. However, don't buy anything that is so sensitive it prevents you from using metal utensils: it means that the surface, such as Teflon, is not robust or thick enough and will wear off with time anyway. If you buy a frying pan, make sure it's big enough and has high sides so that the food does not come flying out in your enthusiasm. This is a sauté pan, from the French, 'to jump' – preferably inside the pan. A large wok is also useful.

OTHER PIECES OF EQUIPMENT

Whisk, sieve/colander, 'Rex' horizontal potato peeler, garlic press, pepper grinder and the modern-day version of the cheese grater – the Microplane – are the minimum. The finest Microplane grater is easy for zesting too. All of these are necessary, plus of course, wooden spatulas, wooden spoons and a metal fish slice. Some sort of casserole dish for long, slow cooking is necessary as well. An assortment of bowls and dishes, from stainless steel to porcelain, is also useful, especially the old-fashioned, light brown bowls with white insides. They're fairly cheap, quite sturdy with ridges on the bottom so they don't skid around and come in a variety of sizes.

OTHER, LESS IMPORTANT PIECES OF EQUIPMENT

- **Food processor:** *Particularly useful for cakes and dough and such like*

- **Juicer:** *If you're into juices, obviously*

- **Bulb baster:** *Like a squidgy syringe and useful for siphoning off fat from the top of a liquid or basting it back on again*

- **Slotted spoon:** *Good for draining off liquid, such as lifting poached eggs from hot water*

- **Meat thermometer:** *For temperatures of the inside of meat and fish to see if it's cooked, if all other means fail (see page 51 for manual methods)*

- **Ice cream maker:** *If you really love ice cream*

- **Blowtorch:** *Especially useful if you like crème brûlée or Italian meringue*

- **Mouli:** *An easy manual blender for soups and mashing things up. Now very cheap*

- **Fish kettle:** *For cooking large, whole fish; you can usually borrow them from a fishmonger, if you really need to, but make sure it fits in your oven*

- **Mandolins:** *Can be a useful as they are super sharp and can cut thinly, so worth getting a good solid one which won't slip; the attachments to a food processor might suffice. You can cut regular slices or julienne matchsticks easily*

- **Julienne peelers:** *These are manual, sharp, cheap and easy to use, producing thin threads of, say, carrot or lemon, from a horizontal blade*

INGREDIENTS

MUST-HAVE INGREDIENTS IN THE STORECUPBOARD

Buy fresh fish and meat when you need them, together with any extra ingredients. The list below may seem long to the uninitiated, but you can always concoct something to eat out of them, if you have the basics. Don't be afraid of trying a recipe if you are missing less important ingredients, because you will learn by improvising.

Olive oil	Plain flour	Soy sauce
Unsalted butter	Cornflour	Pancetta or bacon
Parmesan cheese	Sugar	Fresh fruit and vegetables
Black peppercorns	Milk	Garlic
Salt	Rice	Onions
Lemons	Pasta	Strong Cheddar
Wine vinegar	Potatoes	Bay leaves
Beans and lentils	Eggs	Fresh herbs
Rapeseed oil	Fresh bread	Dried mint and thyme
Herbs and spices	French mustard	Chicken stock cubes
Dried chillies	Canned anchovies	

HELPFUL PROCESSED INGREDIENTS

Even speaking as a fresh food fanatic, there are a few manufactured foods which are invaluable, but would be out of place in a good restaurant, where everything would be fresh and cooked from scratch. The ingredients I have listed below are just for everyday convenience, which means that reasonably good food can be prepared quickly, every single day.

Pasta sauces: Pasta sauces, particularly Loyd Grossman's tomato, tomato and basil, and puttanesca sauces, are about as natural as you can get out of a jar. If the worst comes to the worst, you can always have some pasta and one of these sauces topped with Parmesan. You can also use them as a base for more elaborate sauces.

Pesto: This is also a good standby (try and find your favourite). You can always make your own with crushed garlic, salt, black pepper, chopped, toasted (browned in a frying pan) nuts, preferably pinenuts or walnuts, lots of freshly chopped basil, grated Parmesan and olive oil. Without recourse to the food processor, this makes a very rough and rustic pesto, but to a certain extent this is what makes it stand out from bought varieties. Add some sort of crisp meat like pancetta, bacon or chorizo with pasta and, voila, you have a feast.

Peppadew sweet piquante peppers: These come in jars from South Africa. They are delicious and can be usefully added to all sorts of dishes or used as a mild sort of chilli hotness. The ones marked 'sweet mild spicy' are hot enough.

Curry/Asian sauces: Undoubtedly it is much better to cook from scratch, but if you really are short of time then choose those made abroad. The best are available in jars bought from Asian supermarkets, such as gochujang. You can use them as a base and add what you need. Try not to rely on them too much. It's very easy to make a curry/Asian sauce from scratch. Remember, there are lots of different types on the market, but most UK mainstream ones are packed full of additives, are often quite tasteless (apart from salt and sugar and monosodium glutamate, of course) and unhealthy. Many supermarkets now stock Asian staples in a reasonably pure form, so there's no excuse.

Frozen pastry: Available in the freezer section of supermarkets. There is puff pastry, which is flaky, and shortcrust pastry, which is not. Be careful not to get a savoury pastry, where they have added too much salt, if you want it for a dessert. To make it taste better, I often dob a little butter onto the pastry shells, prior to cooking. The ones you can get in France are superior, but now you can also buy butter-intensive English ones. Do have a go at real pastry though – it's not difficult (page 212).

Filo pastry: This is also great for a many-layered pastry, like apple strudel, Greek tiropita or Indian samosas. In Chinese supermarkets you can find a pastry especially for dumplings and little wrapped things like wonton, which is also very versatile.

Chinese sausages: I used to buy these directly from Chinese restaurants such as Poon's in Soho or Chinese supermarkets, as they are a great standby. They are rather like reddish, sweet and spicy salami and can be kept forever (well, not quite), and when thinly sliced with rice and stir-fried vegetables, they are quick, easy and delicious. It's best to add them to the top of the rice when it is nearly cooked and then they will stay moist.

Frozen peas: A great and useful standby. In fact, dare I say it, they often taste better than fresh, especially when fresh peas have been picked too late and kept on the shelf too long, so they are old, hard and distinctly unsweet. Once they are picked, apparently, the sweetness starts to turn into the floury carbohydrate of old peas, so the moral of the story is – eat peas as soon as you can. Not really on the food front but knowing the kitchen to be the most dangerous room in the house, they are also very useful for amateurish first aid, such as sprained ankles and burns, because they will mould themselves to the body and are instantly available.

Convenience, processed food and takeaways: Try to avoid any ready-made meals, anything else out of a jar (unless you check the ingredients), takeaways (unless it's a good restaurant or takeaway) and frozen meals, because they always contain rubbish and are a con. Just look

Chinese sausages

at the ingredients: ten to one there is always some glue and some sort of added binder or bulking-up ingredient as well as palm oil, a heavy, saturated fat, which is one of the worst added fats in terms of health. There is now the additional concern that vast swathes of virgin rainforest are being destroyed to make way for palm oil production. Avoid anything that says 'hydrogenated oil'. There is also often far too much added salt and sugar in convenience foods, again to make them appear to be more attractive than they, in fact, are. Monosodium glutamate (MSG), often appearing in Chinese food, is also called a flavour enhancer and is a cheap way to introduce some sort of taste to an otherwise dull product.

Make a vow once to avoid any processed food, when you do a shop, and see the difference in the price. I'm as guilty as anyone when it comes to distraction, but if I'm careful, I can save lots of money.

Do watch for sugar substitutes as there are an enormous range of sweeteners, such as aspartame, although some might be useful for use in small quantities, such as xylitol, made from birch tree sap and stevia, made from the stevia plant. Many artificial sweeteners (added ingredients instead of table sugar) such as fructose, lactose, sorbitol, mannitol and so on, may have a laxative effect, in some people, so best to check them personally.

'Lite' or 'light' meals or ingredients are sold as slimming aids, because they may contain less sugar, fat or salt. However, these are also a con, because they are often bulked out with water or glues. The manufacturer then receives the same or enhanced money for the product just by adding water. You can do the same yourself and save money, or even better, make the dish correctly, but just eat a little less. For instance, Lite Coconut Milk is coconut milk with 50 per cent more water added. No wonder it is 'light'; it makes 'light' of our pockets.

In *In Defence of Food* by Michael Pollan, he encourages us to avoid anything making food claims that our grandparents wouldn't recognise and advises us to avoid 'food-like substances', which are 'roughly a bunch of chemicals and a thickening agent masquerading as a meal'.

However, the future may hold some more pleasant surprises on the healthy eating front. Nanotechnology heralds the time of, say, mayonnaise, with the interesting taste of olive oil on the outside of a molecule masking the baubles of water on the inside. The body is fooled into thinking that the first taste runs all the way through the mayonnaise, whereas the water is there to bulk it out and make it healthier. We can't quite vouch for it until we taste it, but you never know... Or is this just some hideous reminder of the future of all food?

MEASUREMENT AND CONVERSION TABLES

Unfortunately, perhaps, my measuring is a bit wayward. I do things by feel and taste, which does not lend itself to precision. I would like to encourage you to be like me, in this instance, since it's much less pressured and enjoyable, but I'm trying to tell you what I'm aiming for and so I would like to give you some sort of guidance.

1 slosh = about 1 tbsp; basically a shake of a bottle of something like wine or olive oil, usually casually converted by the overzealous into a few sloshes

1 dab = about ¼ tsp; how much you might get on the end of a knife – this is usually the measure of things like butter or spices

Pea-size/walnut-size, etc – pretty obvious

25 g = 1 oz

100 g = 4 oz (or ¼ lb) – this is more like 110 g in reality, but it's easier to think of figures rounded up or down

200 g = 8 oz (or ½ lb) – this is more like 225 g or a pack of butter

450 g = 1 lb

150 ml = ¼ pint = 1 cup

200 ml = 1 mug

275 ml = ½ pint = 1½ mugs

A large tub of yogurt or cream is usually 284 ml for some strange reason. It must have been a convenient measure pre-decimalisation

Standard size medium cans in the UK are usually in a 400 g can, while its drained contents may only be 235 g

OVEN TEMPERATURES

140°C	120°C fan oven	275°F	mark 1
150°C	130°C fan oven	300°F	mark 2
170°C	150°C fan oven	340°F	mark 3
180°C	160°C fan oven	350°F	mark 4
190°C	170°C fan oven	375°F	mark 5
200°C	180°C fan oven	400°F	mark 6
220°C	200°C fan oven	425°F	mark 7
230°C	210°C fan oven	450°F	mark 8
240°C	220°C fan oven	475°F	mark 9

TECHNIQUES AND BASIC RECIPES

PEELING

Peeling vegetables is a chore, so try to make it as fast and efficient as possible. Use a sharp knife or buy a 'Rex' horizontal swivel-bladed potato peeler (page 237), or one of its copies. This is just the point when you need a glass of some wine and friends to watch and chat, or even help. Round items, such as potatoes, just need the peeler to do the work. A peeler is good for hard vegetables like carrots, parsnips and so on. Sometimes you can buy cleaned vegetables that don't need peeling, such as carrots and potatoes, but you will have to check. New potatoes can often be cleaned, without peeling, with a pan scourer.

CUTTING

If you want to cut any vegetable into slices or smaller dice or cubes, then one rule should help – always cut the round vegetable in half (or quarters or whatever) so that you can put the flat, cut plane onto the chopping board to stop it slipping and save your hands and your temper. Onions are one of the easiest vegetables to cut up painlessly. One way to get foolproof chopped onions is to use the flat surface to your advantage. Peel the onion, top and tail it, slicing off the hard bits at the ends, then cut vertically in half from top to toe. Put the flat plane onto the chopping board, then hold the onion with one hand, with your nails turned in, and your knuckles exposed like a claw and slice the onion, from top to toe, with slices as close together as you can, using your knuckles as a distancing piece and keeping the basic shape together. Reassemble the half-sphere by prodding back into the shape. Turn the whole onion (or the chopping board) round by 90 degrees, keeping its basic shape and cut the same thin slices at right angles, holding on with one hand. The onion will fall into reasonably (if you have kept your slicing even) sized small chunks. This is finely chopped or diced onion. Roughly chopped is the same process, but each slice is about 1 cm apart. Very finely chopped means you must take the finely chopped onion and chop through using vertical strokes, pushing the whole lot together in the middle of the chopping board. Chefs tend to keep the pointed part of the knife on the board and lift the back up and down. I find that it misses too much of the food and find it easier to lift the whole knife up and down. But then, I'm not a chef. Herbs are treated in the same way.

Mirepoix is a mixture of carrots, onions and celery, and perhaps leeks, and if it is to be served as a vegetable, it must be regular and perfect. If you use it for a sauce that's going to be cooked over a period of time, after which the herbs and vegetables will be sieved out, then you don't have to be so careful.

Carrots need to be peeled then cut in half to give a flat surface and then cut into lengthways strips and perhaps chopped, or cut into diagonal chunks. All vegetables can be cut up into lengthways strips like this – it's called julienne in French.

For perfect squares you must turn the long, thin strips, collected together, sideways and cut through at a 90-degree angle.

You can peel ginger by cutting down four sides so that it is roughly square, taking off the nobbles and dimples separately, running the knife down the corners then slicing finely, keeping the basic square together. You can collect any wayward slices and put them back into the neat square pile and cut through them sideways to get matchsticks out of them. All knobbly or round fruit or vegetables can be cut safely like this.

Celeriac is bigger and tougher to get into the julienne phase, as cutting is difficult, so you usually peel and quarter it, then cut through into thin slices, then cut through the slices into matchsticks. Here a mandolin, a food processor, spiraliser or a julienne peeler might be a better choice. Have a go anyway.

BOILING

You can cook just about anything in boiling water. However, it's best for things that have a strong taste, or are robust in texture, such as pasta, vegetables and meat. Anything that's in a sealed container, such as cans or plastic pouches, can be heated up in hot water or a microwave. It's no good for delicate textures which may fall to pieces, such as delicate fish. It may also make things, well... watery.

I would generally bring water to the boil, then put the things in to cook and add salt, if necessary, to taste, because then the cooking process is rapid and immediate, rather than gradual. Other cooks feel that potatoes, for instance, need to be put into cold water which is then heated. I suppose I baulk at gradual heating up because of the years of suffering soggy vegetables, like cabbage, which were cooked this way, and left too long in the warm water.

I rarely add salt because there is always plenty in the accompanying sauce but do what you prefer. It's healthier to do without salt. Remember you can always add salt at the end, but it's much more difficult to take it away. If you are boiling to reduce the water in a cooking liquor, the taste is more concentrated at the end, so it's even more important to add salt at the end to avoid being over-seasoned.

Nicholas Clee in *Don't Sweat the Aubergine* maintains that ground pepper in the cooking process goes acrid in time, the opposite of Carbonara promoted in the *River Café Cookbook*. To be on the safe side, add it at the end, like salt. Some recipes may call for adding whole peppercorns to the food as it's cooking, which don't go acrid but add a frisson of spice when crunched. Test when the food is done by trying it from time to time.

Boiling is very close to poaching, except in poaching, the water is just simmering – tiny bubbles instead of a walloping great rolling boil. You may also have more flavours added to the basic liquid (this is usually water but can be wine or stock) in poaching, where you want to let the food taste of the simmered liquid, for example, peaches simmered in red wine or chicken cooked in stock.

BOILED RICE

This is perhaps an impure example, because my method only starts with boiling then progresses to simmering and ends up steamed. But still. I don't want to preach but please don't cook rice any other way: other methods are more complicated, apt to go wrong, make for more washing-up and are tedious. My method, which is, of course, not mine to appropriate, is foolproof. An Iranian boyfriend of mine taught me. His mother taught him prior to coming to the UK to study, to ensure his survival.

Basmati rice is the best for savoury dishes, except for dishes like risotto and paella. Here you should use rice which breaks down a little, such as Arborio or Carnaroli, so that it becomes sticky and gluey. Basmati rice will cook so that the grains stay separate and ungluey and Thai Jasmine rice is also very good. Don't bother with precooked, or other commercial brands, because they cost more and are not as good. If you buy rice by the small sack, it lasts for ages and is a good money-saver. Tilda is the most common make of basmati available in most shops now in the UK. This is standard white rice. Brown rice is a bit more robust, seems to take ages to cook and you usually need to boil it.

FOR 2 PEOPLE

- a handful of white rice per person, preferably basmati

- ¼ tsp salt if you really must (I never add salt; you can do without quite easily)

Bring a small amount of water, about 5 cm deep, in a small pan with a lid to the boil.

Wash the rice in a sieve, rinsing away any starch that might make the rice sticky; you don't need to take too long. If you value your teeth, then be extra careful with non-commercial brands, washing through and sifting out bits of stone.

Put the rice into the boiling water, then pour out enough water so the rice is just covered, plus by 3–4 mm. Reduce the heat to very low and cover with the lid. Don't stir. It should only take about 12 minutes. **DON'T STIR.**

Go back and test it once or twice. If it has completely dried out but is not yet fully cooked, add a very small quantity of water, 1 tsp at a time. If it's very dry this will hiss and envelop you in a cloud of steam. Put the lid back on, shaking off any condensed moisture on the inside of the lid and continue until it's cooked and each of the grains is separate. If you watch it carefully at this stage, you can tell by looking if it's done – the surface is flat but with little plug holes where steam has come through.

Rice can be cooked slightly ahead of all the rest of the food and you can heat it up again by adding a very small amount of water, covering with the lid and cooking over a low heat until piping hot. It often sticks on the base, but don't worry, a little more water will ease it off. In Iran they let the rice cook and dry out a little, then make a hole in the centre down to the base of the pan, add a large knob of butter and some oil and keep it cooking over a low heat with the lid on, so that the bottom layer crisps up and becomes golden: you get the perfect combination of textures – white and soft together with crisp, yellow and buttery.

BOILED POTATOES

Cook as for all boiled items (page 43). Make sure the potatoes are roughly the same size, cutting up larger ones into four, at least, and medium ones into two. New potatoes only need cleaning by rubbing with a scourer and you can leave on most of the skins, which is where the vitamin C is, unless you need them to be perfectly white and pure. Old potatoes, however, do need peeling. Use the best tool in the world – a 'Rex' (page 237), a horizontal swivel-bladed peeler that you pull towards you.

Boiled potatoes will take about 20 minutes to cook depending on the size of the potato. Boil the water in a large saucepan, at least twice the size that the pile of potatoes looks as if they need. Make sure the potatoes are all under the water. Cover with a lid and simmer, checking them from time to time to test them. If a sharp knife seems to penetrate reasonably easily then cut one in half, take a small slice, eat it and if it's cooked, it's done. If you overcook them they will start to disintegrate and go floury at the edges. Strangely enough, microwaved potatoes taste sweet. You need to cook them on high, just with a little sprinkling of water, for about 7 minutes, then test and complete the cooking according to how many you are doing. A big bowlful may take another 5 minutes. For extra flavour, roll them around in a little olive oil or butter, sprinkle them with coarse grains of salt and add fresh herbs such as parsley before serving.

BOILED PASTA

Boil water in a large saucepan that is sufficient to cover about three times the volume of the pasta. Add the pasta and stir around so that the individual pieces are separated. If it's long and wrapped up, like spaghetti, then you'll need to unravel it by swishing it about with a fork or chopsticks, as it softens in the hot water. If it's difficult to fit in, then let it down into the water a little at a time, where it will soften and bend to allow more in. Again, anyone other than me will add some salt, and I am sure all Italians cook with salted water, but, as I've said before, I try to avoid it if possible. Pasta is made from dried flour and water, so as it cooks the flour takes in the water and expands. It is difficult to predict how much the pasta will swell, so read the instructions on the pack, although manufacturers tend to overcook their pasta, for some reason. It should retain a bit of a bite, cooked al dente in Italy. If it's overcooked, it will go glutinous and slimy. Test it about halfway through the instructions' time then watch it for a few more minutes. Keep testing until you think it's done. Pour into a colander and unless you are serving it immediately, sprinkle on a few drops of olive oil and stir it around, so that the pieces of pasta are kept separate. Try and serve it straight away. The Italians are particularly fussy about which shape pasta goes with which sauce, an art which I've never been able to fathom. Experiment and come up with the ones you like unless you dutifully follow an Italian guide. Try wholemeal pasta for a healthier change.

ROASTING, BAKING AND OVEN COOKING

We're talking whole things here, like roasted meats and so on. Ingredients in pots or casseroles are covered later. Baking and roasting gives food a brown, crisper outside with a soft inside. Larger items such as roast joints of meat may need to be cooked in the oven, because they need a longer and gentler cooking to ensure the middle is done.

BAKED OR JACKET POTATOES

Called as such to distinguish them from roast potatoes. Baked potatoes are possibly the easiest things to cook, but they take an age and need a whole hot oven for an hour or so, so only contemplate it if you've got other things to do in the oven, or you're willing to use all that hot air. New potatoes – no good for baking – are small because they are the first crop and are available in early summer onwards, so use bigger, old potatoes – varieties like Maris Piper and King Edward, which work a treat for baking. These varieties are left to grow bigger and lifted later in the year. They are then traditionally stored through the winter until the new potatoes are ready in the spring. Store these somewhere cool and dark.

Clean the potatoes, if necessary by scrubbing or scouring and taking out the eyes (the sprouting points that show up as black depressions). Discard green ones, which are poisonous, but you can cut out the smaller green bits if they are not too big. Prick all over with a knife and dry them.

You can rub them with olive oil and salt, if you like. Place on a heatproof baking tray, rack or tin and cook in a hot oven at 220°C (200°C fan oven) mark 7 for about 1 hour, depending on size. You can cut them in half to save time cooking. Test by squeezing the sides and if they easily give, then they are done. Cut in half and dob with some butter, black pepper and salt. Add grated cheese if you want, or whatever you have, to make it into a more elaborate or substantial dish.

I have to say that baked potatoes taste reasonably good in the microwave. Although you lose the lovely knobbly texture of the roasted skins, they come out soft, sweet and fleshy. If you bake them in the microwave, it is much quicker. Cook them for 6–7 minutes on high, test, turn them over and cook for a further 3–5 minutes depending on size and number. Remember to prick them first and cover with a plastic lid or dish to avoid exploding potatoes spattering on the inside of the microwave.

If you have a combination microwave (an oven with microwave, grill and conventional oven settings) you can experiment with microwave and convection heating at the same time until you can achieve the perfect baked potato, keeping the sweetness of the microwaved variety with the texture of the earthy skins of the baked type. I've cooked them for about 10 minutes on high in the microwave until soft, then finished them off in a conventional oven for 20 minutes or more on 220°C (200°C fan oven) mark 7 until the skins go wrinkly and crusty.

ROAST POTATOES

The classic British dish is roast potatoes, traditionally popped in around the meat while it is roasting. Since roasts are not always de rigueur these days, and you may like to have the potatoes independent of the meat, then this is the way of doing them. Preheat the oven to 200°C (180°C fan oven) mark 6. Bring a large pan of water to the boil. Peel the potatoes. Old potatoes, such as Maris Piper and King Edward, are usually the best, but there are other less obvious varieties which are sold as 'floury' and good as roast potatoes because they crisp up – unlike potatoes that are 'waxy' which are sold for salads. Cut in half if small and quarters or sixths if big. Add them to the boiling water, reduce the heat, cover with a lid and simmer for 15–20 minutes until they are starting to soften but are not fully cooked. This is called parboiling. Drain and shake them about a little, so that the sides soften and come apart. These bits will become the lovely crisp, golden, crusty edges to the potatoes as they are roasting.

Add some fat to a large roasting tin, enough to at least coat the base of the tin. Fat in the good, old days would be the dripping, collected from the tin from the last roast meat, which, because of the way we live, is no longer collected and revered as it would have been. Lard is the purified fat from meat, which can be bought in shops, but again, mainly because of the health problems associated with the saturated fat in lard, is not often used. Goose fat (which ostensibly is the best fat for potatoes) is as far as I can go, and apparently, contrary to expectations, has a very low saturated fat level, so is relatively healthy. Or duck fat. Try them for yourself and see what you prefer. My usual fat of choice is a light, thin olive oil, because I like the taste, but any cooking oil, as long as it's not old and rancid, will do. Try groundnut, sunflower or safflower, which work well and have higher burning points. Don't use butter as it burns easily.

Heat the oil in the roasting tin, add the potatoes and move them about in the oil until coated, then roast in the oven for 45–60 minutes. Look and turn the potatoes over once they start browning on the bottom, every 15 minutes or so. They start to feel light and rattle around a bit when they go crispy. You may need to add a little more oil. If they don't look as though they are going to get round to browning and you're running out of time, then increase the oven temperature to 220°C (200°C fan oven) mark 7 for the last 15–20 minutes and they should brown up in time for the rest of the meal.

Whatever you do, be careful when reheating or frying roast potatoes. For some reason, other potatoes, such as boiled and mashed potatoes, can be successfully reused, but roast potatoes sometimes have an acrid, bitter taste when recooked. Try a piece first and if in doubt, give them to the dog.

VARIATION ON ROAST POTATOES – LEMON ROAST POTATOES

This is a lovely Italian take on roast potatoes. The result is not the real, crispy roast potatoes we love so much, but a zestier flavour, with a few crispy edges.

SERVES: 4 OR 2 IF YOU ARE VERY HUNGRY

- old potatoes, peeled and cut into quarters or eighths

- juice of 1 lemon for 3–4 potatoes

- a splosh of olive oil

- a few lemons, cut into chunks

- salt and ground black pepper

- freshly chopped parsley to garnish

Preheat the oven to 200°C (180°C fan) mark 6.

Mix the potatoes and lemon juice together in a bowl, then spread them out in a large roasting pan with the olive oil and lemon chunks. Sprinkle with salt and pepper, then roast in the oven for 30–40 minutes, turning them occasionally, until cooked and crispy around the edges. Garnish with parsley and serve.

ROAST MEAT

Meat, such as beef, lamb and pork, will come in ready-to-cook joints, on and off the bone. It takes a shorter time to cook if the bone is still in, because the bone acts as a conductor, or heat store, and cooks the meat from the inside as well.

There is a theory that you should sear the meat first in a tin with some oil over a high heat for as long as it takes to brown on all sides. This can be done in the oven or on the top of the hob, depending on your roasting tin or pans. As soon as it is brown, then reduce the oven to the required temperature and roast away (see chart below). There is also another theory that this doesn't make any difference. If there is plenty of fat in the joint or around the meat, it's difficult to brown the meat apart from the ends anyway, so there's not much point. In this case, I would just put it into a hot oven pan (so that the timing is exact) with a little olive oil to stop it sticking immediately and cook away. Personally, if it's a matter of really dark brown on the outside and pink, pink, pink in the middle, then pre-brown it.

Always let your meat rest at little after cooking and before serving, somewhere just warm, not hot, so that the cooking stops but the juices inside retreat to the centre and don't run out, which may make the meat drier than necessary. Five or 10 minutes resting time is OK for chicken and up to 20 minutes for beef, lamb or pork. A large piece of beef may be OK left for 15–30 minutes. Cover loosely with foil as necessary to keep the heat in.

PORK

It is always recommended to cook pork thoroughly because of potential disease problems. Luckily, because of the quality and taste of pork fat, particularly if marbled through the meat, or cooked with its crackling on, pork doesn't tend to dry out with extended cooking, so you don't need to be too particular. If, for instance, the crackling is not cooked, and is still pliable and pinkish-brown, then you can turn the oven temperature up for the last 20 minutes or so, and you won't ruin the meat. Some perfectionists insist on taking the crackling off, leaving the joint and fat behind in a warm place, while the crackling is moved into a hot oven to finish crisping up.

BEEF AND LAMB

Beef and lamb need a fair amount of moisture inside to prevent them drying out, so they are generally cooked well on the outside but inside are nicely pink, tasty and moist. Some would say bloody. Don't be put off, this is the tastiest bit, and remember that the French generally use shorter cooking times than the British, so if you ask for well done (which I don't recommend) in England, it will be viewed as inedible in France. It's very useful to know how much the meat weighs, but often, you lose the details of the weight of the meat if buying at butchers, or you accidentally throw the wrapping away, or you don't have any scales, so you may have to improvise to know when it's done. If you have a meat thermometer, then follow the instructions and wait until the centre reaches the correct temperature for doneness. Otherwise, use the ad-hoc method of one-who-is-without-gadgets. Insert a metal skewer into the thickest part of the meat, wait a minute for it to warm up to the temperature inside the meat, then test it by holding it to your lip (which is more sensitive than your hand or mouth). If it's cool, the meat is very rare, lukewarm, it's rare, warm, it's medium and if it's hot, it's ruined. If you know the correct weight, then you can cook the deboned meat as below.

COOKING TIMES

	RARE	MEDIUM	WELL DONE
BEEF	180°C (160°C fan oven) mark 4 10–15 mins/500 g	18 mins/500 g	25 mins/500 g
LAMB	200°C (180°C fan oven) mark 6 12 mins/500 g	16 mins/500 g	20 mins/500 g
PORK	180°C (160°C fan oven) mark 4	30 mins/500 g	Not Advised

If the bone is still in, then you need to cook it a bit less, since the bone conducts its heat into the centre of the meat, so take off 5 minutes per kilo from the overall cooking time. If you use a fan oven, which are much quicker or seemingly hotter, you need to take off about 5 minutes a kilo, or cook at a lower heat, say 160°C (140°C fan oven) mark 3 instead of 180°C (160°C fan oven) mark 4. This is where you need to know your oven and try other methods to check for doneness. If you use a thermometer, then insert it into the thickest part of the meat and use the table below to see if it is cooked:

COOKING TEMPERATURES – IS IT DONE?

BEEF AND VEAL	Rare	50°C
	Medium Rare	55°C
	Medium	60°C
	Medium Well	65°C
	Well Done	70°C
LAMB	Medium Rare	55°C
	Medium	60°C
PORK	Medium	60°C
FISH	Medium	50°C
POULTRY	Legs	75°C
	Breasts	65°C

Given all the possible variations, I recently cooked a piece of beef of 2.55 kg, without a bone. It came out very rare after 45 minutes, and rare after 65 minutes in a 200°C (180°C fan oven) mark 6, so that may help you make comparisons. Gordon Ramsay showed another simple method on TV – he said that a rare piece of meat would feel like someone's cheek if lightly pressed, a medium cooked meat would feel like a chin and well done would feel like a forehead – go on, try it, it works. Try prodding your meat with your finger and see if you're right.

One thing that affects the cooking is how fresh the meat is and how it has been kept. I've ordered a beef fillet before, which came shrink-wrapped when I picked it up at a local butcher, and when I came to cook it, out came a lot of watery blood, which made me suspicious that it had been kept frozen, and it was now defrosted. I tried to dry it off, because you can't get wet things to brown, but even with a high heat, it only turned mid-brown. My fan oven finished it off, and when I came to take it out, I found it was overcooked (at least to my taste). The moral of the story is ensuring that you take the meat out of its wrapping well in advance, and if it isn't dry, allow the surface to dry out, then use kitchen paper to mop up any remaining moisture. A fridge will dry it out as well, but better still, refuse it if it has been pre-frozen.

ROAST POULTRY

Chicken is generally thought to be sufficiently cooked when you pierce the leg/body junction and the meat juices run out clear yellow, not pink at all, or if you twiddle the drumsticks and they move in their sockets. You can also hear that they are cooked – the meat starts throwing out bits of fat, which you can hear pinging away in the heart of the oven. Big birds like geese and turkeys can be treated in the same way for doneness as chicken. Other birds, however, do not abide by such rules, probably because if you overcook them, they start to toughen, and surprisingly quickly, because they have less fat within the meat. Smaller game birds, such as partridge and quail, can be cooked very quickly, so that they are brown on the outside and pink inside, or you can cook them very slowly over a length of time in a casserole with stock and wine, plus aromatics and vegetables, which stops them drying out. Duck and pheasant need about 30 minutes in a hot oven, while grouse, widgeon, partridge, quail and pigeon need about 15 minutes and teal and snipe need even less.

THE VERY BEST WAY TO ROAST A CHICKEN

The absolute minimum you need to do with a roast chicken is to salt and pepper inside the cavity but herbs, particularly marjoram, tarragon, thyme and parsley all go well with chicken and can be put into the body cavity with a halved lemon before roasting. Hugh Fearnley-Whittingstall swears by a simple recipe like this one, but adds butter under the skin as well.

SERVES: 4

- 1.35 kg chicken, giblets removed and retained for stock
- a little olive oil to coat the pan
- juice of 1 lemon
- a handful of fresh herbs, particularly tarragon, parsley and marjoram
- 1 whole head of garlic, unpeeled and halved, plus a few whole cloves (optional)
- a few large knobs of unsalted butter
- salt and ground black pepper
- 2 medium onions, sliced
- 1 mug of chicken stock
- a few sloshes of dry sherry, dry vermouth or dry white wine

Preheat the oven to 170°C (150°C fan) mark 3.

Dry the outside of the chicken, then pour enough olive oil into a large roasting pan to coat the base. Add the chicken, then pour half the lemon juice on to the outside of the chicken, and the other half into the cavity along with the herbs, the spent lemon halves, the halved garlic head, salt and pepper and a knob of butter. Smother the outside of the chicken with more butter and sprinkle with salt and pepper. Roast for about 1 hour, then put the onions under the chicken, turning them about in the buttery juices. You can also add a few whole garlic cloves, with their skins left on, if you like. Put the chicken back into the oven and continue roasting for a further 30–40 minutes.

About 10 minutes before the end of the roasting time, add the chicken stock to the pan plus a good, few sloshes of sherry and continue roasting. If the chicken is well done at this stage, then remove it from the oven, keep warm and finish the onion sauce on the hob. If the chicken is nearly cooked but still pallid and white, increase the oven temperature for the last bit of cooking. The skin will usually turn golden by the end of the cooking period. If you get to the point that the garlic cloves are soft and squishy in their skins and the onions are brown, but the meat is not ready, then remove the onions and garlic and keep warm and let the meat cook for a bit longer. Once the chicken is done, keep the meat covered in foil in a warm place for 10–15 minutes so the juices retreat into the centre of the bird before you carve it.

FLAVOURINGS FOR ROASTED ITEMS

Here are some of the classic combinations that seem to work.

Beef	Horseradish sauce, bouquet garni (parsley sprig, bay leaf and thyme sprig tied together with string or in large pieces), mustard and crushed black pepper
Lamb	Rosemary, oregano, marjoram, mint, parsley
Pork	Sage, bay leaves
Fish	Fennel and dill, which are both vaguely aniseed-ish
Chicken	Tarragon and marjoram

SAUCE FOR ROASTED MEATS – DEGLAZED SAUCE (SAUCE DEGLACÉ)

This is the simplest sauce. Lift the meat and drain any juices from it into the roasting pan. While you are resting the meat in a warm place – say, the oven with the door open slightly – you can make the sauce and finalise the vegetables. Remove all but the last tbsp of fat from the roasting pan, but not any of the meat juices. Discard any badly burned bits, but scrape up any of the meaty, sticky bits that remain in the pan. Add 1–2 mugs of liquid, this can be stock and/or wine (white for chicken, red otherwise), or dry vermouth or, if you really must, water and boil down, reducing the sauce to a syrup, while scraping up all the meaty bits on the base of the pan, then swirl in a knob or two of butter and it's ready. Pour some of the sauce over the meat and put the rest into a warm sauceboat for the table.

If you want something slightly more elaborate then you can add finely chopped onions (preferably shallots or spring onions) to the cooking fat and cook them until just soft and beginning to brown, before adding the liquid. You can also add 1–2 tbsp port or Madeira to enrich the sauce or you can add chopped parsley or other herbs, or you can add cream. Many French sauces will ask for a large amount of butter to be whisked into the sauce before serving, adding to the unctuous, creamy luxury of a well-made sauce: this process is called *monter au beurre.* Whatever you do, don't add any salt until the end, as this amount of concentration of flavour will exaggerate any taste, including salt.

GOOD-QUALITY RICH WINE SAUCE BASED ON MEAT WITH HOMEMADE STOCK

(This sounds dull...but isn't, I assure you.) The one essential for excellent sauces is a homemade stock, which gives a richer, more refined and certain taste, and for me is the cornerstone of a good dish. You can still ask for bones from good butchers – beef, veal, chicken or game bones are best, with a few pork bones (usually too sweet to be used exclusively). I wouldn't recommend lamb, since its fat is too cloying for some. Keep the giblets as well, if you can find them. It is customary and polite to buy some other meat from proper butchers, at the same time as you ask for bones. Ring up beforehand so they can save you some and ask them to chop the bones up for you, so at least they can fit into your pan. You need to make a big panful out of them. If you're short of bones then buy some cheap meat to add, such as belly pork with some bone in, or spare ribs, and if you're really short, then add any small pieces of meat, bones, giblets and carcasses that you might have accumulated. This is strictly verboten when it comes to a classic sauce, and really frowned upon by some chefs, but beggars can't be choosers and this might be the only way you get to try making a real stock. I would improvise, if I were you.

PLAIN STOCK

- enough meat and or/poultry bones to nearly fill a large pan

- giblets from poultry, especially chicken (optional)

- a few sploshes of olive or vegetable oil

- 1 large carrot, roughly chopped

- 1 large onion, roughly chopped

- a few celery sticks, chopped (optional)

- unsalted butter

- a few fresh parsley sprigs (about 10)

- a few fresh thyme sprigs (about 6) or use dried

- 3 bay leaves

- 2 garlic cloves, unpeeled

- 6 black peppercorns

Put the bones and meat bits into a large saucepan or roasting pan with the oil and brown them either in the oven or on the hob. If you have some giblets then sort through them and remove any manky bits, particularly the yellow bile, wash and dry them, then brown them separately.

Empty the bones and meat into a large saucepan and cover with cold water. Bring close to the boil, skimming off any scum that rises to the top with a slotted spoon, then reduce the heat and simmer for 5 minutes.

Meanwhile, brown the vegetables in half oil and half butter in a separate pan, then add them to the bones with the herbs and flavourings. Simmer gently for 2–3 hours topping up with more boiling water so that the bones are always covered and skimming off any scum occasionally. If you think that you've got the most flavour out of the ingredients, then strain the liquid through a sieve into a large bowl and leave to cool. As it cools slightly, the fat will rise to the surface, so wait and carefully spoon it off. You can use a bulb baster (page 33) to siphon off any fat.

When the stock is cool, store it in the fridge, where the fat will congeal at the top and form a protective layer, which can be scraped off easily later if you want. If it's got a thin layer of fat over it, it will last for several weeks in the fridge. If not, then you will need to boil it up every 3–4 days. You can always freeze it. It will mostly thicken up into a jelly, having extracted the collagen from the bones. Have no fear of this, though. When it is needed, this stock can then be boiled down to concentrate the taste for further sauces.

RED WINE SAUCE

- 1 bottle of red wine (the choice is yours but remember that this will be the background taste of your sauce, so don't be too mean)

- 1 bouquet garni (a few parsley and thyme sprigs and 2 bay leaves, tied together with string or in large pieces so they can be removed easily)

- ½ pan of plain stock (page 56)

- salt and ground black pepper

- a very large knob (more like 1 tbsp) unsalted butter

Add the wine and aromatics to the plain stock and boil until it is about half the volume. Taste and adjust the seasoning. Add the butter, swirl around and serve.

Supermarkets now sell fresh stock, but it is always criticised by the foodie press. I think it may have to be a question of needs-must; if you haven't got the time or inclination to make your own stock, then I suppose this is better than nothing. If you're really tired/broke/busy you can use a chicken stock cube to make a basic 'stock', then add the wine and aromatics to produce a passable sauce.

MORE SAUCES – VARIATIONS ON THE SAME THEME

Add sautéed, finely chopped browned mushrooms and onions and you have Sauce Duxelles. Add finely chopped onions, browned in butter, vermouth, mustard and parsley and you have Sauce Robert, and so on. Some of the classic French sauces are based on a little flour to thicken them, before the liquid is added. This is out of favour now – the good were very good but the bad, like the 'Bisto' ones, were horrible. At present, most restaurant sauces are thin in consistency and based on reduction; boiled down to evaporate off the water and thicken them to a thicker, more syrupy consistency. They are generally stronger in taste and so often in restaurants you may only get odd dabs of them, plopped around the edge of the plate. Some chefs are now going in the opposite direction and not thickening the sauces at all, just presenting the cooking liquor as if that's good enough. 'Plain' is the nice way of putting it. Well, I like good, thick, syrupy sauce, enough to enjoy, separately in a pool. I tend to be more generous and pour out a puddle or let people help themselves; it's better to keep things simple and clean, well planned and sensitively put together, rather than overly fussy.

ROAST FISH

Fish is the easiest thing to spoil by overcooking – you must cook it for such a short time that it is imperative that as soon as it is done, it is removed from the heat or the oven, filleted and deboned as necessary, and served immediately onto preheated plates. Make sure the vegetables are prepared ready to go at the same time as the fish. If necessary, cook the sort of vegetables that can stand around, without spoiling at the end. Heat up the plates so that everything can go to the table at the same time and the fish doesn't go cold.

Fish, when uncooked, is partly translucent, just greyish-white and soft to touch. It should be gutted, its fins and scales removed and with the head cut off unless it's cooked whole. When fish is cooked, it turns opaque, goes bright white and has some resistance to touch.

If fish is already filleted and has an even thickness, then it can be cooked on the hob. The simplest way is to shallow-fry it (called pan-frying now) gently over a medium heat in oil or an oil-butter mix. Be generous with the oil-butter, spooning it over and over the top of the fish to help an even cook.

Oven baking is important for larger pieces of fish or whole fish, when a gentler overall heat is necessary, so that the whole fish can cook through gradually. Cook the fish approximately at the rate of every 2.5 cm of thickness for 8–9 minutes in an oven preheated to 190°C (170°C fan) mark 5 or 12 minutes for every 500 g. It's difficult to be precise and it may be easier to keep testing and tasting until you have a feel for it. Unless you plan to take the whole fish to the table before you cut it up, you can always try a little piece from the whole fish, and no one will be any the wiser. Or, if you're serving individual filleted pieces of fish, you can sully one piece and make it yours when you come to serve it. It should be easy to lift off the bone with a knife – if it still sticks to the bone then it is undercooked and should be opaque rather than translucent when fully cooked.

ROAST VEGETABLES

Most vegetables are gorgeous if they're roasted in the oven. This method of cooking seems to intensify their natural sweetness, as the sugars in the vegetables begin to caramelise (called the Maillard reaction) transforming them into something altogether wonderful. Onions, carrots, aubergines, courgettes, red peppers, tomatoes and asparagus are all great. Cut them into thin slices, rub in olive oil and roast in dishes or roasting tins. They all need different cooking times, so just watch and lift them out when they are brown and done, turning as necessary, then keeping them warm until serving.

Aubergines, unless cut very thin, may need more time and more olive oil. They are cooked when the pale green inside flesh becomes blackened or brown and is very soft to the touch of a fork, which can easily pierce it. If they show any resistance and remain the same greenish, whiteish colour they are uncooked and bitter to taste. If you cut them very thin, they are much quicker to cook, but also burn quickly as well, so keep an eye on them. Nicholas Clee in his book *Don't Sweat the Aubergine* naturally goes into cooking aubergines in great depth. He is bothered about the old maxim that all aubergines should be cut up and salted 'to draw out the bitter juices', which preceded all aubergine recipes, once upon a time. We think that aubergine varieties must have been improved, by their commercial growers, because this is obviously quite unnecessary now. Avoid any instructions that demand presoaking, salting, setting out in the midday sun (as our Greek friends insist upon), squeezing out the juices, bitter or otherwise, and drying or frying in vast quantities of olive oil.

If you cut the aubergines into chunks, about 1 cm thick (at the most), rub them in your hands with olive oil and put them into a roasting tin in an oven preheated to 200°C (180°C fan oven), mark 6, they should take about 45 minutes to cook through. If you slice them very thinly, about 5 mm and rub with olive oil, they will cook in about 15 minutes. Both methods will need watching and turning regularly. Aubergines are delicious as they are, or with salt and pepper and, even better, sprinkled with a dressing of garlic, lemon juice, olive oil, pepper and salt as in the recipe below.

LEMON GARLIC DRESSING FOR ROASTED VEGETABLES

FOR ½ MUG OR SMALL BOWL OF DRESSING

- 1–2 garlic cloves, peeled

- 1 tsp salt

- a good few grinds of a coarse pepper grinder

- juice of 2–3 lemons

- olive oil in proportion to the lemon juice of about 3:1

Crush the garlic then put into a small bowl with the salt and pepper and mash together for a minute or two with the back of a spoon until the garlic becomes a purée and the salt dissolves. Add lemon juice and olive oil, then taste and adjust the seasoning – it often seems to need more salt than usual to counteract the acidity of the lemons.

Mix liberally with any of the roasted vegetables, preferably lukewarm, and serve as an antipasto.

SMOKY AUBERGINE DIP

This is a delicious, smoky Middle Eastern dip or purée, sweet and savoury at the same time, rather like moutabal from Syria. The basic variations of aubergine purée exist in a few Mediterranean countries, usually those with an Ottoman background, so you can find this basic recipe with any of the following added, such as tahini, thyme, chillies, yogurt, onions, tomatoes, ginger and parsley. It may be known as sultan's delight, hunkar begendi, baba ganoush or sometimes just aubergine cream.

MAKES: A BOWLFUL

- 4 medium aubergines

- 3 garlic cloves, crushed

- 2–3 tsp salt

- ground black pepper

- juice of 3–4 lemons, to taste

- 1 tbsp tahini mixed with some olive oil to thin a little (optional)

Roast the aubergines over a flame either on a gas hob or barbecue. On the hob, leave them hanging over the flame, on the metal supports, moving them around, so each part is cooked until the skins are blackened and blistered and the flesh is soft when pierced with a fork. This makes a right mess of your hob, with bits of black skin and ejected watery liquid all over the place. Just relax and resign yourself to a good clean up afterwards.

Peel off the charred skins, scraping the hot flesh out into a dish, then using a knife and fork, mash it up until it is a creamy, coarse paste. You don't need to be overzealous with this, as little bits of blackened skin don't ruin the dish. It can be made quite lumpy. Add the garlic, salt, pepper and lemon juice to taste. It seems to be able to take quite a lot of salt and lemon juice, without overseasoning the dip, so try it and be prepared to add some more. Stir in the tahini, if you like. If you like a smoother consistency, then whiz it in a food processor or blender until smooth.

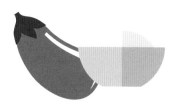

BAKING

This is a mongrel category used by different people to mean slightly different things. Baked can mean cooked in the oven, but then overlaps with roasting, so a few items may be in both categories. Baking, as a term, in Britain, is mostly associated with desserts such as cakes, which are dealt with separately later under puddings. Bread making is also referred to as part of the baking tradition, in fact, it was often used by previous generations, where the woman of the home might be described as a 'good baker'. The TV series *Bake Off* has suddenly resurrected the term and baking has begun to be fashionable again. The savoury use of the term 'baking' is covered under the roasting and oven-cooked sections of this book.

FRYING AND SAUTÉING

Frying is British while sautéing is French. It sounds better in French and describes the desired action more accurately. *Sauter*, meaning 'to jump', describes the way you can cook food. Food is quickly cooked in oil over a high heat either in a frying pan or a sauté pan (one with higher sides). Vegetables such as potatoes, mushrooms, onions and carrots lend themselves very easily to sautéing, while on a day-to-day basis, many of our meals start off with a sauté, beginning with onions and then progressing on to small chunks of meat, adding other vegetables, aromatics and flavourings, according to the needs of the recipe.

The term 'frying' has the poor connotations associated with all fried food, in that the food is often left to cook in an over-large amount of undesirable fat. At best this can be the light tempura batter of Japan, cooked in clean and tasty oil; at worst, battered Mars Bars cooked in last Monday's fat.

Deep-frying employs a pan with high sides, previously the ubiquitous chip pan of British households, with generally old oil, preserved from week to week. This would have been lard or the dripping from the last roast in most houses. Inside the pan was an open-meshed sieve-cum-basket with a handle for draining off the fat. More recently, there have been purpose-made deep-fryers, set into the work surface as an expensive extra in modern fitted kitchens. These are more like smaller versions of the same type used in fish and chip shops and restaurants. They are used for any food, particularly a high volume, like chips, or those which need to be able to move around so that they brown evenly.

Shallow-frying, as its name suggests, uses less oil, coming part of the way up the food. Falafel or meatballs need a fair amount of oil, but don't need to be deep-fried; they can be rolled around easily so they suit shallow-frying. Again, the art of basting the food in the pan with a spoonful of the oil, over and over, becomes an important part of the cook's repertoire. When extra butter is added to this fat, the process is called 'monter au beurre' in the French kitchen.

Other oils that have a higher smoking point than olive oil are useful for quick searing. These include sunflower, groundnut, rapeseed, coconut and avocado. Beware, however, generalised RBD (refined, bleached and deodorised) oils sold often as 'vegetable oil'.

HOMEMADE CHIPS

Use the right kind of potato, certainly an old potato, and a variety such as Maris Piper or King Edward. Peel and slice them nice and big, then wash and dry them. If you don't dry them, the first part of the cooking will only be boiling off the water that coats them and they will end up partially steamed. Heat the fat, lard or beef dripping for the purist, olive oil for others, groundnut oil or whatever for the rest. Rick Stein cooks with goose fat. You must be generous though: without enough oil the potatoes tend to catch and burn on the edges where they are in contact with the pan. Drop in a small piece of potato and if it just starts to bubble, then the fat is

sufficiently hot. Carefully lower the chips in using a slotted spoon, sieve or chip pan holder, a little at a time, so you don't disappear in a cloud of steam and the bubbles make the oil boil over, set the house on fire and so on, then reduce the heat to medium and cook for 5–10 minutes until the potato is cooked, but before it starts to colour. Remove from the pan and drain, blotting them with kitchen paper to remove as much fat as possible, then leave them to cool.

When you're ready to eat them, repeat the process, this time keeping the heat up, so they start to colour. In this way you should get a lovely crisp, golden outer skin and a soft, mellow inside.

PAN-FRYING

I wasn't aware of exactly what pan-frying was until I thought about it.

It's slowly crept into the restaurateur's lexicography as a separate, mysterious and fashionable way of describing frying, that is, normal frying to you and me done in a frying pan. Having said that, there are some basics to pan-frying that can be learned. Contrary to sautéing, which involves lots of action, and in the case of a chef, deft pan-shaking and flipping of food, pan-frying requires some static non-action. The food is meant to cook through a little and 'catch'. This is not to say burn, so you can't totally relax, but you must learn to stop prodding and turning and leave the thing alone. You may just ease it carefully off the base to turn it with a fish slice, for instance, but no more. The point here is to let the food cook gently, and go brown, rendering those crunchy extra tasty bits on the outside. I'm thinking of a nice fish fillet

here, or a steak, potatoes, mushrooms, seafood and so on.

The fat in which the food is cooked is often central to the end result, both in taste and look, so you don't want any nasty, burned bits. Cooking with butter, plus a little olive oil to lower the burning point, gives a gorgeous, lingering, luxurious quality to the cooking. You should add a large knob of butter, or perhaps more depending on how much you're cooking in your pan, plus a splosh of olive oil, then heat it until the foaming of the butter begins to die down and goes quiet. Add your food, then after a moment, ease the food off the base with a fish slice and leave it to brown, spooning over the fat to help to cook the item, before turning it over to cook the other side.

PAN-FRIED PHEASANT BREASTS

This recipe is a slightly more exotic take on pan-frying using only the lean meat of the pheasant breasts with a strong, meaty sauce made from the rest of the pheasant. Cut the breasts off the pheasants, cutting with a sharp knife against the bones and removing the giblets. Look through the giblets and find any remnants of the bile duct, attached to the liver, which is yellow, cutting off any bits that may be accidentally left. The bile duct tastes revoltingly bitter and taints any food it encounters, so wash the liver after you've cut out the gall.

SERVES: 2

- 1 onion, finely chopped
- 1 carrot, finely chopped
- ¾ bottle of red wine
- 1 bouquet garni (2 bay leaves, 1 dsp fresh thyme and parsley sprigs tied together with string or large pieces so they can be removed easily)

- 5–6 black peppercorns
- oil, such as walnut, hazelnut or olive or ½ oil and ½ unsalted butter or butter, enough to make a depth of at least 1 cm
- 2 pheasant breasts separated from the rest of the carcass (see intro)
- vegetables of your choice to serve

Fry the onion and carrot in a frying pan until soft and brown, then transfer to a large pan and put to one side.

Put the carcass, bones and giblets into the frying pan and fry, turning them over for 5–10 minutes until browned. Transfer the bones to the pan with the onion and carrot, then add the red wine, bouquet garni and peppercorns. Bring to a simmer, adding a little water if the bones are completely covered, and cook until the liquid has evaporated by about half. Taste and if it is starting to taste good, strain the contents through a sieve into a clean pan and continue boiling down until it starts to thicken.

Taste: it is amazing that even without any salt it tastes concentratedly savoury.

Heat the oil, or mixture of butter and olive oil, or just olive oil in a frying pan until it is sizzling but not quite smoking. If using just butter, wait until it starts foaming, then add the breasts and brown for 2 minutes, moving them around in the pan, turning them over and over, basting with the oil. Reduce the heat and sauté for 2–3 minutes on each side. Test by cutting through one and tasting it. At the same time, continue cooking the sauce down until it becomes syrupy. Serve the sauce with the meat and any vegetables you like.

SAUTÉED PORK OR WILD BOAR WITH RICH MUSHROOM SAUCE AND APPLES

This is a lovely autumn or winter dish where the meat is quickly sautéed and added to a mushroom sauce. Use pork or wild boar steaks, preferably not too lean and from a good butcher. Supermarket meat will inevitably be prepared only to look good without any fat marbling and will be too uniform. Without any fat the meat will cook too quickly and overcook and become tough. Serve with roast or sautéed potatoes and carrots. Prepare the vegetables and start cooking. When the potatoes are nearly done, start the main meat part of the recipe.

SERVES: 2

- a small handful of freshly chopped mushrooms, such as cèpes (France)/ porcini (Italy) or the equivalent dried per person
- 1 onion, finely chopped
- unsalted butter and oil to cook
- pork or wild boar steaks, cut into bite-size chunks (adjust number needed to size of steaks available)
- 4 bay leaves
- 10 black peppercorns
- 1 cup of dry Martini or dry white wine
- 1 dsp dried bouillon powder or 1 chicken stock cube crumbled into ½ cup of boiling water
- 1 tbsp freshly chopped sage
- 1 apple, peeled, cored, thinly sliced and halved

If using dried mushrooms, put them into a heatproof bowl and cover with boiling water. Leave to stand for 20 minutes, then strain through a sieve, putting the soaking liquid to one side. If using fresh mushrooms, wipe them clean with a cloth or kitchen paper and cut into chunks.

Meanwhile, gently fry the onion in butter and oil in a large frying pan over a low heat. Add the meat, increase the heat to fairly high and sauté, stirring it around and turning it over and over so it doesn't burn, until just cooked.

Remove from the pan and keep warm.

Scrape up the meaty bits on the base of the pan with a metal fish slice. Add a little more fat (half butter and half olive oil) and sauté the mushrooms if using fresh ones until soft. Add all the remaining ingredients, including the reconstituted dried mushrooms and the sieved mushroom water, if using, and bring to a simmer. Cook until it is reduced to a sauce. Keep tasting. When the accompanying vegetables are cooked, stir the meat into the sauce and serve.

POACHING

You can poach food in simmering liquid, with tiny bubbles, not the rollicking great roll you associate with boiling, so that soft and sensitive ingredients, such as eggs, don't break up. Each recipe might have a different liquid base.

POACHED EGGS

The intention is to just cook the white until opaque and firm, while the yolk remains soft. You can use little poaching cups over an individual poaching pan, but you can do even better without, since in poaching cups they always end up uniform, with a tendency to overcook. The aim is to try to prevent the white from breaking up and leaving streaming edges and to achieve as neat as possible a shape. The white should be cooked, and the yolk just cooked, so that when pierced the yolk will ooze out. Obviously using really fresh eggs from happy hens sourced locally will help tremendously. Supermarket eggs are often very old and of suspicious parentage. To poach eggs, simmer some water with vinegar at about 1 tsp per 500 ml. Carefully lower the eggs into the liquid, putting them each into a separate cup or bowl if you are not confident of lowering them into the water straight from the shell. The cracked shell can easily catch on the side of the yolk and break it, so it's best to be cautious. Cook for 4 minutes, then remove them with a slotted spoon if you have one. Rinse carefully with warm water to get rid of the vinegar. I don't know exactly what purpose the vinegar serves, but this is recommended in most French cookery books and therefore must have some good reason, I hope. They also recommend swirling the water around and teasing the egg strands together with a fork or chopstick as you lower the egg into the water, but this needs patience. Restaurants tend to trim the errant fronds with a knife before service.

GRILLING

Grilled food is put onto a heatproof dish or plate, a rack or foil and then grilled under an overhead grill. Again, other nationalities use slightly different terms – the Americans, for instance, say that grilling is always used under food and broiling from above. The food needs to be a consistent thickness, and not too thick, like filleted fish, so that the centre can be cooked without the outside burning and drying out. Meat and fish of up to 2.5 cm thick can be successfully grilled. Grilling is also often used to finish something off, like a cheese topping which needs melting and browning, or a breadcrumb top, which goes golden and crunchy.

BARBECUING AND GRIDDLING

This is like grilling, but outside in the case of barbecuing using charcoal for heat and added smoke, which makes food taste delicious, and inside in the case of griddling. Barbecuing is considered cancer-inducing, but as long as it's not every meal, I can't imagine it being a huge deal. The problem is to get the inside of the food cooked, while still retaining a reasonably unburned outside. If the coals are dying down and completely white, then it might not be too bad in that there may not be too many flames to burn the food. If the food spits while cooking, then the fat released will drop onto the coals and come back into the flame, which will burn the outside. Arm yourself with a water spray to damp down any flames that are out of control. Make sure the water spray has not just been used with something like weed killer though, as ours always seem to be.

Charred vegetables have made a recent impact on the gastronomic scene, since everything seems to be improved by cooking on a barbecue, although they can be easily cooked on the griddle if there's no barbecue lit. Meat is delicious cooked on the barbecue. The better the meat, the easier and quicker it is to cook, as it can take an outside browning and retain an inside juiciness. Sausages, hamburgers and kebabs are obviously suitable options. Things that need a long gentle cook are better in the oven, or a barbecue designed for long cooking. Kebabs made with tender lamb, pork, steak or chicken marinated for extra taste are easy because you can turn them around for even cooking, but they are time-consuming to thread onto skewers if you're dealing with a lot of guests. Some organic butchers make up lovely kebabs, but they are more expensive bought ready-prepared. Vegetables, such as onions and peppers, are good on skewers too.

Hamburgers are improving now as the supermarkets cash in. I tend to like the ones with more ingredients, because they seem to retain moisture better than the pure meat ones, but this comes down to personal taste. For a homemade hamburger, I mix the meat, which is not too lean, with a few breadcrumbs, a grated onion, some lemon and herbs, including mint and parsley, and spices. Italian-flavoured ones feature toasted fennel and perhaps cumin, chillies, garlic, paprika, salt and pepper.

Marinades that contain lemon juice, garlic, salt and pepper always taste great, and a few herbs like rosemary, oregano and marjoram enhance that Mediterranean taste and smell which conjure up Greek islands and that lovely time after a hot day, when the barbecues are just starting for the evening and the sun is going down in a turquoise vapour.

If you fancy an ersatz tandoori chicken, you can marinate it in a sauce made from garlic, hot paprika, lemon juice, turmeric, coriander, chillies (de-seeded and thinly sliced), salt and pepper. Leave to stand for about 30 minutes before cooking, then mix in some plain yogurt. Even if you don't have a barbecue, you can use this recipe and cook the meat in a frying pan.

Robust fish is also OK on the barbecue, but something a bit chunky with large flakes or small, whole fish are best, such as tuna or swordfish steaks. Prawns, scallops and monkfish are also good. Sardines work well. Rub with olive oil to help prevent the fish from sticking, or, even better, use a purpose-made fish clamper to help turn the fish over. Sprinkle with a little salt. Some experts advise cooking in foil, but that really defeats the object, because you can't get any of the smoke in.

Griddling is similar in that it produces burned-in lines where the food hits the hot bars, but griddles are usually used indoors over a hot hob. The slightly burned taste is there but not the charcoal, woody taste of barbecue coals.

BRAISING, CASSEROLING AND STEWING

Casseroles mean three things to the traditional British: not only the method of cooking, but also the resulting food and even the container they are cooked in. The containers are usually oval or round ovenproof dishes. They can be earthenware or heavy-duty steel, such as the well-made French 'Le Creuset'. The Spanish have a range of orangey-brown glazed pottery, for cooking in the oven, which are not only cheap but can be used to sauté food on top of the hob without shattering. This saves washing-up. Don't try to use them in the microwave, as they may end up with a crack, or like mine, scalloped at the edge, as if bites have been taken out.

The great, unsung joy of casserole cooking is that the main part of the meal is cooked all at the same time in one container. Easy, quick to prepare and not much to wash up. A casserole used to be the mainstay of middle-class cuisine in the UK. It's largely out of favour now, probably because long, slow cooking is considered impossibly long-winded for modern life. But the era of slow cooking is making a comeback, and of course, in France, it never really went away. Classic dishes like Coq au Vin (page 194) and Boeuf Bourguignon (page 197) are still gorgeous, easy and loved by everyone. There is a movement towards very slow cooking now, called, quite aptly, Slow Food, endorsed first by the Italians and by some of our greatest chefs, like Heston Blumenthal, where dishes are cooked for a very long time over very low temperatures. Of course, AGA divas have never really cooked otherwise. My oven is a bit too fierce for this extra slow cooking, but one-pot cooking for 2–3 hours always produces something really good.

Cheap cuts of meat can be used in slow cooking, since they become tender and tasty in the long run. Even restaurants are now returning to older, traditional British recipes, using these cuts of meat. Personally, I want to see dishes in the top restaurants, which I cannot or will not cook at home. Well, not very often, that is. If we had a background of bistros or relais throughout the country, as in France, as our basic standby, lowest common denominator, then I would be quite happy to see them use cheap cuts cooked slowly and authoritatively, and the results be served simply. But in the more expensive restaurants, I would still like to see their superior expertise and flair put into something that I would not cook myself.

Casseroles are essentially the same as stews, but somehow to me even the word 'stew' has the awful connotations of school cookery lessons; a collection of meat and vegetables merely put together in water and cooked until thoroughly tasteless and inedible. I remember one particularly dour Lancashire Hotpot, where some gristly grey meat and spiritless vegetables were unceremoniously dumped into a casserole of hot water, which has put me off for life. Modern school cookery does not seem to me to be any better; there's just more emphasis on health and safety, regulations and neatness, which may form part of the curriculum but should not become the overwhelming focus of it. I suppose the name says it all – Food Technology for heaven's sake.

Braising is a similar word, meaning different things to different people. Supermarkets tend to use it to imply a superior sort of stew. Simon Hopkinson sees it in an altogether different light, as he doesn't add much liquid to the ingredients, as most of it comes naturally out of the meat and vegetables, while it's just simmering away.

STEAMING

Steaming involves cooking in something porous over simmering water. You could cook in a colander over a pan, at a pinch. I have a very cheap, aluminium Chinese steamer from an Asian supermarket, which are three interlocking aluminium pans with holes in their bases to let the steam through and a lid for the top one to contain the heat. You simply cut up the food, pop it into one of the compartments, fill the bottom one with some boiling water, put the lid on and put it on the hob. The bottom water simmers, letting the steam rise through the compartments. It has the advantage of gentle cooking, so if you have anything delicate, which may disintegrate on boiling, then steaming is better. Everything is less watery, so broccoli in particular is very good steamed. The problem with boiled broccoli is that it retains the hot water between its florets, and can be easily overcooked, or it is just too watery to accept any sauces or flavours you have cooked for it. Broccoli is even better (because there is no residual water in it) microwaved, but the recipe below showcases steamed broccoli.

GAYE'S BROCCOLI SALAD

This is one dish that gives children a really good impression of vegetables. They can see fresh, bright green broccoli pepped up with toasted walnuts and vinaigrette, dusted with a coating of grated Parmesan. Chilli and/or raisins can be added, for extra zizz.

SERVES: 2

- 1 head broccoli, cut into florets, stalks reserved and chopped
- a large handful of walnuts
- 1 garlic clove, crushed
- salt and ground black pepper
- 2–3 tsp mustard, preferably Meaux or other French mustard
- a few sloshes of white wine vinegar
- 1 tbsp olive oil or walnut or similar exotic oil for the dressing
- 1 red chilli, crumbled (optional)
- a handful of raisins (optional)
- 2–3 tbsp grated Parmesan to serve

Cook the chopped broccoli stems for 2–3 minutes ahead of adding the florets. Steam the broccoli until just cooked or simmer it for 3–5 minutes in boiling water. You can even microwave it on high for 2–3 minutes. If you want to aim for presentation, then you should plunge the broccoli into icy water to stop the cooking process and preserve the greenness.

If the broccoli is just for ourselves, I make sure it's lukewarm as the flavour is better at this temperature. To try to rid myself of the water I usually shake off as much as possible then lay the florets on kitchen paper, so that any excess moisture can drain off. If it's a warm day, I put the plate of broccoli, nicely spread out, into the garden, so that any remaining water droplets are evaporated by the wind and it cools down a little, while I toast the walnuts in a dry frying pan. As soon as the walnuts start to colour I shake the pan about, so they turn over. They should be brown, but not burned.

Gaye's broccoli salad

I make the dressing at the same time in the final serving bowl. Mash the crushed garlic into a paste with a little salt and pepper, then add the mustard, thinning it slightly with the vinegar and then stirring in the oil to make a quite thick dressing. This will stay on and coat the florets better. Add the broccoli and toss, stirring it around to coat every floret. Taste and adjust the seasoning. Add the walnuts, which will sizzle as they hit the dressing, then add the chilli and raisins, if using, and stir until combined. Serve with Parmesan on top.

STEAMED FISH

Steamed fish is greatly loved by the Chinese, because it is pure and preserves the flavour of the fish. The Chinese aluminium steamers are very useful for this. It's incredibly easy. Either cook in a steamer or over a lidded saucepan with boiling water in it. A flat fish such as sole and plaice need only 5 minutes whereas a whole fish or a fillet of something like sea bass, bream or salmon will take 12–15 minutes. You can put thin ribbons of fresh ginger on top or inside as it's cooking. Garnish with fresh coriander and splash with soy sauce and rice or wine vinegar and a dash of sesame oil before serving.

STIR-FRYING

Stir-frying with the help of a wok (again, very cheap to buy) means that you can cook things crispy, such as vegetables, with very little fat. It is obviously a Chinese cooking technique which has become very popular in the West, as we have become more adventurous.

You need to use a lightly flavoured oil, such as peanut/groundnut, corn or rapeseed and then cook the vegetables in the order of length of cooking time needed, starting with any of the following: onions, then carrots, then French beans, then ginger and/or chillies, then garlic (which can easily burn, so watch it and keep stirring), mangetout, beansprouts, baby corn and finally, pak choi, which needs only seconds.

Use the wok over a high heat, stirring with a metal slice to lever any bits off the base of the wok, turning the food over and over rather like large-scale sautéing. If you're very proficient then turn the food over by flipping it, chef-style. It all starts to sizzle and steam, sounding quite menacing, but keep going. The vegetables should be slightly browned at the edges and not quite cooked through. Add a splash each of soy sauce, wine vinegar, dry sherry, a pinch of sugar and then any meat you might want to add. I usually marinate some cut up chicken thighs in the flavourings, as I'm cooking the vegetables, then toss the whole lot in together.

If you use thinly sliced Chinese sausages then you should add them near the end of the vegetables. Even better is to lay them over the cooking rice, allowing the juice to permeate down through the rice in the pan. In this way the sausages are virtually steamed, which makes them a better foil for the vegetables. The aim is to cook quickly, sealing in the flavours and then serve immediately. Again, it's best to get the rice on and finished before you even start to cook the vegetables (see page 37).

PARBOILING OR BLANCHING

Parboiling is part boiling, cooking to a certain stage to retain the essential characteristics of the food. It is then finished off in another form, such as parboiled potatoes which are then roasted. It also cuts down the overall length of cooking time. In addition, you can cook some things ahead of time and then finish them off just before serving.

Blanching is similar, but the aim, from the French *blanc*, is to keep the colour of the ingredient and a bit of the crunch. The vegetable is boiled for a short time, say a couple of minutes, then put into a sieve and immediately plunged into a bowl of iced water to stop the cooking process. A classic French recipe may even call for acidulated iced water – water with a squeeze of lemon. The aim is to remove as much water as possible to preserve the flavour, by either letting them dry in a colander outside, or with kitchen paper or a combination. If I'm cooking vegetables to add to a salad for instance, I may blanch them first and dry them off to allow the salad dressing to stick to them. Carrots, green beans, mangetout, leeks and particularly broccoli are obvious candidates for this treatment.

MICROWAVING

The microwave is the bête noire of the gourmet fraternity, mostly for good reason in that it has allowed people to forgo cooking and depend, sometimes and frighteningly totally, on warming up mediocre ready meals in the microwave. It's used without discretion by a large proportion of the catering trade too. I remember once being served in the Blue Boar Motorway Service Station just north of London on the M1, a portion of soup. It being the early days of microwaves, its operation was rather beyond the dim wit serving me, and when she handed it to me, it had been put into a polystyrene cup, which had slowly and painfully melted down around the soup, so that it and the soup became the diameter of a small plate. Resembling the first ham-fisted attempts at throwing a clay pot, it lay dejected and misshapen, but the ever-proud dinner lady seemed oblivious to its lack of function and edibility and continued to proffer it up to me like that.

But I break with tradition and say that sometimes the microwave can be used not only usefully but sometimes creatively. At best, a combination microwave, which can be used as a small conventional oven, a grill or a microwave, can save time and money. I even produced a very creditable Chocolate Nemesis from the *River Café Cookbook* in a microwave, when I had nothing else to cook with. This recipe is well known to be almost impossible to cook, probably because restaurant quantities can't be easily translated into family quantities. Recommendations from the manufacturers say the best food for microwaves tend to have sugar or fat in them, and this is why cakes are a natural.

Because food cooks so quickly in a microwave, it's important that the parts are of equal size, so you don't find some of the bigger items still undercooked when the smaller ones are ready. It's easy to overcook, so be timid at first. On full heat, first the food will heat, then it will cook very quickly, then it will dry out. Completely dry, that is. The last stage, before it burns down the house, is when it approximates to a new type of warfare. However, used with caution, the microwave can produce good food, and I maintain that microwaved potatoes and vegetables are particularly yummy. If you cover vegetables with something plastic, pierced clingfilm or cook in the pierced plastic bag (if you've bought them from the supermarket), they cook almost by an advanced steaming method. Unless they are liable to explode, you can prick them and just plonk them on a plate to cook, if the above plastics are not available. Don't use any metal in the microwave including foil or it will tend to arc, causing menacing flashes and electrifying sounds.

Obviously microwaves are very good for heating up food, particularly in their containers, which saves washing up. Similarly, you can use them on a conventional setting, more quickly heating up the smaller volume of the microwave, which saves heating up a standard oven. Here are some of the foods I use for microwaving.

JERUSALEM ARTICHOKES

These look like knobbly versions of that gorgeous potato variety – the mis-named, pink fir apple – which we can sometimes find in our shops. These Jerusalem artichokes are pure delight, best eaten before they even reach the table, whole in your hands, the outside still earthy and textured, and the inside squidgy and almost oozing out. Make sure they are clean and don't hide dirt within their outer folds. Don't bother to peel them, then cover and cook on high for about 5 minutes. Slice and flavour with vinaigrette or butter and salt.

CAULIFLOWER AND BROCCOLI SALAD

These are particularly good to microwave because you don't need special precautions to avoid any water clogging the indentations. They come out cooked but not soggy, ready to receive any flavourings. Again, vinaigrette, particularly one that has some thickness to it like a mustardy, garlicky vinaigrette on the just-warm vegetables transforms them into something sublime. Cut into florets, ensuring they are about the same size. Place on a plate or dish so that they're evenly spread out and cook on high for about 3 minutes.

This is also where, contrary to the preceding pages, I have to admit that supermarkets have got something right. If you buy the bags of chopped mixed vegetables, such as carrots, broccoli and cauliflower, then all you need to do is pierce the bag in a few places and microwave on high for about 2½ minutes. Serve with butter, salt and pepper or leave to cool slightly and pour over some vinaigrette. You can also easily add them to a curry, if you like.

WINTER SALAD

A salad of broccoli, cauliflower, asparagus, Jerusalem artichokes, rocket, feta and chilli dressed with vinaigrette and accompanied with some fresh bread, such as ciabatta or sourdough, is delicious. I say winter salad, because I've just made it in December, but this relies on unseasonal vegetables such as asparagus and rocket. To make this, microwave the vegetables, except the rocket and chilli. It doesn't matter in what order because it is all served warm. Assemble all the ingredients, crumbling the feta and mixing in a very small amount of very finely sliced mild red chilli, depending on strength and dress with vinaigrette. Heat the bread if not super fresh, by running wet hands over the surface then heating it in an oven preheated to 200°C (180°C fan oven) mark 6 for 3–4 minutes until its vigour and crispness is restored. Never do this in a microwave – always an oven.

VEGETABLE CRISPS

Parsnips are particularly good as crisps and are traditionally used to accompany pheasant and partridge, but you can use almost any hard vegetable like carrots, swede, beetroot and, of course, potatoes. The virtue of this recipe is that, apart from the small amount of oil to prevent sticking, there's no need to use any oil at all. Peel the outside of the vegetable of your choice, then slice it as finely as possible. If you use one of the horizontal peelers I love so much, you can get very fine slices without much effort; keep peeling so that you are left with lots of thin layers of the vegetable. Spread them out on a plate, smearing them with a little olive oil first and microwave on high. Try for 2 minutes, then add on increments of a minute until you get all the residual water out of the vegetable and you are left with a crisp, sweet, curl of vegetable. Flavour with salt.

MASHING OR PURÉEING

Mashing is a coarse purée, so, of course, a purée is finer. Mashed, as in mashed potato, is exactly how it sounds. You pound up the cooked whatever, usually a vegetable or fruit, with a specialised implement, such as a potato masher, but you can do it with a fork, and then add flavourings, which for potatoes might be butter, milk or cream, salt and pepper. Mashed potato these days has become altogether more exciting in some hands, with the addition of further flavourings such as horseradish or Parmesan or, more exotically, truffle oil. The mashed potato is more than likely to be puréed into a consistently smooth texture (unfortunately likened to wallpaper paste, for some), and is one of many restaurant favourites now.

To achieve this texture at home requires some gadgetry. A food processor, a blender or at least a Mouli is necessary, so that all the lumps are eliminated, and the creamy texture is accentuated by the addition of flavourings.

Restaurants will go further in the quest for ultimate taste. They bake the potatoes in the oven until very brown and crunchy on the outside, then they spoon out the insides into a potato ricer and squeeze the potato out over a horizontal sieve. Then, using a spatula, scrape it across back and forth, through to a pan below, so no wonder it tastes so smooth. It's then beaten with cream and lots of butter until it forms a ball with some elasticity in it, then further flavourings can be added.

I like garlic mashed potato, where I boil a whole head of garlic with its ends chopped off (say about 1–2 cloves for every big potato) in with the potatoes for about 30 minutes until they are soft and squishy. The long boiling tends to soften the flavour, so don't be put off by the quantity. Squeeze out the garlic and mash it up into a purée with a spoon with a little salt. Mash the cooked potatoes, adding butter, milk, cream or crème fraîche, and pepper, then add the garlic and stir it all together. Taste and adjust the seasoning. It's a bit like Aligot, another potato recipe (page 150).

Fruit purées are usually cooked gently, so you can sieve out pips, skin, stalks or stones, and then add sugar as necessary. You can easily pass them through a sieve if they are reasonably soft like raspberries, without the need to even cook them first, or you can blend them in a blender, or purée them in a food processor. This is useful for a dessert sauce, or to be mixed into other desserts like ice cream or custard.

PICKLING

A pickle is a food preserved in brine (salt or salty water) or an acid, like vinegar or lemon juice, and occasionally citric acid with some sugar. Pickling has come back into the fold recently. It does have a bit of an image problem though, as we can still remember the very strong vinegary tastes of things like pickled onions and pickled eggs. For a bowlful of mixed, colourful, pickled vegetables to be served, say an hour or several days later, follow the recipe below.

- 2 medium carrots, peeled and diagonally sliced
- ½ cucumber, halved and cut into chunks
- 1 red pepper, cut into chunks
- 1 medium-hot red chilli, sliced
- a few sploshes of white wine vinegar or apple vinegar, about 3–4 tbsp
- ¼ mug of water
- squeeze of lemon
- 2 dsp sugar
- 2 tsp salt
- about 10 black peppercorns
- a handful of chopped dill

Pickled carrots and cucumber

Combine all the vegetables with the flavourings, turning them over when you remember and eat them on the side of a main dish. You can use any robust vegetable, such as very finely sliced cauliflower or radishes, cut wafer thin. This is where a mandolin is useful.

FERMENTATION

Some fermented foods are pickled, while some pickles are fermented. Fermentation is the process of converting carbohydrates to alcohol or organic acids (using yeasts) under anaerobic conditions. Beer, wine and vinegar are obvious examples of fermentation, but now more exotic food options, including kimchi (fermented hot cabbage from Korea) and, the more prosaic, sauerkraut from Germany are available. Yogurt is probably the best known and widely used fermented food, but foods such as kefir, kombucha, tempeh, natto and miso are all fermented foods on the culinary rise.

WHAT CAN YOU DO WITH AN EGG?

Understanding how eggs cook and interact with other ingredients is perhaps the core of cooking well. They keep for a long time, are nutritious, quite cheap and are now not viewed as contributing to raising cholesterol as much as we formerly thought.

Eggs are so useful. To a certain extent mastery of the full repertoire of the humble egg will bring about a fullness and versatility that no other ingredient alone will command. Eggs are at the centre of a number of important sauces; they will help food to rise, increase its lightness by introducing bubbles, make dishes set and enrich others.

THESE ARE SOME OF THE THINGS YOU CAN DO WITH EGGS:

- *Boil*

- *Scramble*

- *Fry*

- *Poach*

- *Make omelettes*

- *Thicken sauces, such as cold mayonnaise or warm béarnaise (page 165).*

- *For hot custard and chocolate pots*

- *Make things set such as custards and crème caramel (page 215)*

- *Make food light and get it to rise, such as cakes and soufflés*

- *Add air and froth, such as meringue, zabaglione and chocolate mousse.*

I've rather assumed that you know how to separate egg yolks from whites, but if not, here goes. Crack the egg over a basin or bowl and some of the white will drip into the basin while you juggle the yolk from shell-half to shell-half, allowing the rest of the white to collect in the basin below. I've also cracked the eggs on a sharp edge, like a cup, but I've heard recently that you can crack them on a horizontal surface too. If you happen to get some shell in the egg mixture you can easily remove it using the empty shell whereas chasing it around the basin with your finger or a knife is pretty useless.

SOFT- AND HARD-BOILED EGGS

One of the few times you need to use less than fresh eggs is for hard-boiled eggs. Use either supermarket eggs, which are inevitably less than fresh, or wait for two-week-old eggs, otherwise you'll find them difficult to peel, because the white does not come cleanly away from the shell. Bring a pan of water to the boil. Lower the eggs in on a spoon so that the water covers them and simmer large eggs for 6 minutes. The white should be solid and the yolk runny. This is, surprise-surprise, a soft-boiled egg. If you want the yolk hard, then give them another minute. If you cook them any longer the yolks start going grey. I personally would rather a softer yolk than too hard, but this is a matter of personal preference.

Simon Hopkinson uses his favourite method for cooking eggs. He says start with the eggs in cold water and then heat to just simmering. Turn the heat off. Leave a soft-boiled egg in the hot water for 1 minute. For a firmer soft egg, leave for 2 minutes and for a hard-boiled egg but runny yolk, leave for 3 minutes. For a hard-boiled egg, leave for 4 minutes for slicing and egg mayonnaise and 5 minutes for a really hard-boiled egg.

If you want to add anything hot to egg yolks you must mix in a little cold water first to stop them going granular and scrambling. The other thing to remember is always add hot liquor to the cold eggs (gradually, of course), not the other way round.

SCRAMBLED EGGS

Assuming that this is only required for breakfast or a quick snack, then it should be simply made and quickly prepared and served without much ado on hot buttered toast. However, there are ways and there are...ways. For instance, from what I've seen on TV, chefs prepare it rather more like a soft omelette, turning it over deftly in a frying pan. I don't like mine like this. I like a very light and frothy, buttery mixture without any hard bits, which is made in a small saucepan and whisked, if possible, as the beaten eggs are gently heated. This has an altogether different texture, and to my mind quite superior; it is not an omelette, nor was ever meant to be. I do wonder if the hotel restaurant version of scrambled eggs is only as it is because it can be so quickly cooked and served, saving the chefs' time. In the pressurised atmosphere of a commercial kitchen I doubt if anyone can justify my slow and dedicated way of scrambling eggs. Anyway, this is my way, so here goes...

- bread to toast such as wholemeal, Granary, ciabatta and sourdough are all wonderful, as you know (fresh as possible)

- 1 egg per person beaten (you can do this in the pan if you're quick)

- a little milk, so for 2 people, 1 tbsp or to make it more luxurious add cream instead (see note)

- salt and ground black pepper

- butter

Note: To make the scrambled eggs even more yummy, add a big knob of butter towards the end of the cooking time. If you haven't got any fresh milk, then you can make do with water.

Cut the bread and get it ready for toasting. Assemble the plates, preferably heating them, and get the cutlery out ready for swift service. Assemble accompaniments such as bacon, chorizo or smoked salmon. Call everyone to the table and get someone else to make the coffee.

Lightly beat the eggs together with a fork or spatula in a saucepan together with your preferred liquid. Add a big pinch of salt and a grind or two of black pepper. Using a whisk and/or spatula, whisk over a low heat ensuring that the edges are kept lifted and stirred around to avoid overcooked hard bits, especially the edges of the pan where it will first harden and cook. A whisk will make it frothier and lighter. As the eggs heat up they will begin to thicken the mixture. Whatever you do, don't leave them at this stage. Keep them moving off the base and edges, otherwise you'll get hard, overcooked bits. Turn the heat right down to the lowest setting. Get someone else to put the toast on or leave it to the end. Keep stirring and whisking and mixing the mixture so that it starts to form granules.

DON'T OVERCOOK IT. Just before it appears to be cooked through but is still a little runny, remove the pan from the heat and move the mixture down to one corner of the pan, lifting the pan up if necessary on one corner. This is to try to reduce the hot surface area with which the eggs are in contact. The eggs will still keep cooking in the residual heat. Beat in the knob of butter, if using. Butter the toast and pile over the scrambled eggs and serve immediately. It should be very soft, with no specific solid bits. This all seems to be a lot of hard work and hassle, and it is, but it's worth it. To make it more of a special meal, add some smoked salmon, grilled smoky bacon, pancetta or chorizo.

FRIED EGGS

Again, this appears to be a mainly breakfast thing, but like scrambled eggs it can always be used as a standby or added to a larger meal. I prefer my eggs cooked in a specific way, which may not be to your taste. All I can do is to ask you to do it my way once and see if it's not better.

I developed this way of frying eggs after some excellent holidays in Greece, where *avga tiganites* became a staple pick-me-up after a long night partying. This was before the advent of cheap-ish olive oil, and the overcoming of our aversion to what was referred to, in a derogatory and chauvinistic manner, as a 'greasy Mediterranean diet'. I know who's had the last laugh.

You need to be generous with your olive oil and add a few tbsp to a pan. The Lune aluminium pans are ideal (page 237). Heat the pan and oil for a minute or so. Crack the eggs carefully into the oil, ensuring they don't break and fry briskly over a high heat. After 30 seconds or so, cut through the egg whites (if they are attached to each other) and try to gently lift each one off the base with a fish slice, so you can separate each egg out from its neighbour, without breaking the yolk. Reduce the heat to medium. With any luck the white edges will have started to crisp and brown. When the yolk is just cooked and the white has turned from translucent to an opaque, milky white, serve immediately with a pinch of salt and a swirl of black pepper.

POACHED EGGS

See Techniques Section on Poaching (page 65)

OMELETTES

Once again, there is a fair bit of tradition and individual preference regarding how to cook an omelette. I like mine soft and squidgy, just done and definitely not overcooked. You can add any amount of individual savoury flavours such as onion, ham, bacon and cheese as long as it's chopped up small enough to be absorbed by the envelope of the egg wrapping. Onions, unless they are spring onions, and bacon should be cooked separately beforehand. My favourite omelette is cheese, because I like the way it combines with the eggs to form a mid-texture, a little like Welsh Rarebit.

MAKES: 2 OMELETTES

- 2 large eggs
- a pinch of salt, 3 turns of black pepper
- 1 tbsp olive oil or unsalted butter, with a little olive oil mixed in
- 2 large handfuls of grated, strong, hard cheese, such as Cheddar

Beat the eggs gently in a bowl with the salt, pepper and 1 tbsp water.

Heat an omelette pan or frying pan over a high heat. Add the oil and let it get very hot. Add half of the egg mixture letting it run all round the pan by tilting it. Add the other half of the eggs and allow to cook through a little until there is definitely a cooked layer on the bottom. Sprinkle with the cheese, then reduce the heat to medium and roll the egg mixture round the sides of the pan so it can cook. Ease the omelette off the base of the pan with a fish slice. When it's becoming solid and you can't see any gelatinous uncooked white, then transfer to a plate by turning one half of the omelette over the other with a slice and sliding it out of the pan and onto a plate. Keep warm.

EGGS BENEDICT

Always a sign of a good restaurant if they offer this for brunch (or lunch for that matter). A liquid emulsion of flavourings and egg yolks warmed to a silky sauce and served on toast with poached eggs on top. Yum. I must say that most restaurants use a commercial packet version and don't make it from scratch.

SERVES: 2

- ½ onion, roughly chopped (could be a red onion or shallots if you can be bothered to peel them, but being sieved out later there is no need to chop precisely)
- 1 tbsp white wine vinegar
- juice of ½ lemon
- a few black peppercorns
- 1 egg yolk
- a large piece of unsalted butter, chopped into small pieces, about 1 tbsp in total
- salt and ground black pepper

Put the onion, vinegar, lemon juice and peppercorns into a large pan and bring to the boil. Cook until it has reduced by half. Strain the liquid through a sieve into a heatproof bowl, then set the bowl over a pan of simmering water, making sure the base of the bowl doesn't touch the water. Add the egg yolk and stir constantly. It should start to thicken a little. Keep stirring and add the butter. It's best to start whisking now, so the butter emulsifies, and the sauce keeps thickening up. Do not allow it to get too hot and start solidifying. Add 1 tsp cold water if in doubt. Remove from the heat and keep warm, ready for the toast and poached eggs. Taste and add salt and pepper.

HOLLANDAISE SAUCE

This is a classic. Often served with eggs, or fish or meat, it's made from warm egg yolks flavoured with lemon juice and gradually thickened with butter to make a thick, creamy sauce. It's rather like a warm mayonnaise.

- 200 g cold unsalted butter, cubed, plus 2 knobs of butter
- 3 egg yolks
- 1 tbsp lemon juice
- salt and ground black pepper

Melt the cubed 200 g butter in a pan over a low heat, then put to one side.

Beat the egg yolks in a heatproof bowl. Add 1 tbsp cold water, the lemon juice and a pinch of salt and beat together for a minute or so. Add a knob of butter. Do not beat. Set the bowl over a pan of barely simmering water, making sure the base of the bowl doesn't touch the water and stir with a wire whisk until smooth and starting to thicken and you start to see the marks of the whisk on the base of the pan.

Remove from the heat and beat in the remaining knob of butter. Very slowly, beat in a drop of hot butter, then add most of the butter, a drop at a time, beating constantly until it resembles thick cream. At this stage you can add the hot butter more quickly, but still carefully, until it has all been incorporated. Season with salt and pepper and a drop of lemon juice. Serve warm. You can keep it over a very low heat or a panful of lukewarm water if you are not serving it immediately.

Restaurants may cheat a little by adding 1 tsp cornflour mixed with a little milk or water into the egg yolks at the beginning of the recipe to stop the sauce separating, or a little of a béchamel or velouté sauce can be added instead. The flour helps the egg yolks support the added fat, so it is less likely to curdle or separate. As in any egg yolk-based sauce, if it curdles then quickly remove it from the heat and beat in 1 dsp cold water. If it refuses to thicken, then rinse out the bowl, add 1 tsp lemon juice and 1 tbsp of the sauce and beat until it creams and thickens. Put it back over a low heat and beat in the rest, a dsp at a time, until thick. Use immediately or store in the fridge covered in clingfilm for a day or two.

Serve hollandaise with poached eggs or fish. It can be embellished with fresh herbs, such as parsley, chives and tarragon. Instead of lemon juice use concentrated flavourings, such as white wine and fish stock, when it is then called fumet de poisson.

Note: Keep a careful eye on the hollandaise and if at any time it goes lumpy, then remove it from the heat and quickly plunge the base of the bowl into cold water to stop it cooking further. While still whisking, add 1 dsp cold water.

SAUCE BÉARNAISE

An absolutely essential, classic sauce for steaks, fish, chicken or eggs. It adds a smooth background sauce to moisten an otherwise simple dish.

- 3 tbsp white wine vinegar
- 4 tbsp white wine or dry vermouth
- 1 tbsp very finely chopped shallots or spring onions or at a pinch ordinary onions
- 1 tbsp freshly chopped tarragon or 2 tsp if dried
- 3 egg yolks
- a knob of cold unsalted butter
- 100 g unsalted butter, melted

- 2 tbsp very finely chopped parsley

- salt and ground black pepper

Boil the vinegar, wine, shallots and tarragon together in a pan until only 2 tbsp are left. Remove from the heat, leave to cool, then strain through a sieve.

Beat the egg yolks in a bowl, adding the sieved, cooled vinegar mixture very slowly. Beat in the cold butter while thickening over a low heat. Beat in the melted butter, a drop at a time over the heat. Beat in the parsley. Season with a pinch of salt and 1–2 grinds of pepper, then taste and adjust as necessary. Serve warm.

MAYONNAISE

Mayonnaise is basically egg yolks mixed with oil to make a liaison of thick cream full of gorgeousness. This apparently, if I can remember my French at school, was created by a French officer, the Duc de Richelieu, after the Battle of Mahon in 1756 in Minorca (where they thrashed the Brits, by the way). There was nothing to eat except for bread and eggs, so the officer ordered the cooks to eke out the eggs, by beating them with olive oil until they thickened, and then flavoured them with salt, pepper and a little vinegar. Hence 'mahonnaise' from Mahon, eventually to become mayonnaise in English. Again, there are some rules to make mayonnaise simple, such as adding the oil very gradually at first, as in all other egg yolk sauces. Another useful hint is to ensure the equipment and the eggs are at room temperature and not too cold and you must keep beating all the time. As you become more adept to making mayonnaise then you can proportionately use more oil to flavourings. You can keep it until ready for use by closely covering and putting it into the fridge. Again, with judicial additions you can transform mayonnaise into various sauces. A favourite is mayonnaise aux fines herbes, which is further flavoured with an assortment of freshly chopped herbs such as parsley, tarragon, basil, chervil, chives and/ or oregano.

- 3 egg yolks

- 1 tbsp wine vinegar or lemon juice

- ½ tsp salt

- ¼ tsp prepared French mustard

- about ½ mug oil (see note)

Beat the egg yolks in a bowl until sticky and thick. Add the vinegar or lemon juice, the salt and mustard and beat again for 30 seconds. Add the oil very gradually, still beating constantly, at first a drop at a time, then more quickly once it starts to thicken. If it gets too thick, add vinegar or lemon juice, a few drops at a time, and taste. If the sauce looks as though it is starting to curdle and separate then beat in 1 tbsp boiling water, a little at a time. If this fails, then start again. Warm another bowl with hot water and dry well. Add 1 tsp mustard and 1 tbsp of the mayonnaise mixture and beat together until thick and creamy. Add the main mixture to the new sauce, a little at a time until it has absorbed the oil and thickened up. Use immediately or store in the fridge for a few days.

Note: Using all olive oil, particularly virgin, may be too strong in terms of flavour. I would suggest a mixture between light olive oil and groundnut oil or even all groundnut, or any other relatively less flavourful oil such as rapeseed. You need about ½ mug in total but keep it in the original bottle or anything from which you can pour out very small quantities, such as an olive oil drizzler.

AIOLI

This is a favourite, southern French mayonnaise from Provence chunkily flavoured with garlic and used for boiled fish, boiled potatoes and the like. You often find it served with fish soup or bouillabaisse.

- 1 slice thick, white farmhouse-type bread or equivalent, crusts removed and crumbled into small pieces
- 1 tbsp wine vinegar
- 4–8 garlic cloves, crushed
- ¼ tsp salt
- 1 egg yolk
- Juice of 2–3 lemons
- salt and ground black pepper

Soak the bread in the vinegar for 30 minutes. Squeeze out the vinegar with your hands.

If you have a mortar and pestle, then pound the garlic and salt with the pestle; if you don't, then do it by hand. Squash it down with a circular motion with the back of a tablespoon, using the salt as an abrasive to mush the garlic into a smooth paste. Add the bread and continue pounding into the paste until smooth. Add the egg yolk and stir around in the paste. Add oil, a drop at a time at first, mashing it into the paste until it has the texture of a smooth cream. Whisk in more oil, a little at a time, until the sauce is thick. Beat in 1 tbsp or so of boiling water, a little at a time, then beat in enough of the lemon juice until it is the consistency of thick cream. Taste and adjust the seasoning. Use immediately or store in the fridge for a few days.

MERINGUES

Meringues are very useful for using up all the excess whites when recipes call for only egg yolks to be used. Unlike the commercial meringues, which seem to have the consistency of ultra-sweet dust in the mouth, good restaurant or homemade meringues are deliciously crunchy on the outside and meltingly soft and gooey on the inside.

There are a few simple precautions to take when making meringues:

- **Make sure that absolutely no part of the egg yolk gets mixed in with the white. If you are at all nervous, do them one at a time into a separate cup or bowl, then add them when you're sure.**

- **Make sure that the bowl is clean and dry and plenty big enough to whisk everything up. If there is a speck of grease in the bowl or on the whisk, then again you may have trouble getting the whites to rise properly.**

- **They are easier to whisk at room temperature, so if you can remember, then take them out of the fridge (if you unnecessarily keep them in a fridge, that is) a few hours before you need them.**

- 2 large egg whites at room temperature

- 100 g caster sugar

- ¼ tsp tartaric acid (optional)

Preheat the oven to 140°C, (120°C fan oven) mark 1. Line a large baking sheet with baking parchment, if using.

Put the whites into a large bowl and whisk with a hand balloon whisk, an electric whisk or the whisk part of a food processor. Start off gently, then whisk more vigorously at the end. When the whites have become stiff and form peaks when you pull the whisk out, add the sugar, a spoonful at a time, whisking between each addition. The aim is to get as much air into the mixture as possible, so it becomes glossy and stiff. Whisk in the tartaric acid, if using (this isn't essential but adds some acidity to the meringue, which makes it fluff out more).

Spoon out the mixture with a dessertspoon onto the baking sheet. Make individual dollops for separate meringues, or a flattened base of about 3.5 cm and cook for 30 minutes. Turn the oven off and leave them to dry out in the residual heat of the oven for at least 4 hours. The outside should be crisp and the inside soft and gooey. Store the meringues in an airtight container or freeze them.

MOUSSES

The basic use of a mousse is to add lightness and bubbles to a sauce, so you can make a mousse of any thick sauce, savoury or sweet. Think of fish mousse on one side and chocolate mousse on the other. If you cool down the basic mousse, it will slightly set to a light, elegant texture. The introduction of a whisked egg white is the central platform to a successful mousse. Here is a classic chocolate mousse. You need a strong, real chocolate base so that it is intense and aromatic, rather than the more creamy and insipid commercial versions.

CLASSIC FRENCH CHOCOLATE MOUSSE

- 4 eggs, separated
- 100 g caster sugar, plus 1 tbsp
- 2 tbsp orange liqueur, such as Grand Marnier or Cointreau
- 150 g plain chocolate (at least 60% cocoa solids), such as Valrhona, Lindt, Green and Blacks, chopped
- 3 tbsp strong coffee
- 150 g unsalted butter, softened
- pinch of salt
- unsweetened cocoa powder, sifted to decorate

First, make the basic sauce or custard, by beating the egg yolks and the 100 g sugar together in a ceramic or heatproof bowl until it thickens and turns a pale yellow, then beat in the orange liqueur. Place the bowl over a pan of simmering water, making sure the base of the bowl doesn't touch the water. Keep whisking the custard so that it warms up and starts to thicken, then stop and beat for a few minutes over cold water until it reaches the consistency of mayonnaise.

Melt the chocolate in another heatproof bowl set over a pan of simmering water, making sure the base of the bowl doesn't touch the water. Add the coffee and stir together. Remove from the heat and beat in the butter, then leave to cool slightly.

Beat the cooled chocolate mixture into the egg yolk custard, a little at a time.

Whisk the egg whites with the salt until they form soft peaks, then add the remaining 1 tbsp sugar, a little at a time, whisking in between until the mixture stiffens to glossy peaks. Stir the egg white mixture into the chocolate mixture, a spoonful at a time, carefully folding it as gently as possible, so not to destroy the bubbles of air. Spoon carefully into a dish or preferably into individual, single ramekins or small glasses and keep them in the fridge until ready to serve. Decorate with sifted cocoa powder.

IF THINGS GO WRONG

OVERCOOKED

Overcooking is not only a problem, but also irredeemable. In adventurous hands you may change it into another dish, disguising it by chopping it into pieces or mincing it and mixing it with something else, but really, it is bad news. 'You can only learn by your mistakes' is the only consoling, if frustrating, advice, so keep prodding and tasting all the way through a recipe, so you don't get caught out.

TOO SALTY

If something is too salty then you either have to make more of the same and bulk it out, or you can disguise it by adding more ingredients. Some ingredients may make salty food more mellow, such as cream, crème fraîche, plain yogurt or fromage frais. You could make it more pungent by adding something hot like chillies, or more acidic like lemon juice, wine vinegar or wine. Your choice will depend on the basic recipe. Sugar may also help – think about Thai food with the sour, sweet, salty and hot formula, and you may be able to confuse the salt taste buds with all the extra flavours. It depends on what you're cooking, of course: some dishes may just not be salvageable in this way.

BURNED

If food is burned in parts, then you have to cut bits out, or if thoroughly burned then you may have to throw it away and start again. Sometimes the burned taste permeates through the rest of the dish, so you have to be careful and taste around the burned bit just to ensure that the taste hasn't corrupted the whole dish. Any very strong sauce, such as a hot chilli sauce might mask the taste a little, but you'll have to try for yourself. If in doubt, throw it out.

TASTELESS

Too mellow, just not enough taste. You could concentrate the sauce by boiling it down but remember not to overcook the core of the dish. If, for instance, you are cooking meat in a sauce, and the meat is cooked but the sauce is too watery, it's best to remove the meat and put it to one side, keeping it warm while you tackle the sauce. You could also consider adding more acidity with lemon juice, lime juice, vinegar or wine, more salt perhaps or soy sauce or fish sauce, more herbs, or tomato purée, if appropriate. The thing is to taste and see what works for you.

THIN

Savoury sauce not thick enough? Whisk in a little beurre manié, as long as flour will not ruin it. This was a common way of thickening up a sauce, when flour-based sauces were more often used, but it is not common now because the floury taste is deemed rather unsophisticated. Beurre manié is a mixture of equal quantities of butter and flour rubbed together with your fingers to form a soft paste. For most sauces you will just need to add a small ball, added in one blob to the hot sauce and then whisk like mad. Even easier is to add cornflour to thicken a sauce. The cornflour needs mixing with a cold liquid like water or milk, depending on the flavours in your recipe before adding to the sauce. Try mixing 1 dsp of cornflour in a cup with a little liquid until it is a thinnish, pourable paste. Pour it all at once into the hot sauce and whisk to avoid lumps, heating it up as it thickens. Add more if it's still too thin. If your sauce is too pure to add flour, then you will have to reduce the sauce by evaporating off the water by boiling it down. The sauce will still remain thinnish, but it will acquire extra taste and a syrupy quality, as it reduces.

WON'T SET

Generally, dishes that don't set are often the imbalance of liquid to setting agent. You probably need some more gelatine or egg yolks. If it's a gelatine-based recipe, try to read on the pack how much more you'll need. It's tricky. You'll just have to try assessing the amount of liquid you have and then calculate how many leaves of gelatine you need to add. First hint is don't use powdered gelatine; always use leaf gelatine.

If you're using egg yolks to set the dish, then stir the main dish, such as custard, into the new egg yolks, a little at a time. Heat the dish through to cook it very slowly over a low heat, as in the main recipe, and allow the yolks to do their work and thicken the sauce.

If the dish is to be served cold, then you may hasten the setting process by putting the dish into a fridge or even the freezer; just don't allow it to freeze.

Always remember that if you're cooking for someone else, unless you announce your mistakes they are unlikely to know exactly what was intended. Just call it something else. Luckily I once got the whole clove of garlic on my plate, in with the fresh pineapple, rather than my guests. My kitchen was very small, so small in fact that when I heated up the hob, the kitchen sink bowl would also heat up.

FOOD PAST ITS SELL-BY DATE

Unlike the culinary end of our ever vigilant, health and safety dominated society, I believe there are plenty of foods past their sell-by dates, which are still viable, and as I always say, I haven't poisoned us yet. I did accidentally poison the dog once, but she lived to tell (if she could) the tale. I don't advocate eating less than fresh food, but sometimes this is all you have. It's better to eat and use what you have, rather than throw it away. Bin scavengers, people, usually youthful and/or impoverished, who raid the supermarket skips for the food thrown out at the end of each day, are living and walking proof that you can live on older food. This efficient way of dealing with food waste has now been outlawed in the name of public vigilance – or stupidity, some might say. Wash it if you can, then smell it and if that's fine try it. Taste a little (unless it needs cooking) and if it appears OK, then use it.

Eggs: Old eggs, as long as they haven't gone off, are particularly good for hard-boiling because they are easier to shell. Otherwise, crack or open them one at a time, so you can isolate the bad one in a cup, adding them separately before you ruin the whole meal.

Bread: Any bread that should be crisp on the outside is easy to revive. As long as it isn't rock hard, then give it this treatment. Wet it on the outside, either by stroking it with water or running it under the tap. Put it into a hot oven until the outside is crisp again and the inside has been softened by the remaining water. This is good with baguettes and ficelles, but even works on sourdough or croissants.

Meat: If it smells off, then don't risk it. I have a very keen sense of smell, so sometimes, when it is just on the cusp I will wash it with cold water and smell it again. You may just be able to catch it in time. Enhance the flavour by cooking it with a sauce or liquid so that it doesn't veer towards the dry and uncertain.

Vegetables: Any vegetable which can be roasted, although shrivelled and limp, can still be used. Tomatoes, onions, peppers, leeks and carrots are all still usable when past their prime. They can always be added to soups to good effect as well.

Anything with a tendency to go mouldy: I know this is heresy to many, and they will throw their hands up in horror, but it is still possible to revive even the most mould-inducing food. Food such as jams, chutneys, yogurt and cream have a thick protective layer of pre-mould on the surface. If you remove this without affecting the food underneath, by taking off a thick layer, then the food underneath can often be salvaged. Again, be scrupulous in taking a big chunk out, smell it and clean up what's left, running round the pot with a clean J-cloth or a piece of kitchen paper. Smell again and use only when you're happy.

Fish: If it's more than a day old then don't risk it. I once had something called Lake Fishes in Hotel Flora on Lake Garda, left by the owners to be run in their absence by two callow youths. They insisted that I didn't know what I was talking about when I sent it back and two minutes later back it came from the kitchen. They tried to tell me that I didn't know what smoked salmon should taste like! Josh Niland in his book *The Whole Fish Cookbook* endorses the theory that only wet fish smell, so he advocates drying fish when you buy them, and keeping them dry. Much of his book requires vast commercial drying sheds for hanging, smoking and treating fish, but you can adapt the theory to the domestic kitchen if you are feeling adventurous.

Any liquids: If they can be boiled, then boil them up regularly for at least a few minutes and this should kill most dangerous bacteria. Stock and soups should be boiled every other day if kept out of the fridge, or every third or fourth day if they are kept in the fridge. These freeze well.

Anything that looks past its prime: Some foods, particularly those with a high sugar content such as chocolate, take on a bloom or harden with age. They are not 'off' in the conventional sense, but lose their textural appeal and need eating up quickly.

Oils and butter: These can be tasted and smelt. They easily go rancid. If rancid, then throw the oils away because the whole lot is contaminated. With butter, you can cut off the outer, darker yellow bit all round then try the inside, which may be still OK.

Leftover food: Keep leftovers in the fridge, covering with a plate or clingfilm as they may make the rest of the fridge smell or dry up. Heat in a microwave and pierce the clingfilm to stop splattering. You may need to sprinkle a little water over the food to re-moisten it, but microwaving will deposit the water in the food in droplets on the underside of a plate or clingfilm. Don't overcook it, but by the same token ensure that it is very hot all the way through. You may need to rehydrate the food by letting it rest in a bowl with some added water until it softens again.

Herbs and spices: It can be a false economy to buy these in large quantities. Spices in particular are best bought and used quickly and preferably freshly ground in a coffee grinder, spice grinder or pestle and mortar. They quickly go off, not enough to kill you, but they lose their potency.

HOW TO KNOW WHEN IT'S DONE

Numerous cookbooks will proffer advice with precise temperatures, but few will give the off-the-cuff advice amateurs need to know.

MEAT

Manual ways (page 52 for Gordon Ramsay's method using parts of the face and for the lips method)

Meat thermometers (page 33)

Length of cooking time (page 51)

FISH

General advice (page 52)

POULTRY

Chicken (page 52-53)

Duck (page 52)

Others, such as teal (page 52)

PART 2

THE
RECIPES

STARTERS AND SIDES

These recipes are suitable to start a meal, if you're intending a traditional three-plus course meal. Or, you might put many together for a buffet, or a party or an informal dinner, to be served on platters rather like a mezze. For some, you just need judicial shopping and assembling; others need a bit more attention.

CRISPY SQUID

OFTEN CALLED SALT AND PEPPER SQUID FOR OBVIOUS REASONS

The main thing to remember about squid and its fellow, octopus, is that squid is smaller and more tender and therefore needs little cooking – octopus is more robust, and so will have many ways, including beating the hell out of it (a favourite of Mediterranean fishermen), to render it edible, usually cooking it like a stew, for a couple of hours.

FOR 1 SQUID

Twist off the tentacles with the head, pulling out the innards. Cut out the hard 'eye', but keep the tentacles. Remove the transparent 'spine' from inside and cut off the side flaps together with any skin you can with a small knife, including the skin on the tentacles.

Wash and thoroughly dry the resulting tube. You have two options – either cut the tube into rings or cut down the side so you can lay it out flat. If it's flat, then slash it on the inside in a criss-cross, diagonal pattern with a sharp knife or even a Stanley knife, with cuts about 8 mm apart. Dry it, or the rings, again to ensure it/they will crisp up. Cut the tentacles into roughly three pieces. Sprinkle all with salt and pepper.

Lay on a very, very hot griddle pan, or a barbecue or even a hot frying pan, if that's all you've got. It will quickly cook and blacken and curl up.

Crispy squid

Cut the torso into strips.

Serve quickly with a slice of lemon and any sauce you rate. It can be added to a salad, or served with beans, or expanded into something more elaborate.

You can make an extra-crispy coating by laying the squid, just before cooking, into a bowl of flour, salt and pepper and cook it in a fairly deep layer of hot cooking oil until golden.

MACKEREL PÂTÉ

Simple, quick, cheap and stunning taste with the oiliness of the mackerel offset by the sharpness of the apple. No washing up needed.

FOR 6 OR 8

- 2 or 3 smoked mackerel fillets in a pack, pre-cooked

- 1 large Bramley apple or 2 smaller apples of any type but better with a 'cooker'

- ½ red onion finely chopped

- 1 tbsp crème fraîche

- 1 flat tbsp green peppercorns – if you have them

- 1 tbsp roughly chopped dill – nice to see the fronds, actually

- juice of 1 lemon

- salt and pepper to taste – mackerel can be a bit salty, so watch out

Put the fish on a board, skin-side down. Remove the skin: put the fish skin-side down and hold onto the tail end. Make a small incision downwards, close to the tail fins, with a sharp knife, carefully, onto the skin but not through it. Turn the knife parallel to the board and slide the knife under the flesh, onto the skin, holding the tail and pull. Slice the mackerel, cutting into small strips and then chop up roughly, depending on the texture you like - it quickly falls apart.

Peel and grate the apple, if you can bear it; otherwise finely chop to avoid adding knuckles to the mix. Add all the other ingredients and stir around.

Serve with good biscuits or nice bread or toast.

I like the variety of texture in the pâté, rather than the overworked, over-smooth sort you get with a food mixer or buy in the supermarket.

Mackerel pâté

FLATBREADS

So simple and you can keep a batch in the fridge for a few days, wrapped in clingfilm. Use as an accompaniment for just about anything, and nothing beats these freshly cooked straight from the pan.

- 450 g flour
- 70 g yeast
- 350 ml water

Mix together, following the individual directions for the particular yeast you are using. Knead or use the dough hook in the mixer for 10 minutes.

Leave to rise in a warm place, in a bowl with a tea towel over it, for an hour.

Take a large golf ball-size piece of dough and roll out flat, in a roughly circular shape, until about 3 or 4 mm thick.

Pop it into a hot pan smeared with a bit of olive oil. Lift off with a fish slice when it looks as if it's starting to colour and turn over to do the other side.

Yummy yum yum.

BAGNA CÀUDA

An Italian take on crudités: a selection of crunchy vegetables which you dip into a strong garlic mayonnaise, as an appetizer or communal starter.

- Any crisp and fresh vegetables which are dippable, such as little gem or romano lettuce, cauliflower, carrot, peppers, endives, radishes, red pepper, celery etc
- jar of real mayonnaise (or as real you can buy) or preferably make your own (see page 86) without too much salt – see below
- 1 clove of garlic, mashed and bashed into a purée
- 5–10 mashed anchovies (fewer if the mayonnaise is already salty, or you can buy anchovy purée, if you can find it)

- add a little lemon juice if you think it needs it
- it probably won't need any salt, because of the anchovies, but you will need some fresh ground black pepper

Assemble all the mayonnaise ingredients above in a central bowl on a platter and surround it with a selection of chopped vegetables.

SOUTH EAST ASIAN CRAB SOUP

This is another version of my Thai soup (recipe later) but adapted for larger overall quantities to be served in small bowls, for more people, as a starter to a larger meal. This one I served on New Year's Eve for 12 people, but you can adapt it as necessary. Each person should get at least one of the pieces of each vegetable, plus a small tower of crab, in the lovely aromatic broth.

FOR 12 SMALL PORTIONS

- large saucepan of boiling water – about 2–3 litres
- flat dsp each of crumbled dry curry leaves, lime leaves and bay leaves
- 1 tbsp pomegranate seeds
- 10 cardamom seed pods
- 10 peppercorns
- 10 sloshes of fish sauce
- 6 juiced limes
- 2 tbsp sugar
- 2 de-seeded finely sliced chillies (add more if you want it really hot)
- 50 mm x 25 mm x 25 mm peeled ginger chopped carefully into matchsticks
- 1–2 asparagus heads for each person, say 15 for 12 people
- 2 large carrots cut carefully into matchsticks
- 8–10 spring onions cut into 10 mm pieces
- 12 mangetout or sugar snap peas
- 12 very small slices of red pepper
- 3 thinly sliced garlic cloves
- 2 mugfuls of fresh crab meat
- fresh chives and coriander for decoration

Cut up all the ingredients in advance if you want, or leave it to when the base is boiling down, if you're confident.

Boil all the first ingredients, except the veg and crab, for 15–20 minutes, or longer if more convenient – it won't spoil. It will turn into an aromatic base for your soup, the pomegranate seeds making it turn red and giving it a delightful astringency. Strain and taste and adjust the seasoning, adding more fish sauce, or lime juice or sugar to taste.

Boil the asparagus in the soup base for about 2 minutes. Then add the carrots, garlic, chillies, ginger and red pepper for another 2 minutes. Lastly, add the spring onions for a half a minute. Serve in small bowls. Add a small dessertspoonful of crab into the centre of each bowl and decorate with chives and coriander.

South East Asian crab soup

CRISPY INDIAN FRIED VEGETABLES

Assorted vegetables cut up, dipped in a spicy batter and deep-fried until crisp. Any amount of different vegetables can be done, served in a big communal platter or individually. This is a lovely easy way of presenting vegetables to people who may not otherwise like them, such as children and picky people. I gleaned this recipe from the family I stayed with in India at a Homestay B and B called Glenora in northern Kerala. As a coffee estate, we were surprised to be served in bed a morning Nescafé, in lovely china cups.

Cauliflower, broccoli, onions, carrots are all easy, but you can substitute what you like. Some, like potatoes for instance, may need a little more pre-cooking time.

FOR A VERY LARGE COMMUNAL BOWL FOR ABOUT 8 PEOPLE

- cauliflower and broccoli cut up into individual florets to make 2 tbsp each veg

- carrots peeled and chopped into thin (say 5 mm thick) slices say 2 or 3 large carrots

- fresh curry leaves (if you can get them) or otherwise a little chopped parsley or coriander for decoration

BATTER

- 1½ tbsp gram flour but I used self-raising quite easily, with a little extra to coat the veg prior to cooking

- 5 tsp semolina

- ½ tsp chilli powder

- pinch turmeric

- ½ tsp salt

- 1 dsp tomato ketchup

- 1 cup water

Boil the veg until nearly tender and drain. Meanwhile, mix all the batter ingredients together.

Dry the veg as best you can and roll in a little flour. Drop the veg into the batter and coat.

Heat some oil, such as groundnut or sunflower, in a frying pan, about 5 or 10 mm high. Lift the veg with your fingers and drop into the hot oil, making sure you don't crowd the pan. Leave for about 30 seconds before you try to turn them over so that they begin to brown and crisp up. Turn over, so they are brown all over. Take out with a slotted spoon to drain off as much of the oil as possible. Put on a plate covered with kitchen paper. Keep warm and do another batch, or serve in batches. Transfer to a hot platter to increase their visual appeal. Mix in something green with them to make them more attractive and serve immediately.

ACHAR – PICKLED ASIAN VEGETABLES

Achar, or pickled Asian vegetables, is a sort of fermented salad from Malaysia and Singapore – hot, crunchy, sweet and tasty. The vinegar is heated to sterilise the veg.

FOR A LARGE JAR OR BOTTLE

- 3 peeled and cubed large carrots

- 1 large onion, chopped very finely

- 1 unpeeled cucumber cut into bite-sized chunks

- small handful of fine green beans, topped, tailed and halved

- ½ white cabbage cut into chunks, removing any stalks or tough bits

- 2 sliced red chillies

- 1 small cauliflower sliced into small, very thin florets

- 3 cloves garlic, crushed

- 1 large handful of peanuts

- 1–2 tbsp groundnut oil

- 1 dsp ground turmeric

- 1 tbsp sugar

- 1 flat dsp salt

- 1 mugful white wine vinegar or cider vinegar

- 1 thin slice of blachan or trasi, if you can hack it* – rotted shrimp paste is not for the faint-hearted – pounded or chopped into a paste. You can never detect it once it's cooked, though

Sterilise the glass jars and bottles you want to use by washing in warm soapy water, drying them and then putting them in a hot oven for 15 mins.

Dunk the carrots, cabbage, green beans and cauliflower into a pan of boiling water to parboil and remove after 1 minute, cooling under a running tap and dry on kitchen paper.

Gently fry the turmeric, garlic, onion and chillies for a minute or so, in some of the oil, turning them over in the pan. Add the blachan and stir around for a further minute, adding more oil if necessary. Add the vinegar, salt and sugar, turning up the heat to boil the contents.

Fry the peanuts in a separate pan. Cool and roughly chop and add them to the pan together with all the blanched vegetables. Put into a large jar and serve them with any dish, like a condiment or pickle. Try and get the veg to be covered by the liquid – this depends on the container you use, so try to get a tall container rather than a flat container. Our traditional Kilner jars are the right shape.

*You can buy blachan from Asian food shops or supermarkets in various forms, and now even our own large supermarkets will sell it. Very pungent. Keep it wrapped up in foil or clingfilm and put it in a plastic tub and it will keep in the fridge.

BEETROOT DIP

– SOUNDS A BIT BORING LIKE THIS BUT IS DELICIOUS
IN ITS SIMPLICITY AND ZINGY COLOURS

This is basically chopped up and partially puréed beetroot, enhanced with garlic and cream and given a whizzy texture with walnuts. Something like this is very popular in Iran, I understand, where it's called Borani.

ENOUGH FOR A LARGE PLATTER OR DISH TO SERVE MANY PEOPLE

- 4 or 5 cooked and peeled beetroots (careful not to buy the beetroot in vinegar or sweetener), chopped roughly

- 1 clove of garlic, squeezed into a purée and mashed further with a little salt

- ½ red onion, finely chopped

- juice and zest of a lemon

- 2 large tbsp of plain yogurt or crème fraîche

- 2 handfuls of walnuts toasted and chopped roughly

- a few big sloshes of balsamic vinegar, or, better still, pomegranate molasses

- salt and pepper and if you like, add a small handful of green peppercorns

- 1 dsp of chopped dill leaving a few fronds for the top

Chop up the beetroot roughly and beat to a purée with a stick blender, or jar blender leaving a few bigger chunks to give a bit of texture.

Crush the garlic and combine with the salt using a spoon to make a fine purée/sauce.

Toast the walnuts and chop up finely, leaving a bit of it bigger for texture.

Mix all the ingredients together apart from the dill fronds for the top.

Taste and adjust the seasoning. Add more vinegar or pomegranate to taste. Add more yogurt or crème fraîche if it appears too strong for you.

Serve in a low, flat platter or dish and sprinkle the dill fronds on top.

Beetroot dip

SALADS AND DRESSINGS

Salads now cover a multitude of variations, and I have put together an assortment, usually based on salad greens, with raw or cooked vegetables, with added ingredients such as bacon, which you can avoid if you are vegetarian. The main attention is drawn on how you dress the salads, as shown in the following pages.

Salads without dressing is life without food for me – you might as well not bother. I would rather starve than eat what the British sometimes (perhaps not so much these days, in the times of foreign travel and more adventurous food exploration) proffer as a salad.

There are, firstly, far too many disparate ingredients – what are grated carrots, tomatoes, coleslaw and cucumber doing mixed up with lettuce? Keep it simple. Make sure that the ingredients go together, and don't just make the whole design confusing and wet.

Generally all the green things go together – lettuce (of varying varieties and types) will go with asparagus, avocado, fresh shelled uncooked garden peas, sugar snap peas and French beans (briefly cooked if necessary). Think of a traditional French green salad. Add to this basic green salad a few more ingredients and it becomes a lovely main course, which probably only needs some good-quality, fresh bread with it, like a proper baguette.

SALAD DRESSING OR VINAIGRETTE

A salad dressing or vinaigrette is a mixture of oil and vinegar (or lemon juice), salt and pepper for dressing salads, so that the acidic part is held in a suspension of emulsified oil. There are some ghastly shop-made dressings now, mainly from the US, with a long list of chemicals and additives, usually with too much salt and sugar in them. Don't buy them.

Apart from the actual dressing, the most important thing to remember is to ensure that every bit of the salad is dry. I find that unless the leaves are dirty all the way through and it's local and has just been raining, it's better not to even wet the leaves, but to flick or rub off any dirt with kitchen paper or a damp J-cloth. Often, the supermarket leaves don't need any washing, since they've been washed in chlorine, for some reason, presumably to extend shelf life, so although we're being gently poisoned, we are saving time. What I don't understand is how I can smell and taste the chlorine in the drinking water at 20 metres, whereas I've never been able to detect the chlorine in bags of shop-bought salad leaves. This promotes a habit I have, of leaving glasses or jugs of water open to the elements, sometimes inside a cupboard, for at least a day, much to the consternation of people who don't know me. This is effective for allowing the chlorine to dissipate off, leaving the water much more acceptable to taste.

If you must wash a lettuce, you can often confine it to the base of the leaves, where it may be muddy, then dry it in a clean tea towel, wrapped up and shaken, or in kitchen paper. The leaves at the top of the plant are less crimpled, so the water is easier to get off. Often, if you remove the outer leaves, which are usually more bashed about and dirty, it reveals a clean and unsullied centre which doesn't need any washing. Don't bother with other gadgets, such as a salad spinner; it's just another impractical gimmick you'll have to wash up. If there is any chance of insecticides having been used, then I suppose you might have to wash the veg.

A VERY BASIC BUT DELICIOUS VINAIGRETTE

Vinaigrettes or salad dressings are generally made with a mixture of oil and something acidic, like vinegar or lemon juice, plus salt and pepper. If you mix them up together, the acid breaks down the oil into smaller particles – emulsifies it, in fact – so that the result is creamy and tasty, lingering over the surface of the greenery of the salads, adding both piquancy and texture to the whole.

You can use any variety of good oils; I plump for the best quality olive oil you can afford, or try a nut oil for a change – hazelnut and walnut are interesting, peanut is almost tasteless and so is best for cooking and rapeseed, which is all the rage at the moment, doesn't have much of a taste either.

Wine vinegars are made from red wine or white wine, the red being slightly softer, which makes a darker dressing, so you might need to watch the colour of the basic salad. There are all sorts of different flavoured vinegars too. For a change, try something like sherry vinegar, balsamic vinegar or cider vinegar. They each have their own characteristic flavour. There used to be a penchant for raspberry vinegar, but through overuse this seems to be rarely made these days.

I remember when I was first taken out to eat in an Italian restaurant (in the era of Chianti bottles in raffia and red and white-checked tablecloths), the waiter would come and mix the oil and vinegar in a large tablespoon, at the table, and present it theatrically to us for our salad. It was the first time I had ever seen anyone making a dressing and found it powerfully exotic. My mother, at the time, tried to pass off a mixture of malt vinegar and sugar, for heaven's sake, as a palliative for limp salads.

- For a basic vinaigrette, mix olive oil and wine vinegar or lemon juice in the proportions of 4:1 or possibly 3:1

- salt and ground black pepper

Place all the ingredients in a large bowl you're putting the rest of the salad in, or, if you're unsure as to the quantity you'll need, place in a screw-topped jar and stir or shake vigorously until emulsified. Taste and adjust the seasoning. You may like it slightly more acidic or more oily, but this depends on taste, the quality of the oil and the softness of the vinegar or lemon juice used.

GOOD, EVERYDAY DRESSING

- 1 garlic clove, crushed
- salt and ground black pepper
- about 1 tbsp white wine vinegar
- 4–6 tbsp olive oil
- salad leaves

Place the garlic in a salad bowl with a few generous pinches of salt and mash with the back of a spoon to a soft paste. Add the vinegar and stir around in the garlic until it is mixed together and the salt has dissolved. Add black pepper and the oil and stir together vigorously. Taste and adjust the seasoning, if needed. Add the salad leaves and toss in the dressing just before serving. To make this salad more substantial, you can add various vegetables, such as thinly sliced roasted red peppers, avocado, fine green beans or hard-boiled eggs to each serving plate.

CLASSIC FRENCH DRESSING

Restaurants will often add a spoonful of boiling water to this dressing at the end to help keep the oil in suspension, so it will last a whole service.

- 1 tsp French mustard
- 1 dsp wine vinegar
- salt and ground black pepper
- 3 or 4 dsp olive oil

Place the mustard in a salad bowl or screw-topped jar. Add the vinegar and a little salt and pepper and mix vigorously with olive oil until it has emulsified. Taste and adjust the seasoning, if needed.

VINAIGRETTE À LA CRÈME

This is a sort of cross between a vinaigrette and a mayonnaise, which may not be too creamy if you use some crème fraîche or yogurt or a mixture. Use in salads, particularly mixed salads, or over fish, eggs or vegetables.

- 1 medium egg yolk
- 1 tbsp cream, crème fraîche, soured cream, fromage frais or yogurt
- 1 mug of Basic Vinaigrette (page 111)
- 2 tbsp freshly chopped herbs, such as parsley, tarragon, chives and dill
- salt and ground black pepper

Beat the egg yolk and cream of your choice together in a bowl. Beat in the vinaigrette, a little at a time, drop by drop at first (use a teaspoon if you're unconfident) so that it doesn't curdle. Add the herbs and mix in, then taste and adjust the seasoning.

THICK MUSTARD DRESSING

A soft and unctuous dressing which is particularly good over vegetables, such as broccoli and beans; you can use French mustard which is mild, so this dressing is particularly good for children who won't eat vegetables. This I know is sacrilege in France, but I sometimes like to add a pinch or two of sugar (in contrast with what I've said before) with this particular dressing, but you can make your own mind up.

- 1 garlic clove, crushed (if you want)
- salt and ground black pepper
- 1 dsp white wine vinegar
- 3 large tsp French mustard, such as Dijon or Meaux
- 2–4 tbsp olive oil

Place the garlic in a small bowl with a few generous pinches of salt and mash with the back of a spoon to a soft paste. Add the vinegar and stir, then add the mustard and stir around. Gradually add the oil, a little at a time, until it is emulsified with the vinegar and mustard. Season with a little pepper and taste and adjust the seasoning, if needed.

SAUCE VIERGE

A great amplified vinaigrette to accompany plain-cooked food such as grilled fish or meat.

- 2 large ripe tomatoes
- 1 tsp red wine vinegar or more to taste
- 1–2 tbsp olive oil
- 1 garlic clove, thinly sliced
- 1 tbsp finely chopped onion, preferably shallot or red onion
- juice of ½ lemon
- 1 tbsp finely chopped basil
- 1 tbsp finely chopped parsley
- salt and ground black pepper

To peel the tomatoes, make little cuts around the top of each tomato and place in a bowl of boiling water for a few minutes, then drain and peel off the skins. Cut in half, de-seed with a spoon and cut the flesh into small cubes. Put to one side. This sounds a bit of a fuss but it makes a neater end product.

Place the vinegar and oil in a bowl and mix together, then add the remaining ingredients, including the tomatoes, and stir to combine. Taste and adjust the seasoning.

SALSA VERDE

Use this bright green, zingy sauce to lighten up fish, meat or vegetables.

- 1 small bunch each of parsley, basil and mint, finely chopped
- 1 dsp capers, washed, gently squeezed out to remove water and chopped
- 1 dsp finely chopped gherkins or cornichons
- 1 anchovy fillet, chopped
- 1 garlic clove, crushed
- 2 tbsp olive oil
- finely grated zest and juice of 1½ lemons
- salt and ground black pepper

Mix all the ingredients, except the lemon zest and juice, together in a bowl. Just before serving, add the lemon zest and juice. Taste and adjust the seasoning. You may not need any salt as the anchovies can be salty.

GREMOLATA

A simple, basic (but delicious) Italian accompaniment for all sorts of dishes – serve it on top of meat, fish or pasta, or as a side. It tastes a bit like a pesto.

- a small handful of fresh parsley
- 1 garlic clove
- finely grated zest and juice of 1 lemon
- salt and ground black pepper
- olive oil

Roughly chop the parsley and garlic by hand or whiz in a small food processor with the lemon zest and juice. Season with salt and pepper and add a little oil to make into a more unctuous, flowing sauce.

ZHOUG

Another take on a green zingy sauce, this time dominated by coriander and used all over the Middle East. Either stir it into sauces or dribble over the top of food.

- a small handful of fresh coriander, chopped
- 2 garlic cloves, crushed
- 3 mildish chillies, such as jalapeños, chopped
- juice of 2 lemons
- ½ tsp ground cardamom
- 1 tsp ground cumin

- ½ tsp salt
- a few chilli flakes if you like it hot (optional)
- a few sploshes of olive oil

Mix all the ingredients together in a bowl. Taste and adjust the seasoning. Serve.

CHIMICHURRI

This is a South American take on the green sauce like Zhoug and Gremolata above. Argentinians and Uruguayans love this sauce over a steak, particularly barbecued meat. Parsley is most favoured as the green herb base, but you can add coriander as well.

- a small handful of fresh parsley
- 2–3 garlic cloves
- ½ small red onion
- 1 mild red chilli
- a few sploshes of red wine vinegar
- ½ tsp salt
- a few sploshes of olive oil

Chop the parsley, garlic, onion and chilli, then place in a bowl and add the remaining ingredients. Stir until combined. Alternatively, blitz in a food processor.

SALADE NIÇOISE

Use crisp lettuce which will take a dressing, such as Little Gem or frisée if you can find it, or some mixed leaves or rocket – try not to wash them, since they rarely need it and it's a devil to get rid of the water afterwards. However, if they're full of dirt, then you might have to. Wipe dry with kitchen paper or clean tea towels. Avoid using iceberg lettuce if possible – it's tasteless and generally used in poor restaurants because it stays crisp. Romaine, Cos, lamb's lettuce and rocket are fine to use.

SERVES: 4

- a handful of very small new potatoes, scrubbed
- a handful of French beans, cooked
- 1 medium egg per person
- lettuce or salad leaves
- choice of dressing, such as a thick garlicky one
- 1 medium can tuna in oil, not brine, or 1 small, undercooked piece fresh tuna, flaked and perhaps mixed with mayonnaise and more lemon juice
- 1 dsp soft, black pitted olives, halved
- a few anchovy fillets, either kept whole or sliced
- salt and ground black pepper

Bring a pan of water to the boil, then add the potatoes, reduce the heat to a simmer and cook until soft. Drain and cut in half. Put to one side.

Cook the beans either in a pan of boiling water until just beginning to soften, or place in a bowl, splash on a bit of water, cover with clingfilm and cook in the microwave on high for 3 minutes or until just cooked. Dry and put to one side.

Cook the eggs in a pan of simmering water for 6 minutes, then remove with a slotted spoon and place in a bowl of cold water. Leave until cool enough to handle, then peel off the shells. Put to one side.

Place the lettuce or salad leaves in a large bowl and toss with your choice of dressing. Place the tuna in the middle with a few halved olives. Arrange the potatoes around the tuna, then add the green beans in bundles across the potatoes, with the halved eggs on each side. Add the anchovies. You can add some of the dressing to the potatoes and beans, if you like, then season with salt and pepper and serve.

CAESAR'S SALAD

Here I don't mean any of the commercial or supermarket renderings we often see; such a far cry from the original. I must credit Rick Stein in his BBC show *The Road to Mexico* for the main thrust of this dish, as he at least visited the original Caesar's Restaurant in Tijuana to glean how they did it.

SERVES: 4

- 1 garlic clove, crushed
- salt and ground black pepper
- 2–3 anchovy fillets, mashed into a rough paste
- juice of 1 lemon
- 1 tsp French mustard
- 1 medium egg yolk
- 2 tbsp olive oil
- 2 tbsp less flavourful vegetable oil, such as rapeseed
- nearly 1 whole small Baby Gem lettuce, cut into large pieces
- a handful of shop-bought croûtons
- 2 large handfuls of grated Parmesan cheese

Place the garlic in a large bowl with ½ tsp salt and mash with the back of a spoon to a soft paste. Add the mashed anchovies, then pour in the lemon juice and leave to stand for a few minutes.

Stir in the mustard, then add the egg yolk and season with pepper. While stirring, gradually add the oil, a drop at a time, until it starts to thicken. Once it thickens, add the oil in a steady stream until it is the consistency of mayonnaise. Unless you don't want to use it immediately you can pour the sauce into a screw-topped jar. It can be stored in the fridge for a few days.

Add 3 tbsp of the sauce to a large serving bowl, then add the lettuce and stir until coated. Stir in the croûtons, then sprinkle over the Parmesan to serve.

ROCKET AND NECTARINE SALAD

This colourful, leafy salad includes nectarines and an orange-based dressing. Make sure the nectarines or peaches are ripe and juicy. Adjust the amount of salad leaves and dressing to the amount of people you are serving.

SERVES: 4

- 2–3 ripe nectarines, oranges or peaches
- 1 bag of rocket, spinach and watercress

FOR THE DRESSING

- finely grated zest and juice of 1 orange juice or ½ lemon
- 1 tbsp olive oil
- salt and ground black pepper

Mix the dressing ingredients together in a salad bowl. Taste and adjust the seasoning, if needed.

Cut the fruit up into segments, peeling as necessary, and add to the bowl with the salad leaves. When ready to serve, toss together until coated in the dressing.

CHICKPEA AND PANCETTA SALAD

This is a lovely combination of chickpeas, chillies and pancetta. Use a combination of green or red chillies or substitute with the small, spicy 'Peppadew' peppers you find in a jar, if you like. As this is a cold salad, it might need more flavourings and seasoning, so taste and add if needed.

MAKES: A LARGE SALAD FOR 8
AS A SIDE DISH

- 10–12 piquillo chillies or smaller medium-hot chillies
- 2 tbsp chopped sliced pancetta
- 2 × 400 g cans chickpeas, drained and rinsed
- 2 garlic cloves, crushed
- salt and ground black pepper
- juice of 3 lemons
- olive oil, to taste
- 3 tbsp freshly chopped parsley

Preheat the grill, then grill the chillies until they are blackened and blistered. Cut in half, scrape out the seeds and chop into smaller pieces if they're hot. Put to one side.

Cook the pancetta in a dry frying pan over a high heat for a minute or so until brown and crisped up. Remove from the heat and put to one side.

Place the chickpeas in a large serving bowl.

Mash the garlic in a bowl or a pestle and mortar, then add 1½ tsp salt and the lemon juice and pound together to a paste. Add to the chickpeas with the remaining ingredients, including the chillies and pancetta, and stir until mixed together. Taste and adjust the seasoning, if needed.

BORLOTTI BEAN SALAD

I happened on these beans in long, dry, shrivelled pods – fresh but dry – obscuring their carmine-and-white-sploshed interior, in the Goods Shed, a permanent indoor farmers' market in Canterbury. I would have passed them by without their sign, not recognising what they were, but knowing borlotti to be Italy's best loved bean, I bought them and found their almost chestnut sweetness and non-squelchy texture a real joy. All sorts of other beans can be treated in the same way, although borlotti are easily the best. For a quick snack or part of supper you can use the three-bean cans (check they're not pre-dressed), rinsed in a sieve to remove the slimy, thickened water.

SERVES: 4 OR 2 IF YOU ARE REALLY HUNGRY

- 5–6 handfuls of fresh borlotti beans or add the equivalent from a can
- olive oil to cook, plus extra to add to the overall taste
- a little dab of butter
- 1 red onion, shallot or ordinary onion, very finely chopped
- 2 garlic cloves, crushed
- 2 rounded tsp ground cumin
- juice of 2 lemons
- 1 tbsp freshly chopped flat-leaf parsley
- 1 tbsp freshly chopped coriander
- salt and ground black pepper

Pod the beans, then cook them for about 2 hours in a pan of simmering water, without salt. Drain and put the beans back into the pan.

Heat a little oil and butter in a frying pan and fry the onion until soft and uncoloured. Add the garlic and cumin and fry very gently, stirring constantly, for a minute or so. Add to the cooked beans together with the lemon juice, more oil, the chopped herbs and salt and pepper and serve lukewarm as a salad. You can mash the beans up a little to let more of the dressing through to the flesh of the bean, which gives it a chunky appeal, if you like.

SUGAR SNAP AND ASPARAGUS SALAD WITH BACON BITS

This is a clever little salad, delicious but perhaps a little too oily for some tastes. The sugar snap peas and asparagus are fried until just tender in the excess bacon fat, so they catch a little and have nice, smoky brown bits to contrast with the crunch of the vegetable. If you're worried about the frying, then grill the asparagus and steam or boil the peas, but it's well worth trying to fry it for once, just to see the difference.

MAKES: A LARGE BOWL FOR 4 PEOPLE AS A MAIN COURSE

- 2 large handfuls of lettuce and/or salad leaves, torn into pieces
- several rashers of smoked streaky bacon, pancetta or good-quality lardons
- olive oil to cook
- a handful of sugar snap peas
- a handful of asparagus, snapping off the tougher base third of each stem
- fresh white bread, such as ciabatta or sourdough or Aligot (page 150), to serve

FOR THE DRESSING

- a big slosh of olive oil
- 3 sloshes of wine vinegar
- salt and ground black pepper

Mix all the dressing ingredients together in a large serving bowl. Add the salad leaves, but don't toss yet.

Fry the bacon in a little oil until crisp, then remove from the pan and cut into strips. Add to the salad bowl.

Add the peas and asparagus to the bacon fat in the pan and fry, stirring constantly, until just beginning to soften. They should be still quite crisp, with a few blackened places. Add to the salad bowl, then toss everything together and serve with the bread or Aligot.

RADICCHIO SALAD WITH PEAR, WATERCRESS AND HAZELNUTS

If you can't find radicchio you can use ordinary salad leaves instead.

SERVES: 4–6

- 1 tbsp hazelnuts or walnuts
- 1 ripe pear
- 1–2 radicchios, torn into large pieces
- 1 small bunch of watercress
- ½ tsp red wine vinegar
- 1 tsp lemon juice
- ½ tsp mustard, preferably French
- 2 tbsp olive oil
- salt and ground black pepper

Lightly toast the nuts in a dry frying pan, tossing occasionally to prevent burning. Remove from the pan and roughly chop. Put to one side.

Peel and slice thinly the pear, then place in a shallow bowl with the radicchio and watercress.

Mix the vinegar, lemon juice, mustard and oil together, then season to taste and pour over the salad. Toss together, then sprinkle the hazelnuts over the top.

BEETROOT, ORANGE AND MINT SALAD

A bright, zingy salad with earthiness, sweetness and aromatics.

SERVES: 4

- 2 shallots or 1 small mild red onion, very finely chopped
- 2 large oranges
- 4–6 pre-cooked beetroot without sugar, sweetener or vinegar, peeled and cut into large chunks (see note below)
- a dash of hot chilli pepper sauce, such as Tabasco
- a handful of salad leaves, such as rocket
- a handful of fresh mint leaves

FOR THE DRESSING

- A big slosh of olive oil
- 3 sloshes of wine vinegar
- salt and ground black pepper

Mix all the dressing ingredients together in a bowl and season to taste. Add the shallots and allow to marinate for an hour or so to let all the flavours develop.

Peel the oranges, top and tail them so that they have a firm flat base, then cut off the skin and pith. Cut off the inner centre white bits, then cut down each segment to release a pure flesh segment. Place in a bowl and put to one side.

Place the beetroot in another bowl. Add some of the dressing, then add the chilli sauce and mix together.

Add the salad leaves to the oranges in the bowl, then add the remaining dressing and toss together to combine. Arrange the salad leaves and orange salad on serving plates and place the beetroot to the side. Sprinkle with mint leaves to serve.

Note: If you want to cook the beetroot from fresh, then cut off the stems and roots, wash them and bake in an oven preheated to 180°C (160°C fan oven) mark 4 for 1 hour, or until tender. Peel off the outer skin. I can't see any point of roasting them in foil, as often advised. You can also boil them, but it's as easy to buy them ready cooked, although not as tasty of course.

PATATAS BRAVAS WITH BEAN SALAD

Patatas bravas is a well-known tapas dish which varies from café to café in Spain. Mine has no claim to faithfulness, and is usually put together with what I have in the fridge. I tend to boil the potatoes, then cut them into chunks and roll them around in a slightly piquant sauce, rather than fry them and serve the sauce over the top. This is done mainly out of sloth, rather than a claim to greater flavour, but it always goes down well. Beans can be cooked as in the Borlotti Bean Salad (page 119), or drain a can of your favourite beans, or your own cooked beans and add the basic dressing/vinaigrette.

SERVES: ABOUT 4 PEOPLE AS A SIDE DISH

- olive oil to cook
- 1 large onion, finely chopped
- 275 g can tomatoes or the equivalent in a passata pouch
- 1 dsp tomato purée
- 1–2 sloshes wine vinegar, preferably sherry vinegar
- 1 flat dsp smoked paprika
- some kick of chilli, either a slosh of Sriracha sauce, 1 small crumbled chilli or 1 tsp chipotle paste
- ½ tsp sugar

- 3 garlic cloves, crushed
- salt and ground black pepper
- about 10–15 small boiled potatoes, cut into bite-size chunks
- freshly chopped parsley to garnish

Patatas bravas with bean salad

Heat the oil in a pan over a high heat and gently fry the onion, stirring occasionally until it starts to colour. Add the tomatoes, tomato purée, vinegar, paprika and chilli, reduce the heat to medium and stir until most of the liquid has evaporated. Stir in the sugar and garlic and cook for about 5 minutes, stirring to prevent sticking and adding a little water if necessary. Season to taste. Add the potatoes and stir until they are coated in the sauce. Garnish with parsley and serve.

CELERIAC SALAD WITH BROAD BEANS

Roasted celeriac with broad beans in a creamy mustard sauce, this is an odd recipe in a way, as I can't remember its origin at all. I think I might have seen the first part of this dish on a TV programme and then decided what to do with it.

SERVES: 4

- 1 whole celeriac, washed and top leaves removed

- oil to smear on an oven tray

- 2 handfuls of fresh or frozen broad beans, preferably taken out of their skins

- ½ carton of single cream taken from a small pot

- 1 cup white wine

- 1 tbsp freshly chopped tarragon

- 1 tsp sugar

- 1 tsp French mustard such as Dijon or Meaux

- 1 tsp capers, rinsed and patted dry

- salt and ground black pepper

Preheat the oven to 200°C (180°C fan oven) mark 6. Now this is the odd bit. Place a whole celeriac on an oiled oven tray in the oven and cook for about 1 hour or until it's shrunken and black. Remove from the oven and leave to cool.

When the celeriac is cool enough to touch, cut it in half and scrape out the soft innards. Chop up roughly. Put to one side.

Have a bowl of cold water ready nearby. Bring a pan of water to the boil, add the broad beans and blanch for 1 minute. Drain and cool in the cold water, then drain the beans and dry.

Place the cream, wine, tarragon, sugar, mustard and capers in a pan, season to taste and mix together, then bring to the boil, stirring constantly. Turn off the heat and leave to cool slightly.

Put all the ingredients together in a large serving bowl or plate.

Celeriac salad with broad beans

123

POTATO SALAD

Here I don't mean the mean-spirited supermarket offering, which mixes potato chunks with commercial mayonnaise and seems to think this is acceptable. If you're making it for a party, then it's well worth using my method, as it is very simple to do and cheap to boot. Use waxy potatoes that won't fall to pieces after they have been boiled. Charlotte, Pink Fir Apple or new potatoes, such as Jersey Royals are delicious as a salad. If you want a bigger bowl then just apportion the ingredients accordingly and keep tasting until you are happy.

TO FEED MANY AT A PARTY

- 1 bag of salad potatoes, about 20–30 small waxy potatoes

- 2 garlic cloves

- salt and ground black pepper

- 1 tsp French mustard such as Dijon or Meaux

- 2 tbsp white wine vinegar

- 1 tbsp honey

- about 2 tbsp olive oil

- chopped spring onions or parsley to garnish (optional)

Cook the potatoes in a large pan of boiling water until soft, then drain and cut into quarters. Put to one side.

Meanwhile, place the garlic in a large serving bowl with 1 tsp salt and mash with the back of a spoon to a soft paste. Add the mustard, vinegar, honey and oil and mix to combine.

Add the potatoes, still warm, to the serving bowl and season with lots of salt and pepper. Let the potatoes absorb some of the sauce, then taste and adjust the flavours, if needed. As this salad cools down, it seems to need more flavouring, so be generous. This salad is best served warm, garnished with spring onions or parsley, if you like.

MERGUEZ AND COUSCOUS SALAD WITH ROASTED VEGETABLES

This can be a small individual salad or can be extended into a large platter scaled up as necessary, with sweet and spicy flavours, vaguely Moroccan in inspiration.

SERVES: 6–8

- olive oil to cook
- 2 large onions, sliced
- 2 red peppers, halved and de-seeded
- 20 small sweet tomatoes or equivalent of flavourful larger tomatoes
- 2.5 cm cube of fresh root ginger, peeled and finely diced
- 4 garlic cloves, crushed
- 2 preserved lemons, finely chopped, as they are pretty strongly flavoured
- 2 large reasonably mild dried chillies, such as ancillo, softened in boiling water and chopped
- 1 dsp tomato purée
- 1 tbsp sherry vinegar
- juice of 1 lemon
- 1 tsp each of ground coriander, ground cumin, ground cinnamon, smoked paprika and ground turmeric
- 2 tbsp fresh or frozen green peas
- 2 tbsp fresh or frozen broad beans
- 4–5 handfuls of medium couscous
- salt and ground black pepper

- 8 cooked fried merguez sausages, cut into pieces about 5 cm long
- 1 small dried chilli, such as Italian chilli, finely chopped
- a handful each of freshly chopped parsley, mint and coriander

Preheat the oven to 180°C (160°C fan oven) mark 4.

Heat some oil in a frying pan and fry the onions until soft and brown. Remove from the heat and put to one side.

In a roasting pan, roast the peppers and tomatoes in a little oil to prevent them sticking until soft and darkened, then cut into chunks and put to one side.

Merguez and couscous salad with roasted vegetables

125

Mix the ginger, garlic, preserved lemons, half the roasted red pepper and the softened chillies together in a large bowl with the tomato purée, sherry vinegar and lemon juice. You can blitz everything together if you like or leave it as individual chunks within the dish.

In a large frying pan, fry the spices gently in a little oil, stirring to prevent burning for a minute or so until they release their aroma. Remove from the heat and put to one side.

Cook the peas and broad beans in a pan of boiling water for a minute or so, then drain and put to one side.

Place the couscous in a heatproof bowl, cover with boiling water and leave until it has swelled up, or cook according to the pack instructions. Drain, if necessary, then place on a serving platter and mix in the tomato mixture and toasted spices. Taste and adjust the seasoning, then add all the remaining ingredients, arranging the sausages and herbs on top.

ROCKET, SWEET POTATO AND PINENUT SALAD

This is one of those sweet catch-alls, which can be easily extended and improvised as necessary. Here, the base leaves, rocket – or it could be any green leaf – are given an added flavour dimension with the addition of soft, sweet potatoes and the crunch of toasted pinenuts.

SERVES: 4

- 1–2 medium sweet potatoes

- 1 garlic clove, crushed

- salt and ground black pepper

- juice of 1 lemon

- olive oil

- a few handfuls of greenery, such as rocket, but can be general salad leaves, pea shoots or lamb's lettuce or even a mixture

- a handful of pinenuts or a nut of your choice

- 1–2 roasted or grilled charred red peppers, cut into long strips

- 2–3 spicy peppers, like Pepperdew ones from a jar, if you have them, halved

Cook the sweet potatoes by halving them (without bothering to take the skins off) and microwaving them on high for 8 minutes. Alternatively, boil them until soft, then drain. Cut the sweet potatoes into chunks and put to one side.

Place the garlic in a large serving bowl with 1 tsp salt and mash with the back of a spoon to a soft paste. Add the lemon juice, then mix in 2 tbsp of olive oil and stir to combine. Taste, then add pepper and the greenery and toss in the dressing.

Toast the pine nuts in a dry frying pan for a minute or two until they are just beginning to colour.

Add the sweet potatoes, peppers and spicy peppers to the serving bowl, stir and taste and adjust the seasoning. Top with the toasted pine nuts and serve. The potatoes have a tendency to soak up the dressing, so be prepared to add more if the greenery needs it.

Rocket, sweet potato and pinenut salad

FRISÉE, AVOCADO, SAUTÉ POTATOES AND LARDON SALAD

An extended salad which is quick, forgiving and delicious. You can use up any additional bits you might have in the fridge and enlarge it for parties. Frisées are enormous, so judge how much you want and cut into pieces for ease of eating – it has lovely fronds of deliciousness.

SERVES: 4

- 8–12 boiled small or new potatoes, sliced

- olive oil to cook

- 1 tbsp cooked and fried smoked lardons, either pancetta, bacon or even chorizo or ham if you want to use it up

- part of a frisée lettuce or salad leaves

- 1–2 ripe avocados, peeled, stoned and cut into bite-size chunks

FOR THE VINAIGRETTE

- 3 tbsp olive oil

- 1–2 lemons

- salt and ground black pepper

Mix all the vinaigrette ingredients together in a large serving bowl, adding 1 tsp salt and a few grinds of black pepper. Put to one side.

In a large frying pan, fry the precooked potatoes in olive oil over a high heat until crisp on the outside, then remove from the pan and put to one side.

Add the lardons to the pan and fry to heat up. Put to one side.

Add the frisée leaves to the serving bowl and toss until they are coated in the dressing. Taste a little and adjust the dressing and seasoning, if needed. It should be quite strong to counteract the remaining ingredients. Add the fried potatoes, lardons and avocado and toss again. Serve immediately.

VEGETABLES AND SAUCES

The recipes in this chapter can be served as main dishes or accompaniments. The sauces are also versatile and can be used as chutneys, side sauces or accoutrements for buffets, parties and main courses.

PEAS

Use frozen peas, which often taste as good as, if not better, than the fresh. Fresh peas, unless you know the source, can be sold too late and too old, when they start to harden and go floury as the sugar in them converts to carbohydrate. Unless you're sure, or they are homegrown, then it's better to stick with frozen.

The simplest way to cook peas is to fill a pan of water, about a third up the side and bring to the boil. Add some salt if you really must, say a couple of pinches for 4 people, then add the peas, sufficient for your own requirements, and boil for about 2–3 minutes until the peas are just heated through. Taste.

Serve with a knob of butter. They will lose their colour and go wrinkly if you leave them to cook for too long or if you leave them for too long before serving. Sometimes, if I want to use them in a salad, I just pour boiling water over to defrost them, then strain, dry a little and serve.

BETTER PEAS

Here, peas are cooked in stock and butter so that as they cook the liquid is reduced down to a buttery syrup, coating the peas and bringing out their natural flavour.

For 4 people, as a side dish, crumble a chicken bouillon stock cube into ½ mug of boiling water in a pan and frisk it with a fork until dissolved, then add 6–10 black peppercorns, 3 bay leaves, 2 tsp sugar and 2 large knobs of butter. Add 4 heaped tbsp of peas to the boiling stock and boil until most of the liquid has disappeared. This will only take about 3 or 4 minutes. Make sure everything else is ready for the meal. When the liquid is really reduced and starts to turn syrupy, then serve the peas immediately. Carrots, green beans, leeks and similar vegetables can all be cooked this way, especially if the rest of the meal is relatively simply cooked, or there isn't a sauce and you want some extra moisture. If the vegetables demand more cooking time then be prepared to add more water to the stock but a little at a time. It's the end syrup you're after.

CARROTS

Apart from the lovely roasted carrot and sweet caramelised carrots, this is another form of cooking which intensifies naturally sweet carrots when you buy them young and fresh.

- allow about 1–2 large carrots for each person as an accompanying vegetable, peeled and cut into 1 cm thick slices either lengthways or diagonally sliced

- a sprinkle of sugar

- juice of ½ lemon (if you have it)

- a sparse sprinkle of ground cumin

- a few knobs of butter

- salt and ground black pepper

You can either microwave all the ingredients for about 3 minutes on high, then taste and cook a little bit more if necessary, or you can roast them in an oven preheated to 180°C (160°C fan oven) mark 4 for about 20 minutes. Alternatively, you can place all the ingredients in a pan with a little bit of water, cover with a lid and cook until tender, adding a little more water, if necessary.

PURÉES

There are all sorts of vegetables, such as potatoes (naturally), carrots, turnips, cauliflower, celeriac and onions that you can make into a purée; the only problem being the consistency, which must never be so over-processed that it resembles the consistency of wallpaper paste.

Peas and beans make an excellent purée. Cook your vegetable of choice first in boiling water until just tender. Drain. Use a stick blender in the pan rather than a food processor, if you want to be sure of the consistency, adding butter, cream, crème fraîche, black pepper and cheese if you want to change the taste. The old-fashioned Mouli graters are excellent for this as well.

Restaurant chefs are using purées more and more. Not only does this purée have an interesting taste, but the texture can provide an added softness within the whole plate of food. Unfortunately, chefs often use them rather indiscriminately, as a smear across a plate. While having some visual appeal (I begrudgingly suppose), this may make them difficult to eat, as they are spread out. Fine on smooth china; appallingly ridiculous on slate, wood or even, once in France, on the rough, absorbent surface of an unglazed tile.

CELERIAC REMOULADE

Celeriac 'cut' into matchsticks with a creamy mustard dressing is traditionally served in winter when other vegetables are thin on the ground. You can buy it all over France in delis and it's now seen in major supermarkets in the UK.

MAKES: 5–6 TBSP

- 1 small melon-size celeriac
- juice of 2 lemons
- salt and ground black pepper

FOR THE DRESSING

- a few tbsp mayonnaise, depending on how big your celeriac is, preferably homemade
- 1 dsp French mustard
- 1 tbsp plain yogurt or crème fraîche (if you have it)

Top and tail the celeriac, then cut off the outside skin to remove all the bumps and folds that may harbour dirt. Cut the celeriac in half vertically, then into quarters, depending on the method of making julienne sticks. Cut into matchsticks or spaghetti strands either manually or use a food processor with an attachment, a spiraliser (if you still have one!), a grater (although you end up with short flat bits including your knuckles) or a mandolin or julienne peeler. Place the matchsticks in a bowl, sprinkle over the lemon juice and add about 1 tsp salt, then leave to soften for 30 minutes or so if you have the time.

Mix all the dressing ingredients together in a bowl, but don't season yet.

Mix the dressing into the celeriac and taste, then season with salt and pepper.

SPINACH

Spinach with garlic, lemon and chilli, it sounds nothing, but tastes yummy. Add some chopped and squashed anchovies if you like, but then omit the salt.

This is one of those convenience foods that are what they say – so convenient it's not worth buying anything else, unless you have oodles of time and patience. Buy prewashed spinach, because washing it takes bowl after bowl of water to come clean, and even then you're never sure, and just one piece of grit will ruin the whole meal. If you wash the spinach yourself, then try and dry it as best you can – it's important to ensure that you're not drowning in water as you cook it, because it's impossible to get rid of the excess water. Spinach has enormous quantities of water within it, so it's very easy to end up with something that looks like a dark green, slimy chamois leather. It cooks so quickly you can't even boil out the water without destroying the spinach, so it's best not to add any unnecessary water. Dry on plenty of kitchen paper or a tea towel. Cooked spinach quickly loses its heat so put the oven on to heat the plates first.

SERVES: 4

- a big knob of unsalted butter (1 tbsp)
- a splosh of olive oil
- 1–2 garlic cloves, crushed
- 1–2 fresh chillies, de-seeded and chopped or 2 pinches of dried chilli flakes, depending on how hot you like it
- 3 anchovy fillets in oil mashed into a rough paste
- 1 bag of washed spinach, about 200–250 g, removing any stalks
- juice of 1 lemon
- salt and ground black pepper

Heat the butter and oil in a large saucepan over a medium heat, add the crushed garlic, chillies and anchovies, if using, and turn them over quickly in the oil without browning – just a minute at the most. Add the spinach, prodding it down as it wilts, if it doesn't all fit in the pan, then add the lemon juice, and season with salt (careful if you're using anchovies) and pepper. Turn it over until it's hot, then serve immediately as it wilts.

LEEKS

Leeks are lovely roasted and probably best cooked like this, but unless you buy pre-cleaned ones, it's important to ensure that any bits of mud are not still lurking in its innermost folds. If it has rained recently, then there will be a tendency for the mud to collect at the bottom of the leeks before harvesting.

To prepare leeks, cut the ends off, removing the really frayed leaves and the bits of root at the other end. One way is to cut the head in half lengthways and swish it about in some cold water to remove any mud. This is foolproof, but you do lose the completeness of the stalk, because by cutting it down, it falls apart. The other way is trial and error, as you have to cut off any leaves that still have mud embedded at their base. I try to cut through a few leaves with a sharp knife and make a vertical slit lengthways down the side of the stalk, but only going through a few leaves at a time, leaving the main stalk intact. Then I chop the bottom off again, removing the dirty leaves and re-examine the base. I then chop the remaining stalk into biggish chunks horizontally, about 3 cm each and roast them on an olive oil-smeared baking tray. This way the leeks go into roundels rather than pieces.

The other way to cook them is to boil them in slightly salted (if you must) water for about 5 minutes until tender. Cook them too much and they start to disintegrate. This is perhaps the third ingredient (other than prepared salads and spinach) that you might like to buy ready cleaned.

VEGETABLES À LA GRECQUE

All sorts of vegetables can be cooked and served in this classic French style. Vegetables such as carrots, leeks, mushrooms and so on are boiled down into an aromatic broth until they are just cooked and the sauce has condensed into a lively syrup. The result is then served, preferably lukewarm or, if you have to, cold. Brill.

SERVES: 3–4 AS A STARTER

- a slosh of oil, such as rapeseed
- 1 tbsp unsalted butter
- 1 small onion or 2–3 shallots, very finely chopped
- 1 carrot, thinly sliced
- 2 leeks, washed, outer leaves removed and cut into 2 cm-long slices
- a handful of French beans, halved
- a handful of small mushrooms, such as button, cut into 1 cm slices
- 1 tbsp white wine vinegar
- 1 cup of white wine
- ½ cup of water
- 10 black peppercorns
- 2 bay leaves
- ¼ tsp fennel seeds
- 5–6 coriander seeds
- a small bunch of parsley
- a few thyme sprigs

Heat the oil and butter in a large pan. Add the onion and stir around for a minute or two. Add the other vegetables, then reduce the heat and stir them around in the pan for another minute or so. Add all the other ingredients and bring to the boil. Reduce the heat to a simmer and cook for about 15 minutes, stirring when necessary until the sauce has reduced down. If at any time the sauce looks ominously thick, just add a little water.

Once the sauce has reduced, remove from the heat and leave to cool. Serve, fishing out the parsley and thyme.

ASIAN AUBERGINES

An unguent hot, spicy and sweet sauce with aubergines from Southeast Asia originally, although now it is more of a version I do with my more limited store cupboard. There are a few mixed metaphors here with Chinese, Japanese and Vietnamese influences, but it works.

SERVES: 2

- ½ mug of vegetable oil, such as rapeseed or groundnut oil

- 1 large aubergine, cut into chunks, about 1–1.5 cm thick

- 1 garlic clove, crushed

- 2 tsp miso paste dissolved in hot water

- juice of 1 lemon or 3 limes

- 2 dried chillies, rehydrated in a little bowl of hot water, then drained and sliced (try ancho or pasilla for a change, plus a hotter one for balance)

- 1 dsp sugar

- a slosh of rice wine

- a slosh of mirin

- a slosh of white wine vinegar

Heat the oil in a large frying pan and gently fry the aubergine chunks until you can feel them softening under your wooden spoon, scraping the disintegrating aubergine off the base of the pan. Add more oil as necessary. They should be golden brown now with no pale bits. Ensure they're properly cooked by testing one.

Make a well in the centre of the pan and add the garlic, miso and sliced chillies; there should be enough residual oil to stop it sticking. Stir around for a minute. If it does start sticking, add a little of the chilli soaking water. Add all the other ingredients, stir around and taste. Balance up the tastes and add more of any flavour you think is lacking.

Note: The choice of chillies make this more interesting than it might have been since the ancho and pasilla chillies have an aromatic, smoky and sweet taste. Being very mild, you might like to pep it up with a 'normal' biggish red chilli (variety unknown) you know and trust, the kind we get from our shops. You can buy more unusual chillies online and sometimes in the bigger supermarkets.

HOT, SWEET AND SOUR AUBERGINES

This is a slight variation of the last recipe with a classic Vietnamese sauce (see also page 145 with salmon).

SERVES: 4 AS A SIDE DISH

- 1 large or 2 medium aubergines
- 1–2 tbsp flavourless oil, such as rapeseed or groundnut
- 2 garlic cloves, crushed
- 3 tbsp fish sauce
- 1 tbsp lemon or lime juice, or wine vinegar if you must
- 1 dsp sugar
- sliced chillies, to taste or 2.5 cm cube of fresh ginger, peeled and chopped
- chopped coriander to sprinkle
- a few sesame seeds to sprinkle

Cut the aubergines into thin bite-size chunks and fry them in a large frying pan in some flavourless oil until beginning to brown. Reduce the heat to low and allow the aubergines to fully cook until they're really soft and brown, adding more oil if necessary. Add all the other ingredients, except the coriander and sesame seeds, stir everything around, then taste and adjust the seasoning. Cook gently until you have a rich, savoury sauce. Serve with the coriander and sesame seeds sprinkled on top.

Note: You can add a splosh of sesame oil with the rapeseed oil, if you like, which is strong and more authentically Asian than, say, olive oil.

RADICCHIO OR RED ENDIVE/CHICORY SALAD

Both of these related red salad leaves are relatively bitter, but have a lovely crisp interesting taste if cooked and served alongside other vegetables with a good dressing. Chicory and endive are basically the same vegetable and the names can be used interchangeably. Radicchio can be also simply cooked by cutting it in half then into quarters, frying slowly in oil and butter until brown and serving with lemon juice and salt.

SERVES: 2–4

- 1 onion, finely sliced
- 1 tbsp olive oil, plus a little extra
- 1 garlic clove, crushed
- finely grated zest and juice of 1 lemon
- ½ radicchio, chopped into large slices or 1 red endive/chicory, divided into separate leaves
- ½ tsp salt
- a few pinches of pepper (try Aleppo pepper or pul biber for a change)
- freshly chopped parsley, to garnish

Cook the onion in a hot frying pan with the oil, stirring around until brown. Add the garlic and briefly turn around. Reduce the heat and add all the remaining ingredients, except the lemon zest and parsley. Stir and taste, then add a little more olive oil to make the dish glossy. Taste and adjust the seasoning as necessary. Serve, garnished with parsley and lemon zest.

CAULIFLOWER THREE WAYS: PICKLED, PURÉED AND FRIED

I don't know quite what it is with food these days, as unexpectedly fashions are created one day and disappear the next. One such fashion – cooking the same ingredient in different ways – is still with us. It could be carrots or potatoes, or in this case, cauliflower. Was it on TV first or in a restaurant? I can't remember. Anyway, in the spirit of the age, I tried out cauliflower just to see. If you have time, start the pickle the day before to intensify the flavours.

SERVES: 2–4

- 1 small–medium cauliflower
- 1 tsp sugar
- salt
- 3 tbsp white wine vinegar
- 1 onion, chopped

- olive oil and unsalted butter, to cook

- 1 chicken stock cube

- a few black peppercorns

- 1 tbsp cream

Cut the cauliflower head into three, then thinly slice one third, cut another third into small egg-size pieces, cutting off the central hard stem, and the last third into small teaspoon-size pieces. Put to one side.

First, start the pickle. Place the sugar, 1 tsp salt, wine vinegar and 1 tbsp water into a bowl and add the thinly sliced cauliflower. Put to one side, preferably overnight or at least while the rest of the dish is cooking.

For the purée, place the egg-size florets in a large saucepan with a little hot water, just enough to make the cauliflower float off the bottom and bring to the boil.

Meanwhile, fry the chopped onion in a slosh of oil in a separate frying pan until soft and browning. Crumble the chicken stock cube into the cauliflower pan, add the peppercorns and swish

around, then add the cooked onion and allow to boil off the excess water until the residue is well condensed. With any luck, this should coincide with the cauliflower being cooked.

As it's cooking, fry the small teaspoon-size cauliflower in 1 tbsp oil and a knob of butter on each side until brown; the edges of the florets will begin to bloom and crisp up. They are delicious at this stage and impossible to resist. Sprinkle with a little salt, then remove from the heat, put to one side and keep warm.

Go back to the cooked cauliflower in the large pan, making sure it's soft, and evaporate off almost all the remaining liquid. Don't let it burn. Using a stick blender, purée the cauliflower into a reasonably smooth purée. Check the seasoning and add the cream.

Drain the pickle, which should have absorbed some of the flavourings, then add a little of the three textures to each serving plate, using them as a separate vegetable, or let them sing as a starter on their own. You could put a small soft-boiled egg, such as a quail's egg, into the centre as a treat.

WHITE-YELLOW ENDIVE/CHICORY SALAD

Known as endive in the UK and France and chicory in the US, this is the adult lettuce plant related to the salad green we know as frisée, with frothy green leaves. Endives or chicory (*Cichorium endivia*) are grown and kept light free, 'forced' when young into the veg bulb we know as endive or chicory. Confusingly, frisée in the UK is often also called endive.

This is really a salad, but I often serve it at parties on platters when trying to feed up to 50 people, so it needs three platters. This is invaluable where people need to be able to eat with their fingers, but are tired of the more usual carbohydrate fare and like the crunch and bite of this useful vegetable.

SERVES: 8 – 2 EACH

- 1 endive/chicory, divided into its constituent parts and cut off the base to get about 16 whole leaves

- about 100 g softish blue cheese, such as Gorgonzola or bleu, such as Saint Agur or Stilton

- 2 handfuls of toasted walnuts, roughly chopped

- chilli sauce either proprietary or homemade

- freshly chopped parsley or coriander to garnish

Divide the endive/chicory into separate leaves and spread out in a circle on a serving dish or platter. Spoon a little cheese into each leaf. Squash in some walnuts with your fingers to stop them coming out, then dribble over the chilli sauce and sprinkle with herbs to garnish.

White-yellow endive/chicory salad

BRAISED RED SPICY CABBAGE

Traditionally, this only really comes out at Christmas, but these days it's become much more of a staple – easy, cheap and plentiful, its latent savouriness is augmented by its spicy, rich sauce.

SERVES: 4–6 AS A SIDE

- 1 medium red cabbage, cut in half from top to toe
- 1 large brown onion, chopped into small pieces
- a large slosh of olive oil
- 1 large tbsp unsalted butter
- 2 garlic cloves, crushed
- 2 cinnamon sticks, about 4 cm long or ½ tsp ground cinnamon
- 2 star anise
- a few grates of nutmeg
- a little bit of five-spice powder on the end of a knife
- 1 clove
- 1 peeled and chopped cooking apple
- 1 mug of boiling water with 1 chicken stock cube crumbled up and dissolved in it
- 2 mugs of red wine, dry white wine or cider or 1 mug of dry white vermouth plus 1 mug of water
- a slosh of dry sherry or red wine vinegar
- 1 dsp pomegranate molasses
- 1 flat dsp sugar
- 3 bay leaves
- a handful of freshly chopped parsley
- 6 black peppercorns

After cutting the cabbage in half, remove as much of the central white stalk as possible. I find that I can make a diagonal cut either side and remove it, mostly in a single lump. Cut off the base again to release the outer leaves. Take off a few of the large leaves and cut either side of their white stalks to remove them. You're aiming to get rid of the really large, hard, difficult-to-cook bits. Finely slice across the halved cabbage, then turn at right angles and cut again to form an enormous pile of shredded cabbage (have heart; it will cook down).

Fry the onion in the oil and butter in a large saucepan over a high heat, stirring constantly until just beginning to brown. Reduce the heat to medium-low and let the onion soften and caramelise. Add the garlic and stir around in the oil for a few seconds, adding a little more oil, if needed. Add the remaining ingredients, except the cabbage, and stir until well mixed. Add the cabbage and stir around in the sauce. Taste and adjust the seasoning, if necessary, then reduce the heat to low, cover with a lid and simmer for

20 minutes, checking from time to time to ensure there's enough liquid, adding a little bit of water at a time, if really necessary. Check, and adjust the seasoning if necessary.

Uncover and simmer for about 20 minutes or until the sauce has almost evaporated. Add a little water. It should be rich and slightly spicy and the cabbage soft and fully tender. Serve.

BROCCOLI OR CURLY KALE, SWISS CHARD, CAVOLO NERO AND CIMA DI RAPA

All these types of cabbages/brassicas are useful winter 'greens', which can be cooked the same way. The cabbages are intrinsically rather bitter and their inner spines can be chewy, but don't let that put you off and if they're cooked well, in a strong buttery sauce, they are delicious. If you wish to make this into a main course you can easily add a few sliced cooked potatoes to the mix towards the end to heat through with the greens.

SERVES: 4–6 AS A SIDE

- 3 big handfuls or 1 bag of kale leaves, about 400–500 g

- 2 anchovy fillets, chopped

- ground black pepper

- ½ tsp pul biber pepper or a few chilli flakes

- 1 large garlic clove, crushed

- 2 very big knobs of unsalted butter

Cut out all the really hard white stems from the raw leaves by cutting down each side of them. Swiss chard can have white, yellow, red or even rainbow stems, which may be thin enough to remain, as they are attractive to serve against the dark green leaves. If they are not too old, you can separate the stems from the leaves and cook the stems first. You'll just have to learn about how old and tough your leaves are, by trying. Throw away the very hard stems and keep any reasonable stems, chopped into lengths of about 5 cm.

Add the anchovies, pepper or chilli and garlic to a large saucepan with 1 big knob of the butter and a slosh of olive oil. Allow to boil while stirring for 1 minute. Add the stems, if you are using them. Add a little water – just enough to cover the bottom of the pan. Cover with a lid and let them steam in the heat for about 3–5 minutes until just tender, adding a little more water if absolutely necessary, just enough to prevent it burning. Add the leaves and turn them over and over until all the leaves are coated in the mixture. Put back on the heat and bring to the boil, stirring occasionally while the leaves wilt and the sauce is reducing. Cook for 3 minutes, then taste and test if the leaves are cooked. You probably don't need a lid now as a lot of the moisture has already come out of the leaves and you won't need any salt, because the anchovies are remarkably salty, but check to see if it needs more pepper.

Serve quickly, adding the remaining knob of butter to the pan. Don't serve cold, as like most vegetables, they are best served hot or at least lukewarm, and like most spinachy things they tend to cool down very quickly.

CORIANDER SAUCE

This bright green sauce, with or without chilli for extra sharpness, is perfect to have on the side of a main dish, curry or to serve with a buffet. Use beetroot leaves instead of spinach, if you like.

MAKES: A MEDIUM BOWL

- 1 large bunch of coriander
- 1 bunch of spinach or ½ ready-washed bag or the equivalent in frozen leaves, about 100 g
- 2 garlic cloves, mashed
- 3 cm cube of fresh root ginger, peeled and cut into matchsticks or chunks if you're blitzing it
- finely grated zest and juice of 1 lemon
- 1 red chilli, finely chopped (if you have it)
- 1 big dollop of plain yogurt
- salt and ground black pepper

Finely chop the coriander and spinach, or use a blender or blitzer. Add all the remaining ingredients and blitz to a reasonably smooth sauce. Taste and adjust the seasoning. Serve or transfer to a container, cover with a little oil, seal with a lid and store in the fridge for a few days.

PEPPER AND TOMATO RELISH
(OR WHAT I CALL MY 'RED SAUCE')

This is a fresh and lively red pepper and tomato sauce, similar to Sriracha but milder and fruitier to serve on the side. If the quality of the tomatoes is good, then the sweetness of the tomatoes comes through, even though they are uncooked.

MAKES: 2 SMALLISH JARS, ABOUT 200–300 G EACH

- 2 red peppers, cut into large pieces
- 1–2 medium-hot chillies, (about 10 cm long)
- 2 trusses of very sweet, best-quality small tomatoes with about 14 tiny tomatoes on each truss, quartered
- olive oil
- salt and ground black pepper
- a squeeze of lemon juice to taste

Preheat the grill, then roast the peppers and chillies under the grill until they go black and charred. Remove and leave until cool enough to handle.

Once they are cool enough to handle, pick off the blackened skin: you don't need to be pernickety, and chop the chillies into pieces. Put the peppers and chillies into a blender with the tomatoes and a little oil and the lemon to help the blades go round. Blitz until everything is smashed up into a rough purée. Season with salt and pepper to taste.

Put the relish into clean smallish jars, pat it down until it forms a smooth surface and pour over a little oil to keep it airtight. Seal with lids and it will keep in the fridge for a long time, adding more oil to seal the top, once you start to eat it.

COURGETTE PICKLE

MAKES: A 500 G JAR

- 1 dsp black mustard seeds
- vegetable oil, such as rapeseed, corn or groundnut oil to fry
- ½ tsp ground ginger
- ½ tsp cayenne pepper
- a few pinches of ground or grated nutmeg
- 1 cinnamon stick, about 5 cm long
- 1 onion, finely chopped
- ¼ cauliflower, cut into small slices
- a handful of runner beans, cut into medium slices
- 3 medium courgettes, cut into bite-size chunks
- 4 tbsp white wine vinegar

- ½ preserved lemon, cut into chunks

- 1 dsp sugar

- 1 tsp salt

Put the mustard seeds into a frying pan with a little oil and stir around for a minute or so until they start popping. Reduce the heat to low and add the ginger, cayenne, nutmeg and cinnamon. Add a little more oil to stop the spices burning and stir around in the pan. Add more oil, then add the onion and stir for a few minutes until it starts to soften. Add the cauliflower, runner beans and courgettes and stir around until they are coated with the spices. Add 4 tbsp water and the vinegar. Increase the heat until it starts to boil, then add the lemon and sugar. Reduce the heat again and stir until the sugar has dissolved. Taste and adjust the flavourings, then add the salt. You may need to add more liquid in the form of water and/or vinegar, so that everything is nicely coated. Serve immediately or transfer to large clean jar, cover with a little oil, seal with a lid and store in the fridge for a few days.

COCONUT SAUCE

A side dish originally intended to be served with a curry, only slightly hot and relatively mild, to offset and complement something more complicated.

MAKES: A SMALL BOWL

- 2 tbsp desiccated coconut moistened in water or the equivalent, if you're feeling energetic, of grated fresh coconut, or frozen grated coconut from Asian shops

- 1 fairly mild red chilli, chopped

- 1 garlic clove, crushed

- juice of 1 lemon

- ¼ tsp sugar

- 1 dsp very, very finely chopped red onion

- 1 dsp plain yogurt

- a small handful of finely chopped coriander to garnish

Mix all the ingredients together in a bowl. Just before serving, garnish with coriander.

QUICK AND EASY MIDWEEK DISHES

The recipes in this chapter are all reasonably simple and often economical; you won't need to cook anything for very long, so they should be quick enough to make in the evening. If they need a bit longer to cook in the oven, it will be the sort of dish that you don't have to worry about too much.

SALMON STEAKS WITH HOT SPICY LEMON SAUCE

The marinade acts as the cooking liquor, so you don't need any oil. This makes a very quick but extremely tasty dish, which will satisfy the most carnivorous of eaters because it's so strong and tangy. Very healthy, it only has some sugar to thwart the hardliners, so it might be a way to tempt the family into eating fish. The marinade boils down to an unctuous, lemony syrup, which you can dribble over the salmon on the plate.

SERVES: 2

- a handful of rice per person or if you're in a rush use supermarket mixed rice/quinoa/lentils in a bag heated in the microwave
- 2 salmon steaks, skinned
- 1 garlic clove, crushed
- 2 tsp sugar or use a sugar substitute
- 3 tbsp fish sauce or 2 tbsp soy sauce (if you must)
- juice of 1½ lemons or 4 limes
- 1–2 chillies, de-seeded and sliced

TO SERVE

- seaweed thins or biscuits as a crispy addition
- green vegetable of choice, such as peas or beans

Put the water on for the rice in a pan and wash the rice in a sieve.

Place the salmon and all the remaining ingredients together in a bowl and leave to marinate for a while if you have the time or inclination, turning it around every now and again to keep coating the salmon.

Add the rice to the boiling water in the pan and empty out enough water to just cover the rice (page 44). Cover with a lid and simmer over a very low heat until cooked. Turn off the heat and cover with the lid to keep warm. Cook the accompanying veg at the same time and keep warm.

Heat a sauté or frying pan over a high heat. Add the salmon and marinade to the pan (it will hiss and steam), then reduce the heat to medium and cook the salmon for 2–3 minutes on each side, depending on how thick it is. If in doubt, open up a bit of the one you're eating and see if it's just got a little pinkness in the middle. If so, it's done. Turn the heat off and leave it in the pan. It will continue cooking in the residual heat, while you serve the rice. If the marinade starts browning and thickening too much, just add a spoonful of water and stir around to keep it from burning. Try not to overcook the salmon or it will stiffen and start drying out – the point of all fish is to try to cook it just enough, so that it retains its moisture, flavour and softness.

Put a few crispy seaweed thins on the side for added texture and serve with a vegetable of your choice.

Salmon steaks with hot spicy lemon sauce

CALVES' LIVER WITH SAGE LEAVES OR BALSAMIC VINEGAR

I love calves' liver with either of these accompaniments. The liver is dark and nutty on the outside and softly pink in the middle. Both versions are vaguely Italian in style. Serve with something simple like peas and boiled potatoes. Some may feel this is a bit exotic or over-expensive for a midweek meal.

SERVES: 2

- a few sloshes of oil
- a big knifeful of unsalted butter, about 6 mm slice
- 1 generous slice of calves' liver each, about 6 mm thick
- salt and ground black pepper
- flour to coat
- about 10 fresh sage leaves or 3–4 tbsp balsamic vinegar
- vegetables of your choice to serve

If you have the time and the inclination, then a side order of thinly sliced, fried, lightly browned, slow-cooked onions goes down a treat with this. If you go down the onion route, cook them in 1 thick slice of butter and 1 tbsp oil to stop the butter burning, until they take on a little colour, then reduce the heat and cover with a lid. Keep a watch over them and stir occasionally, adding more butter if it appears to be drying out. When the onions are soft and brown, heat a separate pan with the oil and butter over a high heat.

Season the liver with salt and pepper and roll in a little flour. Add the liver to the pan and cook for about 1 minute on each side, but allow it to sear and brown on the outside. Remove from the pan and keep warm while you add a thin slice of butter to the pan and either add the sage leaves or balsamic vinegar. Reduce the heat to low. The sage leaves will shrivel as they cook, so remove them from the heat immediately after a few seconds. If you're using balsamic then the vinegar will hiss and steam while it concentrates, but allow it to cook for a couple of minutes, then serve it over the liver, or combine with the onions to enhance their sweetness. Serve with vegetables of your choice.

QUICHE LORRAINE

It sounds awfully mundane, but when it's good, and fresh, the pastry is crisp and melting and the inside is warm and just set, it's a great dish. Never eat it in a pub or restaurant unless you know the chef. Serve this quiche with a salad, and if possible, don't let any remaining quiche go solid in the fridge: don't ever serve it cold. Same goes for any pastry. At the very least, warm it up a little in the oven before you serve. Don't heat pastry in the microwave as it will just go soggy or harden if left too long.

SERVES: 4

- 1 savoury shortcrust pastry shell (page 212)

- a few rashers of bacon or ham, cut into bits, or lardons

- 3 eggs

- 1½ cups of single cream or half milk and half cream

- ½ tsp salt

- a few grinds of black pepper

- a pinch of ground nutmeg

- 10–15 pea-size pieces of butter

Preheat the oven to 180°C (160°C fan oven) mark 4.

Line the pastry case with the pastry, then prick the bottom of the pastry with a fork to stop it rising and weigh down the bottom with buttered foil, greaseproof paper or baking parchment and fill with some dried beans. You can buy ceramic baking beans if you like. Bake for 8–9 minutes, then remove from the oven when just beginning to colour. Remove the beans and paper and prick the bottom of the pastry again. Return to the oven for another 2–3 minutes (for a partially baked shell) or 7–10 minutes (for a fully baked shell). For this recipe, we need a fully baked shell.

Meanwhile, fry the bacon in a pan, then arrange it in the base of the pastry shell.

Beat the eggs and cream together with salt, pepper and nutmeg and pour the mixture into the pastry shell. Dot the top with butter and cook in the oven for 20–30 minutes until beginning to colour on top and the pastry edge is brown. The eggs will make the filling rise, so it's best to eat it now, as it will sink if you leave it.

SPICY THAI CHICKEN WINGS

Easy marinated chicken wings, with a spicy sauce.

MAKES: 12 CHICKEN WINGS

- 2–3 spring onions, roughly chopped

- 2 garlic cloves, crushed

- 3 cm square piece fresh root ginger, peeled and finely chopped

- 2–4 lemongrass stalks chopped, using the inner softish bits only

- 1–2 fresh red chillies, chopped

- juice of 4 limes or 2 lemons

- a few sploshes of fish sauce

- 1 tbsp coconut cream, thinned with a little boiling water or coconut milk if you have it

- 12 chicken wings (get the best you can afford and they'll probably be bigger and meatier)

- watercress or rocket

- oil (you could use sesame oil if you have it for extra Asian flavour)

- salt and ground black pepper

If you want an even, thick sauce, then blitz the spring onions, garlic, ginger, lemongrass and chillies together. Thin them down with the lime juice (reserving some lime juice for the salad dressing), the fish sauce and coconut cream. Otherwise, just add them all to a bowl and mix together. It won't hurt if it's not a smooth paste. Add the chicken and leave to marinate in the sauce for an hour or so if you have time.

Preheat the oven to 180°C (160°C fan oven) mark 4.

Transfer the chicken and marinade to a roasting tin or flattish casserole dish and cook in the oven for 30 minutes, or until crisp and brown.

Meanwhile, dress the salad leaves with the reserved lime juice and the oil and season with salt and pepper. Be heavy on the lime juice and light on the oil.

Serve the chicken with the dressed salad leaves.

ALIGOT WITH SALAD

Janet Theophano, in her book *Eat My Words* waxes lyrical about this, maintaining it must be eaten alone (by itself, not by yourself), but I think it needs to be served with a salad. Aligot is an elaborate, delicious version of garlicky, creamy mashed cheesy potatoes, where the cheese melts into elastic strings within the potatoes.

SERVES: 4

- 12 small old potatoes or 8 medium or 4 large, such as King Edward, Desiree or Maris Piper, peeled and cut into halves or quarters

- 50 g unsalted butter

- 3 garlic cloves, finely chopped or crushed

- a small tub or about 200 ml single or double cream or crème fraîche

- 250 g mozzarella, cut into smallish pieces. You can use all sorts of other cheeses, but they are better if they are the stringy type, so that when they melt they go into long strings. Use the stronger Cantal or Gruyère if you prefer

- salt and ground black pepper

Boil the potatoes in a large pan until soft, then drain and mash. Put to one side.

In a large frying pan, add the butter and heat it gently. Add the garlic, reduce the heat right down and stir around, not letting the garlic take on even a hint of brown, for a minute or two. Add the cream and allow to heat through until just bubbling.

Stir in the potatoes until the cream mixture is thoroughly amalgamated. Add the mozzarella and keep stirring vigorously so that the cheese begins to heat through and melt and the potatoes don't start to catch on the base of the pan. The potato will coalesce into a sticky ball with the cheese making long strings within the potato. Season with salt and pepper to taste and serve.

SPICY CHICKEN THIGHS WITH CHICKPEAS

The spices from the chicken mixed with the chickeny juices give an extra kick to the chickpeas. It's quick. It's easy. It's delicious. If you leave the skin on the chicken it will crisp up and go gooey with the soy sauce and sugar. Timings are fairly imprecise, because it's easy to leave without it being ruined, so you can relax. If you buy very small thighs, you may need to shorten the cooking time.

SERVES: 4 (OR 2 VERY HUNGRY, GREEDY ONES)

- 4 chicken thighs with skin on and bones in

- 2 garlic cloves, crushed

- 2 tbsps of soy sauce

- 3–4 tbsps of Thai fish sauce, or 1 slosh of soy sauce and 6 anchovy fillets, finely chopped

- juice of 2 lemons or 5 limes

- 1–2 dried red chillies, crumbled or 2 medium fresh ones, finely chopped

- 10 black peppercorns

- 1 flat tbsp sugar, plus extra to sprinkle

- 400 g can chickpeas, drained

- chopped parsley or coriander to garnish

- cooked rice to serve

Spicy chicken thighs with chickpeas

Preheat the oven to 180°C (160°C fan oven) mark 4.

Arrange the chicken side by side in a fairly upright casserole dish (see note). Rub the crushed garlic into the skin and underneath the thighs with your hands. Add 1 tbsp of the soy sauce, then add the fish sauce, lemon/lime juice, chillies, peppercorns and sugar and rub well into the skin and flesh. Cook in the oven for about 50–60 minutes. The chicken should be beginning to cook and soften but not brown. After about 30 minutes, add the chickpeas and stir around to coat. Put the chicken back in on top (it's been partially marinated in the flavourings, so now the marinade will flavour the chickpeas and give the chicken time to crisp up on top) and add the remaining soy sauce over the skin. It will mainly run off, but keep going. Sprinkle a little sugar over the skin, then put back into the oven and continue cooking for 30 minutes or so until the skin is golden and crunchy. Don't be too deterred if the skin even blackens a little, because it seems to be indestructible.

Garnish with chopped parsley or coriander and serve with rice.

Note: The chicken thighs should sit side by side in a fairly upright casserole dish so the flavourings come up the side of the chicken and won't dissipate sideways during cooking. If this does happen, the chicken will not taste of much of the flavourings and the liquid will also tend to evaporate leaving the chicken high and dry.

CHICKEN THIGHS WITH TARRAGON

A quick and easy chicken dish with its natural accompaniment – tarragon.

SERVES: 4

- 4 chicken thighs (or more if you need), with bone and skin left on

- about 1 tbsp butter

- a splash of olive oil

- 1 lemon

- a large handful of fresh tarragon, chopped

- salt and ground black pepper

- 1 tbsp crème fraîche or any cream or yogurt

Preheat the oven to 180°C (160°C fan oven) mark 4.

Place the chicken in a roasting tin with a big of knob of butter and the oil to stop it burning and roast for 45 minutes or until the chicken is brown. Add the lemon, the remaining butter and the tarragon, then bring to the boil in the tin on top of the hob. Alternatively, transfer to a large saucepan (if your oven pan can't be used on the hob) and turn the chicken around in the cooking juices for a few minutes. Season with salt and pepper. Taste and adjust the seasoning if necessary and serve, stirring in the crème fraîche to give a creamy sauce.

SPICY SMOKED TOFU

This is a crunchy, zesty curry, more akin to Vietnamese food. You can substitute chopped chicken breast for the tofu, if you like. Very clean and fresh. Serve with rice and vegetables of your choice. I tried it with roasted asparagus tips because I had to use them up.

SERVES: 2–3

- 225 g pack of smoked tofu, cut into cubes

- 1 garlic clove, crushed

- 2.5 cm cube of fresh root ginger, peeled, thinly sliced and cut into matchsticks

- 1–2 largish shallots, finely chopped or use mild red onion, or even a plain brown onion

- 1 tsp smoked paprika

- 1 tsp ground cumin

- 2 tbsp soy sauce

- a few sloshes of fish sauce

- 4–5 curry leaves

- 4 tbsp dry sherry

- juice of ½ lemon

- 1 tsp sugar

- 1 small fresh red chilli, de-seeded (if you're worried about the heat) and chopped

- a handful of rice per person

- vegetable of your choice

- freshly chopped parsley, coriander or mint to garnish

Marinate the tofu in the remaining ingredients, except the rice and vegetables, for as long as you can, even if it's only for 5 minutes. You can leave it for 24 hours.

When ready to cook, cook the rice following the instructions on page 44. When the rice is cooked, turn off the heat, cover with the lid and keep warm.

Prepare and cook any vegetable of your choice.

Add the tofu and marinade to a saucepan and bring to the boil, stirring everything around to coat the tofu. Reduce the heat to a simmer and cover with a lid. Cook for about 10 minutes, stirring occasionally, if you can until the sauce has reduced a little.

Place the rice on serving plates. Taste the tofu and sauce and adjust the seasoning, if necessary, then add to the rice with any vegetable of your choice on top and garnish with herbs.

MINESTRONE

This gorgeous, comforting Italian winter soup is a far cry from the watery offerings from the old-fashioned Italian trattorias we grew up with in the UK. My friend Clare and I announce the official start of autumn with our first minestrone. I can tell the weather's getting cold when I'm found wandering around the supermarket muttering the ten ingredients like some demented bag lady. I've found that it doesn't really matter whether you have precisely the right ingredients, but at least for the first time, I'll give them to you correctly. This is the real Italian soup, as laid down by Nigella Lawson, but it's not for the faint-hearted – a real Jeykll and Hyde. This recipe produces a thick, gloopy, brown, not very endearing-looking soup, but taste it and it takes on an ambrosial quality. In fact, you can't stop eating it, especially alone in the kitchen, when it's just lukewarm. But at least it's full of vegetables and goodness; you can use up your old Parmesan rinds and feel virtuous. To improve the presentation I tend not to mix in the Parmesan, but rather make a heap of it on top of each bowlful, surrounding it by a swirl of olive oil and a generous scattering of black pepper.

MAKES: ENOUGH FOR 6–10
PORTIONS

- 2 tbsp olive oil

- 1 large onion, chopped

- a few celery sticks, finely chopped

- 1 large or 2 medium carrots, finely chopped

- 2–3 small–medium potatoes, peeled and roughly chopped

- 3 medium courgettes, chopped

- a handful of French green beans, cut into 3 pieces

- 2 medium leeks, thinly sliced

- 1 small Savoy cabbage, halved, white stalky bit removed and rest finely sliced

- 1 chicken stock cube dissolved in 1 mug of boiling water

- 10 black peppercorns

- 3 bay leaves

- a few Parmesan rinds (if you have them)

- 1 large tbsp grated Parmesan per person

- 400 g can cannellini beans, drained and rinsed

- a handful of small-size pasta, such as little macaroni or orzo

- good-quality extra virgin olive oil

Heat the olive oil in a very large pan and fry the onion over a high heat until soft and brownish, stirring round and round to avoid it sticking. Reduce the heat, add the celery, stir around and add the carrots. Add a little more oil if it starts to stick and continue adding and cooking the next vegetable.

After the cabbage has been added, pour in enough water to just cover the vegetables, plus the dissolved stock cube, peppercorns, bay leaves and Parmesan rind, if using. Cover with a lid and bring to the boil. Once boiling, reduce the heat and simmer for about an hour, stirring once in a while to prevent sticking.

Add the cannellini beans and pasta, adding a little water if the mixture in the pan looks completely thick and sticky (the pasta needs some liquid to help it cook and swell). Serve as soon as the pasta is cooked in a generous-sized bowl for each person, with a dome of grated Parmesan, pepper and an outer ring of extra virgin olive oil on top.

This soup can be reheated success-fully, but don't expect it to last very long, because it is so delicious as it cools the family will dive in and there will be nothing left.

Note: You can cut up the vegetables in the order of the ingredients list while the last vegetable is cooking and then add it to the pan.

SPICY SWEET POTATO AND PARSNIP SOUP
WITH AROMATIC COCONUT

This is a real mongrel of a dish, but surprisingly effective. My family groaned as I started to boil the potatoes and parsnip – 'Ugh, they'll go all mushy' – but loved it at the end. You can substitute ordinary potatoes for the sweet sort, and I daresay any mixture of veg would suffice, but at least I have tried this and it worked. The hot, spicy vegetables sit in a pool of aromatic coconut milk, so it's a sort of two-headed soup, one thick and one thin with contrasting tastes and textures. The garlic and ginger are only partially cooked, so that they retain a bit of bite, helping to give some crunch within the softness of the potatoes and parsnips. This soup is so easy you can leave it to cook and you don't need to concentrate on it.

SERVES: 6–8

- 6 sweet peeled potatoes (could be ordinary ones if necessary) cut up into chunks

- 3 very large parsnips, peeled, and cubed into bite-size chunks

- 2–3 tbsp frozen peas

- 4–5 tbsp oil, such as groundnut or corn oil (coconut oil would add a bit of flavour, if you have it) to fry

- 3 garlic cloves, thinly sliced

- 2.5 cm cube of fresh root ginger, peeled and sliced

- 1 tbsp ground cumin

- 1 tbsp ground coriander

- 1 tbsp ground turmeric

- 1 tsp dried red chillies crumbled or equivalent fresh chopped

- 6 fresh or frozen curry leaves

- a little milk to stop anything sticking

- 1½ chicken stock cubes

- 10 lime leaves

- 1 tsp sugar

- 100 g creamed coconut

- fish sauce if necessary

- freshly chopped coriander to garnish (if you have it)

This will taste a million times better if you use fresh spices and grind them yourself at the start, but I know it might be a last-minute meal with whatever is left in the cupboard, so just adapt the recipe to your individual circumstances and feel good about it.

Boil the potatoes and parsnips in a large pan until just tender, but not disintegrating. This will not take long, because they are cut up so small. Add the peas right at the end and leave for a minute or so until the peas are heated through. Drain the potatoes, parsnips and peas and stir them around a little in the colander to dissipate the steam, stop them cooking and try to dry them out a bit. Put to one side.

Using the same pan, heat the oil and briefly fry the garlic and ginger for 30 seconds or just enough to coat them with oil. Do not overcook. Add the spices and stir them round quickly for no more than 30 seconds so they cook through a little. Add a little more oil, if necessary. Add the cooked potatoes and parsnips, turning them over in the aromatics, trying not to mash them into a pulp. Add a little milk to stop any sticking and reduce the heat to low so the mixture stays hot.

Meanwhile, in a medium pan, bring 500 ml water to the boil. Crumble a stock cube into the water and swish with a fork to dissolve it. Add the lime leaves, sugar and coconut and leave to simmer while you get the serving bowls out. Taste and adjust the seasoning, adding the extra ½ stock cube or some fish sauce if it tastes too watery, or more water if it's too salty. Taste the potatoes and add salt if you think they need it.

Serve by adding a ladleful of the coconut milk to the base of the bowl, a large dollop of the potato mixture into the centre of the bowl and garnishing with coriander.

PASTA CARBONARA

This is simple, quick and cheap (assuming you have a lump of Parmesan on hand). As long as you have some sort of lardons, bacon or chorizo, it can be adapted, but pancetta is better or even guanciale (dry cured pork cheek) favoured by Romans. This recipe is adapted from the first *River Café Cookbook*, via Chrissie, a friend, so it's now a long way from an authentic Italian recipe. In fact, given the whole recent hoo-ha about carbonara in the media, it might be more judicial to call it something else.

SERVES: 4

- a large handful of pancetta, smoked bacon or chorizo (see note)

- a little olive oil to cook

- ground black pepper

- enough pasta for 4, about 2–3 large handfuls, such as linguine or funnel-shaped pasta, but if you haven't got it, use whatever you have

- 5 large tbsp finely grated Parmesan

- 1 large egg

- 1 small tub of crème fraîche, plain yogurt, cream or milk, about 4 tbsp

Get all the plates, forks and table set at the beginning – you'll see why at the end. Fry the pancetta in a large pan in oil with a good few turns of pepper until crisp.

Meanwhile, cook the pasta, drain and put into the pancetta pan. Stir the pancetta and pasta, then stir in half the cheese. Place the pan over a very low heat, add the egg and stir around briskly until it is broken up, so it doesn't have time to set. Add the rest of the cheese, then add the crème fraîche and stir around to combine. The low heat will heat the egg sufficiently to allow it to start thickening the liquid. Turn off the heat. Taste and adjust the seasoning, if necessary and serve. It doesn't seem to like to be kept waiting and tends to separate a bit if you leave it waiting at the end without serving, hence setting the table early...

Note: It's best to use Italian pancetta, cut into little pieces, otherwise you can use smoked bacon or chorizo. A handful is enough, as it's only there to give taste and some colour. Supermarkets sell ready-cut smoked lardons these days, but the quality is variable, and I often wonder if they're just using up their rubbish on us. Anyway, beggars can't be choosers. Good butchers, such as our local farm butcher or Lizzie's, The Black Pig in Deal, Kent, sell their own bacon. The smoked back is simply delicious, but streaky will give you a yummy crispness. It is thick and flavourful, and enhances a simple carbonara wonderfully. Many supermarkets promote Dutch bacon, which is generally rather wet, pink and lifeless in comparison with great local bacon. Why pay for someone else's water? Check out a good butcher near you for some and see the difference. Commercial bacon contains a lot of water and will form a sort of claggy steam in the pan, which you have to evaporate off by boiling. This wet bacon will be hard to get to crisp up.

THAI CHICKEN AND NOODLE SOUP

This is not an authentic Thai recipe since it is totally made up, but it gives the idea of that sweet, hot and fresh soup which is so easy to conjure up. You can use almost any combination of meat or fish with vegetables with varying degrees of success. I'll show you one of the best ways, but you can really substitute as you wish.

SERVES: 3

- 2 skinless, boneless chicken thighs, cut into bite-size pieces

- a few sloshes of fish sauce

- a little soy sauce

- a little sugar

- unflavoured oil, such as peanut, rapeseed or sunflower

- 1 small carrot, cut into matchsticks

- about 10 sugar snap peas or any green beans, cut into chunks

- 1 chilli, thinly sliced

- 1 garlic clove, thinly sliced

- 1 pak choi, sliced into chunks

- a handful of bean sprouts

- 1 chicken stock cube dissolved into about 300 ml boiling water or ½ dsp miso paste

- 1 layer of noodles

- 400 ml can of coconut milk

- a few fresh or frozen lime leaves can be added plus a spoonful of fresh ginger cut into matchsticks

- a handful of freshly chopped coriander and basil (Thai basil if you can find it) to garnish (see note)

Marinate the chicken in the fish sauce, soy sauce and sugar for 10–15 minutes, or overnight if you have more time.

In a large saucepan (not a wok, because it might make the soup taste metallic), heat a large splash of oil and stir-fry the vegetables, except the pak choi and beansprouts, adding each one separately and stirring around. Don't let the garlic colour or burn. Add the chicken stock and bring to the boil. Add some hot water if necessary to cover the ingredients, then add the chicken and noodles, closely followed by the pak choi, beansprouts and coconut milk and stir-fry until the chicken is cooked through. Garnish with coriander and basil and serve.

Note: Thai basil is obviously more authentic in taste, is beautiful and very fragrant, with an aniseed overnote. You can buy fresh bunches from Asian shops if you ask, since they're often lurking in a fridge.

PASTA WITH SWEET ROAST VEGETABLES AND LEMON CHICKEN

I started out wanting to cook a noodle dish, but having assembled everything I found there were no noodles in the larder, so this had to become a pasta dish – another of my happy accidents. It is decidedly untraditional for Italian purists, but seemed delicious to my family and me. It may sound longwinded, but it's simple. You don't have to stand over it; you can go and do something else. Basically it is oven-roasted vegetables with lemon and garlic chicken put together with pasta, with the juice from the chicken giving the background flavour to the pasta.

SERVES: 3–4

- about 30 cherry tomatoes or 10 medium tomatoes quartered, or 5 large, cut into large chunks
- 3 leeks, outer leaves removed and cut into 4 cm lengths
- 2 carrots, sliced lengthways then into batons
- 1 red pepper, halved, de-seeded and squashed flat
- 1 small, hot chilli, split lengthways and seeds scraped out (keep the stalk on to give you something to grip without having to touch the flesh) or more less fierce ones to taste
- olive oil to cook
- lumpy dried pasta, such as fusilli or orecchiette
- 1 skinless, boneless chicken breast or thigh, cut into chunks
- 2 garlic cloves, sliced
- 2.5 cm cube of ginger, peeled, finely sliced and roughly chopped
- finely grated zest of 2 lemons
- juice of 3 lemons
- salt and ground black pepper
- a handful of freshly chopped parsley

Preheat the oven to 150°C (130°C fan oven) mark 2.

Roast the tomatoes, leeks, carrots, red pepper and chilli in a roasting dish with a slosh of olive oil to stop them sticking, giving them a stir every now and again until tender. Remove the vegetables as they cook. As the chilli is small it will cook the quickest, so remove this first.

Put the pasta on to cook 5 minutes before you think the vegetables will be ready.

Sauté the chicken in a scant tbsp of olive oil over a high heat. After a minute or so of stirring around, add the garlic, ginger and the lemon zest and juice. Add salt and pepper to taste and try a little piece of the chicken. If it's done, then remove the pan from the heat immediately. You don't want to overcook the chicken because it will start to harden and dry out.

Drain the pasta and transfer to a large bowl. Add the chicken and all the bits to the pasta and stir around. Add the roasted vegetables and chilli (which will need chopping up a little), then taste and adjust the seasoning. Pour on a little more olive oil as you feel right. Although this sounds ordinary, it's extraordinary how the discovery of little bits of deliciousness in the form of caramelised vegetables make this a star-studded pasta dish.

YUMMY FRIED CABBAGE OR BRUSSELS SPROUTS WITH GARLIC AND PANCETTA

This may sound impossible, or even a breach of trade descriptions, but I assure you that it's true. Because the cabbage is so removed in texture and taste from the norm, it becomes something 'other'. Extremely easy, cheap and quick for a simple mid-week meal and great served with baked potatoes. Brussels sprouts can be cooked in a similar way with added chestnuts as an extra treat.

MAKES: ENOUGH FOR 6–10 PORTIONS

- 1 small Savoy cabbage or use 10–15 Brussels sprouts

- 4–8 rashers of smoked streaky bacon or pancetta

- 2 tbsp olive oil

- a very large knob (1 tbsp) of unsalted butter

- 1–2 garlic cloves, chopped

- salt and ground black pepper

- baked potatoes to serve (optional)

Cut the cabbage in half, then make diagonal cuts around the white central stalk and remove it together with any particularly manky outer leaves. If using Brussels sprouts, then prepare them similarly, cutting off the bottom stalk and any dirty leaves and halving them. Shred the remainder of the cabbage into thin slices, cutting out any stalky bits as you go.

Cut the bacon into small strips at right angles to the fat and remove the rind if you have it.

Heat a little olive oil in a large saucepan and fry the bacon until crisp. Add the cabbage and a little more oil and half of the butter, then increase the heat and stir it around, allowing the cabbage to catch a bit and go brown in places. When it's nearly done, going limp, a bit brown but still retaining its crunchy essence, create an opening in the centre and add the remaining oil and butter. Add the garlic to the centre, then reduce the heat and keep stirring in the central hole for a minute or so, so the garlic begins to cook but does not brown. You don't want it burned. Stir all the ingredients together, then taste – the cabbage should taste sweet and buttery. Add a little salt (perhaps there may not be need for salt, but add it if you think it needs something) and lots of pepper. Taste and adjust the seasoning. Serve with the potatoes, halved and buttered or with crème fraîche or whatever you fancy.

Note: If you are serving this dish with baked potatoes or whatever, then cook them first and leave in a warm place while you prepare the rest of the dish. If you microwave the potatoes then you can turn them on to 'conventional' oven and crisp up the skin a bit while you wait for the cabbage.

INDIAN-SPICED POTATOES, SPINACH AND LAMB

This dish is a lovely combination of spices, garlic and butter, which makes the spinach delectable and the potatoes rich – the lamb is really there as a background taste or to convince any men, like my husband, that their carnivore traits are being assuaged. You can substitute any leanish meat or pancetta or bacon or eggs, although, of course, you would be straying from any remaining authenticity. I actually used a piece of rump steak I wanted to use up from the freezer. You may see this dish on a restaurant menu as a version of aloo gobi. To make it easy and to save time and cut down on washing-up, it's all made in one large pan; it might sound laborious and long-winded, but it's really simple.

SERVES: 2

- 1 small piece of lamb steak or fillet, fat and gristle removed and cut into chunks (you only need a handful of meat if at all)
- 2–3 small potatoes each, according to taste and hunger and potato size, halved
- 1 onion, finely sliced
- 1 tbsp unflavoured oil, such as peanut, rapeseed or sunflower
- 1 large tsp ground cumin
- 1 large tsp ground coriander
- 1 large tsp paprika
- 6 cardamom pods, bashed with something heavy like a knife sharpening steel to open them
- 1 large tsp black mustard seeds
- 2.5 cm cube of fresh ginger, peeled, sliced and chopped
- 1–2 medium-hot chillies, de-seeded and sliced (more if you like as you can always taste it near the end and add a little dried chopped chilli, if you want it hotter)
- salt and ground black pepper
- 2 large knobs of unsalted butter (and a bit more, if you want to make it gorgeous, but very calorific; if you're desperate not to eat butter then add some more oil)
- 4 garlic cloves, crushed
- 300–400 g spinach, prewashed as it's such a pain to remove the dirt
- juice of 1 lemon

Season the lamb chunks with a little salt and pepper and put to one side.

Boil the halved potatoes in a large pan of water until cooked and soft.

Meanwhile, in a large sauté pan, slowly fry the onion in the oil until very soft and just about to colour. You can use a large saucepan, but it's more difficult to toss the food around, and it may seem steamed rather than fried. Add the cumin, coriander and paprika, then reduce the heat and stir around to avoid burning, adding a little more oil if necessary. After 2 minutes, add the cardamom pods, mustard seeds, ginger and chillies and stir around over a gentle heat for another 2 minutes. If you need to wait for the potatoes, remove the pan from the heat.

When the potatoes are cooked, drain and cut them into quarters, then add to the main pan and cook over a medium–gentle heat, moving them around so they are well coated in the aromatics and onion. Sprinkle over a little salt to taste.

Separate out the vegetables, so that there is a hole in the middle of the food. Add a knob of butter, then stir the garlic into the middle of the hole. Briefly stir around, then push into the main mixture. Make another hole in the centre of the mixture and add another knob of butter. Add the meat and fry until it has just enough time to colour the outside of the meat but no more. It will continue cooking while the spinach cooks around it. Add the spinach, turning it over so that the onion and potato mixture comes to the top and the spinach heats through and begins to wilt. You might have to do the spinach in 2 batches because it's so bulky at first. Squeeze the lemon juice over the spinach with a sprinkling of salt and pepper.

To be seriously indulgent, add another few knobs of butter, then taste and adjust the seasoning and serve.

Note: Don't overcook the spinach. Good-quality spinach will retain its freshness and not disintegrate into a slime, if you just toss it over and over in the pan.

CAULIFLOWER CHEESE

Leeks, broccoli or any other vegetable can also be used: a classic béchamel or velouté sauce is incorporated in this recipe.

SERVES: 2–6

- 6 black peppercorns
- 3 bay leaves
- 1 chicken stock cube, crumbled
- 1 cauliflower, cut into florets
- 1 large onion, chopped
- 1 dsp oil
- 3 knobs of unsalted butter
- bacon, chorizo or salami, cut into small pieces and enough to make up 1 tbsp meat (if you have it)
- 2 tbsp flour
- 250 ml cooking liquor, milk and/or cream and/or crème fraîche
- 150 g grated cheese, such as strong Cheddar or Gruyère, plus Parmesan if you like for the taste
- salt and ground black pepper
- extra cheese and/or breadcrumbs to finish (if you have some)

Bring a large pan of about 250 ml of water to the boil adding the peppercorns and bay leaves. Then crumble in the stock cube, whisking well to dissolve it. Add the cauliflower. Tip out some water if necessary so that the water is only just halfway up the cauliflower and boil for 10–15 minutes until the cauliflower is just cooked and soft enough to eat but still a bit crunchy. Drain in a colander set over a pan to retain the hot cooking liquor. Bring the cooking liquor to the boil to condense the flavour.

Meanwhile, in another frying pan, fry the onion in the oil and 1 knob of butter until soft and just beginning to brown, then add the bacon, chorizo or salami, if you are using it, until they are just cooked. When you're a bit more used to the recipe you can cook the roux in this pan, but for clarity I have kept the sauce and meat separate.

In another large pan, heat the remaining butter gently until frothy. Add the flour and stir around for about 2 minutes, so that the mixture comes together into a stiffish paste, coming away from the sides of the pan and the flour is cooked and loses its raw taste. It shouldn't colour or start to stick. Add a little more butter if necessary. This is called a roux and can be the starting point of every classic flour-based white sauce, not only in France, but, for example, on the top of a Greek moussaka, and so on. If it cooks a little more and becomes smooth and light golden brown then it is the foundation of a brown sauce.

There are two ways of making the sauce.

The first needs a little practice and time, in that the liquid, milk or cream is added to the roux, a very small amount at a time, quickly stirring the mixture around at each addition, to prevent lumps. You can add cold liquid this way.

The second way is more foolproof, but requires more washing-up as you need an extra pan. Here is the second way which is what we are using in this recipe:

Make the roux as above, adding a little more butter as it's cooking. At the same time, heat whatever liquor – stock, cauliflower cooking liquor, milk, wine-stock combo – you're using in a separate pan until it boils. When they're both hot, quickly tip the liquor into the roux, stirring constantly with a whisk and you'll end up with a smooth thickened sauce. You add hot liquor this way.

This produces the basic sauce.

Back to the cauliflower. Add the cheese to the sauce and let it melt down and flavour the sauce. It should taste really cheesy, rather than just a slightly savoury white sauce, so be prepared to add more cheese at the end if necessary. Most people including restaurants serve it rather bland. Taste and adjust the seasoning, then add all the other ingredients.

If you want to serve it at the table in a serving dish, then you can finish it off under a hot grill, adding a layer of cheese and/or breadcrumbs to brown over the top.

SEA BASS WITH BÉARNAISE SAUCE

These are baked whole so it's extremely easy and great when really fresh.

- small sea bass, about 15 cm long and 1 each to be generous, cleaned

- olive oil

- enough garlic cloves, crushed to add ½ clove to each fish

- enough chopped parsley to add half a tbsp to each fish

- 1 lemon, sliced

- salt and freshly ground black pepper

Preheat the oven to 180°C (160°C fan oven) mark 4.

Remove the scales from the fish, by rubbing a sharp knife at 90 degrees to the skin to slough off the scales, then cut the fins off. Or better still, get the fishmonger to do it for you. It's important to get all the scales off, as they have an awful effect if you find one inadvertently while chewing. Wash the fish inside and out and dry the outside with kitchen paper.

Smear a little olive oil immediately under the area the fish will take up on a baking tray or piece of foil. Stuff each cavity with ½ crushed garlic clove, half a tablespoon of chopped parsley, a slice of lemon and salt and pepper. Dribble a little olive oil over the skin and season with salt and pepper. Arrange on the baking tray or foil and cook in the oven for 15–20 minutes until the skin is slightly golden and crisp which you can easily peel off and the flesh (if you're unsure) comes easily away from the bones. Peel off the skin or leave it to individuals if you can trust them not to complain. I tend to make things as easy as possible for any family members distrustful of fish, and skin and fillet them ready for combat. Modern presentation favours leaving the skin on fillets, but do what you really want for yourself. If you want to fillet them then, like any whole fish which isn't flat, turn it on its side, run a sharp knife halfway down the side on the lateral dark line (if it has one), along its length, cutting through until you hit bone. Peel back the skin if you don't like it or it's not crisp enough. Put the knife against the bone at an angle and carefully detach the fillet from the bone at the top and then the bottom. You've then got 2 clean fillets. Turn the fish over and do the same on the other side leaving 4 fillets in total and a clean bone.

SAUCE BÉARNAISE

An absolutely essential, classic sauce for steaks, fish, chicken or eggs to add a smooth background sauce to moisten an otherwise simple but dry dish. Best to make this first and keep warm while you're cooking the fish, so you're not distracted.

MAKES: A MUGFUL

- 3 tbsp white wine vinegar
- 4 tbsp white wine or dry vermouth
- 1 tbsp very finely chopped shallots or spring onions or, at a pinch, 'normal' onions
- 1 tbsp freshly chopped tarragon or ½ tbsp if dried
- 3 egg yolks
- a knob of cold unsalted butter
- 100 g unsalted butter, melted
- 2 tbsp freshly chopped parsley or tarragon (second lot)
- salt and ground black pepper

Boil the vinegar, wine, shallots and the 1 tbsp chopped tarragon for a few minutes, or until only 2 tbsp are left, then strain and leave to cool.

Beat the egg yolks, just like making Hollandaise, adding the strained, cooled vinegar mixture very slowly. Beat in the cold butter while thickening over a low heat. Beat in the melted butter, drop by drop, over the heat. Beat in the remaining herbs. Season with a pinch of salt and a grind or two of pepper. Taste and adjust as necessary and serve warm.

SEARED TUNA IN CHILLI OIL WITH TOMATO SAUCE AND FIG RELISH

If you don't have any chilli oil, then marinate the tuna with some chopped chillies in a tablespoon of olive oil, say one for each of the steaks, depending on your taste and the strength of the chillies.

SERVES: 2

- 2 tuna steaks about 1.5–2 cm thick
- chilli oil
- 5 large fresh tomatoes (skinned and de-seeded) or some ready-made tomato sauce or even 1 can plum tomatoes
- 1 medium onion, finely chopped
- oil to cook
- 5–6 new potatoes, scrubbed, halved or quartered according to size
- a handful of capers. If the salted variety then drain, wash and squeeze out
- 3 anchovy fillets, cut into large chunks
- 2 tbsp fig relish or 2 figs, sliced
- a splash of wine or balsamic vinegar (if you have it)
- 2 bay leaves and 5 black peppercorns
- ½ tsp sugar
- ¼ tsp salt
- 1 tbsp freshly chopped coriander
- 1 tbsp freshly chopped flat-leaf parsley
- a few snipped chives to garnish

Marinate the tuna in some chilli oil for as long as you can, even 5 minutes before you cook.

Cut a small circle down and around each stalk end of the tomatoes to remove the stalk end and any sepals. Make a small cut at the base end and put into a bowl of boiling water. After about 5 minutes the skin should start receding from the cuts so you can peel it off. Remove the tomatoes from the bowl and peel off the skins, then halve, remove the remaining core and seeds and chop. This might seem a bit of a palaver, but it makes for a cleaner end result and should only take a few minutes.

Fry the onion slowly in oil in a frying pan over a low heat, stirring from time to time, until soft. Add the tomatoes and any juice lying on the chopping board and let it slowly cook through, evaporating off the water and becoming thick. Keep stirring and don't let it catch like I did once. Distracted by a game of football, I had to resurrect the sauce with more sugar, more salt, tomato ketchup and a little Loyd Grossman together with some chopped spring onions.

After about 10 minutes pick out the chillies from the fish and add to the tomato sauce, adding a little water if the sauce is becoming too thick.

About halfway through the cooking process, of say a total of 45 minutes, boil the water for the potatoes and start cooking them.

Add the capers and anchovies to the tomato sauce and taste and adjust the seasoning.

When the potatoes are tender, drain and keep warm in the same pan with a knob of butter.

Heat a frying pan or griddle until very hot.

Heat the plates, easy in a microwave.

Put the fish into the pan with a little oil to prevent the fish sticking. If you've got a griddle pan with ridges then you'll come out with impressive and professional dark char-lines. You can watch the sides for 'doneness' as it gradually turns from dark to light. When it turns light halfway up the side, then turn over. Each side should take about 1½–2 minutes, but here you can adjust it so that it is just seared and dark pink in the middle, or fully done (as some picky people prefer) when it all turns light browny pink all through.

If you don't have any fig relish, then briefly fry the sliced figs, add a splash of vinegar, the 1 tsp of sugar and salt and pepper and stir around until everything is coated. Remove from the heat and put to one side.

Add the chopped herbs to the tomato sauce, then serve the sauce first in a small roundel with the fish on top, pouring over a little chilli oil around the plate – sometimes your hand might slip at this stage, but don't worry; it will be wolfed up. Sprinkle the fish with a little salt and scatter the snipped chives over the top, then put the potatoes on one side and a nice dollop of fig relish or the fresh figs on the other side.

BROCCOLI, CAULIFLOWER AND CARROT CURRY

Sounds a bit prosaic, but really tasty. A quick and easy curry that can be adapted to almost any vegetable. Here, I'm using a bag of prepared broccoli, cauliflower and carrots, which will serve 2–3 people. It's a cheat I know it, but at least it's a vegetable and nearly fresh, and available from all supermarkets. You can always use fresh, local vegetables if you can afford the time to shop for them.

SERVES: 2–3

- ½ onion, roughly chopped
- oil, such as peanut or sunflower to cook
- 1 bag of supermarket veg or any of your own choice, such as carrots, broccoli, swede, butternut squash, green beans and so on to make up about 3 or 4 tbsps
- 2 garlic cloves, mashed
- 1 small fiery red chilli, de-seeded and finely chopped or crumble 2 dried ones instead
- 2.5 cm cube of fresh root ginger, peeled, finely sliced and chopped
- 6 small tomatoes, or the equivalent, roughly chopped

- ½ block of creamed coconut (usually comes in 200 g blocks), chopped into 4–5 pieces

- salt and ground black pepper

- 1 tbsp ghormeh sabzi or methi leaves (see note)

In a large pan, gently brown the onion in some oil of your choice.

Microwave the bag of vegetables by making a few slashes in it with a knife, so that the steam does not build up too much and cook on high for 3½ minutes. Try a bit and cook a little longer if necessary. It should still retain a bit of bite.

Meanwhile, add the garlic, chilli and ginger to the frying pan, reduce the heat to a simmer and stir around the pan so they don't stick. After a minute or so, add the tomatoes and cook until they have fallen apart and become a mush,

stirring constantly. Add the coconut. If the mixture is too thick and it's beginning to stick, add a very small amount of water, milk or cream, then taste and adjust the seasoning, adding salt as necessary. Stir in the ghormeh sabzi if you are using it, or methi leaves, then stir in the vegetables and serve.

Note: A really lovely addition to almost any curry is ghormeh sabzi, which I have found in Asian shops. It is a blend of chopped herbs containing parsley, chives, fenugreek and coriander leaves. The real delight is that, although all the herbs are relatively common these days, this zingy, authentic combination gives it a unique and delightful fragrancy, mainly from the fenugreek leaves. If you can't find it, then use some dried methi leaves, often called fenugreek in the west. If you ever see it fresh in Asian shops, it's worthwhile buying and trying. ghormeh sabzi is also the name of the famous Persian herb stew. My pack of ghormeh sabzi is packed by Greenfields, 25 Crawford St., London.

SPICED STIR-FRIED PORK WITH RASPBERRY- SWEETENED SOY SAUCE

This is a mid-week standby; easy to cook and quick to prepare. Soy sauce is often sweetened with sugar in Chinese food, but here I used some leftover raspberry coulis and some crème de framboise from the larder, which never seems to get used up. If you haven't any raspberry coulis hanging around, which is most probably the case, then squish a big handful of defrosted frozen raspberries through a sieve with a little icing sugar.

SERVES: 2–4

- about 100–200 g lean pork, cut up into chunks per person, depending on how you feel

- a handful of rice per person

- ½ large onion, chopped

- 1 tbsp oil, such as rapeseed or groundnut oil

- a handful of mangetout, cut into diagonal chunks

- 1 large carrot, peeled and cut into small batons

- 3 baby sweetcorn, cut into chunks

- 1 fairly mild chilli, thinly sliced

- 2.5 cm cube of fresh root ginger, peeled, sliced and cut into matchsticks

- 1 dsp cornflour mixed with a little cold water into a smooth, milky paste

- a few sploshes of soy sauce, wine or rice vinegar or dry sherry if you have it or water (if you must)

FOR THE MARINADE

- 1 tbsp each of teriyaki or soy sauce and wine vinegar

- 1 tbsp soy sauce

- 1 dsp caster sugar

- 1 dsp raspberry coulis

- 1 dsp crème de framboise

- 2 garlic cloves, crushed

- a smidgeon of five-spice powder (a little pile at the end of a knife or a small shake, if you can trust yourself with an open spice jar)

Mix all the marinade ingredients together in a large bowl, then add the pork and leave to marinate in advance if possible, but it doesn't really matter.

Cook the rice according to the instructions on page 44.

In a wok or large frying pan, stir-fry the onion over a high heat in the oil. When the onion is just about to catch, add all the other vegetables, including the ginger, and stir-fry until they are nearly done but still crunchy.

Check the rice and if it's ready, then turn off the heat and cover with the lid to keep warm.

Move the vegetables to the sides of the wok and add the meat and marinade all in one go into the centre, boiling down the liquid as the meat cooks. When the meat is just cooked through, stir in the cornflour mixture. This thickens the background sauce. If it gets too thick, then add a few sploshes of soy sauce, wine or rice vinegar or dry sherry or even water. Serve immediately. The rice should be done at about the same time. This is not classic Chinese cuisine, in that the meat and vegetables would normally be cooked separately and kept warm, but time is short and if you cook over a high enough heat and move the vegetables out of the way, you should still achieve a reasonable and yet delicious stab at it.

TARTIFLETTE

A really indulgent creamy, cheesy, layered potato dish which reminds me of many skiing holidays, since this is a speciality of the Haute-Savoie region of France, with many variations on the same theme coming from other Alpine regions. The Swiss have their version and this is mine. Being a rich combination of potatoes, bacon and cheese with cream, it is delicious but calorific, so is normally confined to the winter months when this sort of comfort food may be more justly deserved, especially after a day spent skiing.

SERVES: 6–8

- 10 large or 14 medium potatoes, peeled if you want and halved lengthways

- 3 large onions, sliced

- half unsalted butter and half oil, plus extra butter to grease

- 12 rashers smoked streaky bacon or 250 g smoked lardons or equivalent in pancetta, cut into small pieces

- 10 slices of salami, cut in half

- 1 garlic clove, halved

- salt and ground black pepper

- 1 big glass of dry white wine

- 1 chicken stock cube dissolved in 1 mug of boiling water

- a big block, about 8 cm square strong cheese, such as mature Cheddar or reserve aged Gruyère or strong (real) aged Gouda, grated (this I might add is in contrast to the French version which only allows Reblochon, so take your pick)

- 2 mugs of double cream or crème fraîche or at pinch, milk

Preheat the oven to 190°C (170°C fan oven) mark 5.

Boil a pan of water large enough to hold the potatoes. Meanwhile, prepare the potatoes and add them to the pan. As soon as the water starts boiling, reduce the heat to a simmer and cover with a lid.

Fry the onions in half butter and half oil, stirring over a high heat at first, then reducing the heat and cooking the onions gently, stirring now and again to stop them burning, until they are a rich, soft, golden colour. Remove from the pan and put to one side.

Fry the meat until crisp, then add to the onions and put to one side.

When the potatoes are parboiled and beginning to soften, about 10–15 minutes, drain, then put the flat cut side of the potatoes down on a chopping board and thinly slice.

Rub a casserole dish, preferably with high, straight sides or a small roasting tin with butter and a cut clove of garlic. Arrange a layer of potatoes laid flat and overlapping in the base of the casserole dish, then cover with a layer of the onion and meat mixture finishing off with the second layer of potatoes, adding salt and pepper to each layer of potatoes. Pour the wine and stock over the potatoes. If you use Reblochon then you need to add the cream over the potatoes and put the Reblochon, cut in half horizontally, on top. If you're using the hard cheese then grate the cheese and mix it in with the cream and spoon it over the top of the potatoes. Cook in the oven for 30 minutes or until the top is sizzling with anticipation.

STILTON AND BROCCOLI SOUP

A classic, but much, much better this way than any other you may have tried. This is one of those dishes that remind me of Christmas when you might be minded to use up the bits of leftover Stilton.

SERVES: 2–4

- 1 large onion, finely chopped
- 1–2 tbsp olive oil
- 1 large head of broccoli, finely chopped
- 1 mug of milk
- 1 chicken stock cube dissolved in 2 mugs of boiling water
- 10 black peppercorns
- 3 bay leaves
- a big chunk of Stilton, about 7 × 7 × 2.5 cm, crumbled if possible
- ½ mug of cream
- ground black pepper
- toasted walnuts to sprinkle (if you have them)

TO SERVE

- rounds of sourdough or baguette, toasted
- 1 garlic clove, halved
- butter

Fry the onion in the oil, stirring over a high heat at first, then reducing the heat and cooking gently, stirring now and again to stop it burning, until it is very soft and only just beginning to brown. Add the broccoli and stir around the pan for 2–3 minutes over a low heat. Add the milk and increase the heat to high, then add the stock, peppercorns and bay leaves and simmer for about 10 minutes.

Taste the soup. The liquid should have reduced a bit and the broccoli should be cooked. Add the cheese, stir and allow it to melt over a low heat. Add the cream and heat through very gently to stop it separating. The broccoli should be small enough to still have some texture within the soup. If you like smooth soups, you can blend or purée it at this point, but I like the immediacy of this version, so I purée a little but leave some lumps. Grind over some pepper, sprinkle with toasted walnuts, if you have them, then serve with toasted rounds of bread, rubbed with a cut garlic clove and then buttered to lie floating on the surface of each generous soup dish.

SALMON IN SOY SAUCE AND MIRIN

This is absurdly quick, very healthy and uses no oil, except for the natural good oils in salmon. The salmon is marinated in this slightly sweet and savoury marinade which cooks down into a glossy, intense coating. Serve with rice and a bright green vegetable. Here I've used peas and made a garlicky crème fraîche sauce – it's certainly not authentic, this mixture of tastes, but somehow it seems to work.

SERVES: 2

- 2 salmon fillets
- a few sloshes each of soy sauce, mirin and sake or soy sauce, balsamic vinegar (or other vinegar) and dry sherry
- 1 garlic clove, crushed
- 1 level dsp sugar or use a small amount of sweetener
- 2 handfuls of rice
- a large handful of frozen peas
- salt and ground black pepper
- a small handful of freshly chopped dill and parsley to garnish

Cut the skin off the salmon. To do this, place the salmon, skin side down, on a chopping board, then slicing with a sharp knife from side to side against the skin and the board, tugging it with one hand to keep the skin taut. This is easier to do if the fish has just been defrosted and is quite cold, and the knife has been freshly sharpened. Once the fish is warmed up it seems to start cooking and the skin and flesh will not be parted so easily. Remove any bones, then place the salmon in a large dish, add the soy sauce, mirin and sake (or the soy, vinegar and wine) together with the garlic and sugar and leave to marinate for as long as you can, or at least while you do everything else.

Cook the rice according to the instructions on page xx. Put the plates to warm in the microwave for 2 minutes on high.

Meanwhile, cook the peas in a pan of boiling water for 2–3 minutes, then drain and keep warm in the pan.

Place the salmon and marinade in a frying pan or sauté pan over a high heat. Wait until it starts bubbling, then reduce the heat to low. Depending on the thickness of the salmon, it should only take 2–3 minutes on each side and the marinade should evaporate down to a thick, savoury sauce. If the sauce looks like it's burning or disappearing completely, add the smallest amount of water and swirl around. Again, it's better to undercook the salmon, as it continues to cook even as you take it off the heat. Taste and adjust the seasoning if needed.

Serve the salmon with the teriyaki sauce dribbled on top and garnished with chopped dill and parsley. The salmon should have taken on the dark hues of the soy sauce on its sides, but still be a little pink in the middle. I have another version of this dish, which is even less authentic, adding crème fraîche to the final sauce, which to the Japanese would be very odd as they do not include much dairy in their diet. This quietens the sauce down, making it less salty. You might like to try it as a variation.

SPICY CHICKEN WITH PINEAPPLE

Normally I would run a mile to escape additions of things like pineapple to a Chinese-style meal: it smacks too much of vivid concoctions, such as sweet and sour chicken, from the worst sort of Chinese takeaways. Anyway, here it works well, because it has no added sugar, so it's not ridiculously sweet, and the pineapple retains its freshness, texture and colour. Again, not totally authentic, but it works well.

SERVES: 2

- 2 skinless, boneless chicken thighs, cut into chunks

- a few sloshes of soy sauce

- 3 pinches of five-spice powder

- 1 handful of rice per person

- 1 medium onion, very finely chopped

- 2 tbsp unflavoured oil, such as rapeseed or groundnut oil

- 1 red chilli, de-seeded and finely sliced (see note)

- 1 small piece fresh root ginger, peeled and thinly sliced

- a small handful of any crunchy green vegetable, such as pak choi, sugar snap peas or fine beans, cut into chunks

- 1 tbsp sesame oil or other oil

- a small handful of fresh pineapple, cut into chunks

- a small handful of freshly chopped coriander or use some dried ghormeh sabzi (page 168)

Place the chicken in a large bowl with the soy sauce and five-spice powder and leave to marinate for 10–15 minutes, or longer if you have the time.

Cook the rice according to the instructions on page 44.

In another pan, slowly cook the onion over a low heat in the 2 tbsp oil until very soft and beginning to brown. (This is the exact opposite of normal stir-fried, crunchy onions.) As the onion browns, add the chicken and marinade and cook until just tender – no more.

Check the rice and turn off when cooked, but leave the lid on to keep warm.

Stir-fry the chilli, ginger and green vegetables over a high heat in the sesame oil, turning the food over and over with a fish slice or spatula so that it does not burn or catch. Add a small splosh of water if it looks like it might be burning.

After 2–3 minutes, when the green vegetable is wilting and softening a little, add the chicken and onion mixture to the wok, turning the mixture over. Add the pineapple and turn around in the wok.

Heat through and serve with coriander on top and the rice on the side.

Note: To finely slice the chilli, halve it lengthways, then scrape out the seeds (unless you like it hot) and slice the flesh thinly.

SPICY MOROCCAN STIR-FRY

This is a bit of a misnomer, in that it is an approximation of what I think is Moroccan. It's more to do with using up bits in my kitchen and adapting what I've got, to what I want. These sorts of dishes benefit from the sort of fridge I operate. There is always an assortment of bits and bobs in various little bottles and jars, half-finished and never quite cleared up. I built this dish up having bought a (yes, just one) sweet potato. Wondering what to do with it, I looked in the fridge and there was some chicken thigh fillet and some leftover spiced Moroccan lemon paste. From the cupboard, I found some ghormeh sabzi and the end of a packet of ras el hanout.

SERVES: 2–3

- 1 large tbsp chopped dried apricots
- olive oil to cook
- ½ medium onion, chopped
- 1 medium sweet potato, peeled and cut into small chunks
- 1 dsp ras el hanout or use a little cumin, 2 whole cloves with 2 heaped tsp smoked paprika or perhaps you might have a bit of leftover ghormeh sabzi herb mixture or harissa sauce
- 1 dsp dried coriander
- 3 garlic cloves, sliced
- a handful of pinenuts
- 1 dsp lemon paste (available from most supermarkets, but if you can't find it use the grated zest and juice of 1 lemon or any leftover preserved lemons chopped up)
- ½ tsp chilli flakes (I admit my hand slipped and it must have been more like 1 whole tsp and it was very hot. Again, even chilli flakes are variable in hotness)
- 1 heaped tsp salt or less if you use preserved lemons as these can be very salty
- a handful of bulgur wheat or couscous per person
- 3 skinless, boneless chicken thigh fillets, cut off any fat then cut into bite-size pieces
- fresh coriander and parsley (optional), to garnish

Place the dried apricots in a small heatproof bowl and pour in enough hot water to cover. Leave to plump for 20 minutes, then drain and put to one side.

In a large sauté pan, add a little oil and stir in the onion over a high heat. Reduce the heat to medium, keep stirring and let the onions go soft. Add the sweet potato and stir around to coat the potato. Cook for about 10 minutes until the potato is just starting to soften. Add the ras el hanout and dried herbs and keep stirring to prevent them burning, but let them cook through a little. Add the garlic and stir for 1 minute. Add enough water to half cover the potato, then increase the heat to high and boil, turning the potato over when you can. Add the apricots, pinenuts, lemon paste, chilli flakes, salt and some of the fresh herbs, if you are using them.

Meanwhile, start the bulgur wheat or couscous. You only need a little because of the starch in the sweet potato. Leave the bulgur wheat to steep in a pan of cold water for 20 minutes to swell up a little, then empty the water, add enough hot water to cover and boil for 2–3 minutes to heat up. Strain through a sieve. When you are more practised, you can add just enough boiling water to cook the wheat, then you shouldn't need to strain it. If in doubt, follow the pack instructions.

Taste and adjust the seasoning to the main dish. The potato should be half-cooked by now. Reduce the heat and leave to simmer for 5–10 minutes until some of the liquid has evaporated and the sauce is thickish and the potato is fully cooked. Increase the heat to medium, adding a little water if it begins to stick, and add the chicken, turning over in the sauce until it cooks. Garnish with the fresh herbs if you are using them and serve with the cooked bulgur wheat or couscous.

GAZPACHO

This would probably not go down well in Spain, since it is very much my version of the classic cold, spicy Spanish soup. However, mine is not in the least bit watery, but quite a strong-tasting soup, which I think is necessary for anything served cold.

SERVES: 2–3

- 1 garlic clove
- 6 largish best-quality tomatoes, preferably peeled (page 114), de-seeded and chopped
- ½ red chilli, de-seeded and finely sliced (choose the variety according to your taste in chillies)
- ½ cucumber, peeled, de-seeded and chopped into cubes

175

- a few slices of red pepper, preferably the sweet sort

- juice of 1 lime

- 2 tsp sherry vinegar or mixture of red wine vinegar and sherry

- 1 tsp sugar

- ½ tsp salt

TO SERVE

- good-quality olive oil

- ground black pepper

- good, fresh bread

It's so easy; ideally, you need a blender or food processor, but you can throw in all the ingredients straight from the fridge. Blend all the ingredients together and cool in the fridge if necessary. Eat it with a swirl of good-quality oil, a few grinds of black pepper and some good, fresh bread. It should be fresh and zingy, cold and refreshing all at the same time.

CHICKEN AND PEAS IN A SPICY SAUCE

This is really a curry, but, unlike authentic Indian versions, it's cooked without oil, butter or ghee (clarified butter), so it's very healthy. There is a purée of onions, garlic and ginger and so on, in which the chicken and peas are cooked together in a large sauté pan.

SERVES: 2

- 1 medium onion, chopped

- 1 garlic clove, halved

- 2.5 cm cube of fresh root ginger, peeled and chopped

- a few pinches of dried chillies or equivalent fresh, de-seeded and chopped

- 6–8 whole little spicy peppers from a jar (sold as mild 'Peppadew' piquante peppers from South Africa, usually available in supermarkets)

- 10 whole black peppercorns

- juice of 1 lemon

- a few sloshes of fish sauce

- 1 tsp black onion seeds

- about 6 curry leaves

- 1 tsp Thai 5 spice seasoning or a large pinch of ground cinnamon and 2 cloves

- 2 skinless, boneless chicken thighs, cut into chunks

- 1 tbsp frozen peas

- rice

- freshly chopped coriander to garnish

Put everything, except the chicken, peas and rice, in a blender and blitz until it is a thick purée. Empty out the purée into a large sauté pan and bubble over a medium heat. Wash the blender out with about 1 cup of water, swilling out the residue at the same time and add to the purée. Reduce the heat to low and add the chicken.

Meanwhile, cook the rice in a separate pan following the instructions on page 44.

Stir the chicken around, then increase the heat to high until it starts bubbling. Reduce the heat to low and leave for a further 5 minutes, watching it so that there's enough liquid, and stirring the chicken around. Add the peas, then increase the heat again and bring to the boil. Once it's boiling, reduce the heat to medium and cook the peas for 1–2 minutes until they are warm all the way through.

Serve with the rice, garnished with chopped coriander.

KEDGEREE

There are so many versions of this dish – a classic, Britano-Indian meal made with rice, aromatics and smoked fish, and mine is just one of the many versions. I like it because the individual ingredients stay separate and tasty, rather than the more bland overview that some chefs like. I add lots of herbs so it looks fresh and green. This dish can easily be served as a starter, or traditionally for breakfast, but seeing as it's relatively wholesome, it's probably best as a main course. The poppy, black onion and mustard seeds are not essential but they give a bite to the rice and make it more visually appealing.

SERVES: 4

- 3–4 handfuls of rice or less if it's a starter
- 1 large fresh smoked undyed haddock or smoked cod fillet (this can be larger or smaller, according to whether you're doing this as a main course or a starter)
- 1 medium–large onion, finely sliced
- 1 tbsp vegetable oil, such as corn, rapeseed or peanut
- 1 tsp black poppy seeds
- 1 tsp black onion seeds
- 1 tsp black mustard seeds
- 1 tbsp unsalted butter
- 2 garlic cloves, finely sliced
- 1–2 mild red chillies, de-seeded and finely chopped
- 1 mug of milk
- 6–7 cardamom pods
- 4 large eggs
- a handful of frozen peas
- 1 tub of crème fraîche or cream, about 300 g
- finely grated zest and juice of 1 lemon
- salt and ground black pepper

Cook the rice following the instructions on page 44.

Place the fish, skin side down, on a chopping board and skin, using a sharp knife almost parallel against the skin. You can usually just pull the skin off, keeping the knife angled down on the board.

Fry the onion in the oil in a large sauté or frying pan until brown.

In another pan, fry the seeds in a little of the butter until spluttering, then add the garlic and chillies, reduce the heat and stir around for 1 minute. Don't allow the garlic to colour, or it will overcook and burn. Empty it all out into the large pan with the onion.

Place the fish in a small saucepan with the milk, a knob of butter and the cardamom pods and gently simmer for a few moments until the fish is white and non-translucent. Remove the pan from the heat and transfer the fish to another warm dish. Keep the pan of milk.

Boil the eggs in a pan of water for 5 minutes, then place them in a bowl of cold water and peel off the shells. Keep them in hot water until final assembly. It is quite difficult peeling the shells off and the eggs are easy to pierce, but try to keep them as much together as you can. Effectively, you have cooked the eggs until they are only just done, and they will be slithery to handle. Alternatively, you can always poach them or really hard-boil them for 6 minutes. I prefer to see the warm egg yolk still liquid for the finish.

Empty the cooked rice into the large pan and stir around until the rice is coated with the onion and seeds. Boil the milk until only 1 tbsp remains, then remove the cardamom pods.

Quickly boil the peas for 1–2 minutes in a pan of boiling water until hot, then drain and stir into the rice. Add the crème fraîche and lemon zest and juice, then stir in the milk and lastly, salt and pepper. Taste and adjust the seasoning. Gently stir or fold in the fish, trying not to let it break up too much, separating it into individual flakes, if you can, and keeping some for the top of the rice. Divide the rice among plates or bowls, add the rest of the fish and place an egg per person on the top of the rice, so that when it is pierced, the soft yolk oozes out over the little pyramid of rice. Garnish with chopped herbs and serve.

Kedgeree

INSPIRED BY A SORT OF TAGINE

This was largely inspired by a friend bringing me back some harissa from Morocco. It came as a medley of ground spices, quite red and pungent, whereas I've only ever known harissa as a prepared sauce before, so I don't know who conned who. The supermarkets now sell their own, sometimes as 'rose harissa' with the addition of rose petals, I presume. I had no onions (shame) so I started with shredded cabbage and it resulted in a fruity, spicy, aromatic mixture of vegetables with unusual textures of pinenuts and sweet potato. I can't claim it is in the least bit authentic, but then the Moroccans argue about the best tagine, which is always personal, and to our taste at least, needs a bit of bite and hotness, together with a mixture of fruit, dried or otherwise.

SERVES: 4–8

- ½ Savoy cabbage, with tough bits cut out and finely sliced

- olive oil and butter to cook

- a small handful of fresh or frozen peas

- 6 small carrots, peeled and rough bits removed and chopped into big pieces

- 1 medium sweet potato, peeled and rough bits removed and chopped roughly

- 3 dsp harissa or use a mix of ground cumin, coriander and paprika with a little chilli

- 2 garlic cloves, sliced

- a knob of fresh root ginger, peeled and sliced

- a few big sloshes of fish sauce or ½ tsp salt

- a handful of chopped dried apricots and pine nuts

- 3 or 4 lamb steaks de-fatted and cubed or 4 chopped skinless, boneless chicken thighs

- a few slices of red pepper, for colour

- 1 tbsp freshly chopped coriander

- 1 tbsp freshly chopped mint

- rice, bulgur wheat or couscous to serve

Fry the cabbage in a large sauté pan in a little oil and butter over a high heat until just starting to brown. Try a bit; it's amazing how even the humble cabbage takes on a new flavour if it's fried rather than boiled. Add the peas, carrots and sweet potato and stir around for a few minutes. Add the harissa or spices and stir for a minute or so, just so that the harshness of the spice powder is cooked a little. Add a little more oil now if the mixture is sticking. If it's a prepared sauce, then it's easier. Add the garlic and ginger, stir around and add enough water to almost cover the vegetables. Add the fish sauce or salt, but watch the amounts as, if you're using a prepared sauce, it's almost bound to have salt already in it. Add the apricots and nuts.

Prepare the rice (see page 44) or start the couscous or bulgur wheat as instructed.

Once the water has started to boil in the main pan, reduce the heat to a fast simmer and leave until the vegetables are just tender and the water has evaporated by about half. Tip in the meat and red pepper and keep cooking, turning the meat over until it is done. Mix in the chopped herbs, then taste and adjust the seasoning. Serve with rice, bulgur wheat or couscous.

ROAST FENNEL, BACON AND POTATOES

This is the sort of meal that appears out of nowhere, sounds pretty basic but is surprisingly tasty. I think the combination of the textures, as well as the tastes, is particularly appetising, and often it can use up bits of food left in the fridge. You can add all sorts of vegetables to it. I once did it with roast asparagus and red peppers, substituting fried spinach (or, in fact, some radicchio from the garden) with a little chilli and garlic for the fennel. This can be served either hot or lukewarm like a salad.

SERVES: 2–3

- 3 medium fennel bulbs, with the outer leaves, which may be beginning to brown, removed and then finely sliced

- olive oil

- 6–10 small new potatoes

- a handful of pancetta pieces or bacon bits or rashers of smoked bacon, sliced sideways into large matchsticks, about 1 cm wide

- 2 garlic cloves, crushed

- a few sloshes of some sort of vinegar, preferably a flavoured type, like apple or balsamic vinegar

- salt and ground black pepper

- a squeeze of lemon juice

- a handful of fresh green herbs, such as parsley or chopped spring onions

Preheat the oven to 180°C (160°C fan oven) mark 4.

Spread the fennel out over a baking tray, coated with some olive oil and roast for about 15 minutes until just beginning to go soft and brown, turning them once or twice in the cooking process.

Meanwhile, boil the potatoes in a pan of boiling water until soft.

Fry the pancetta or bacon in a frying pan until the fat is crisp.

Drain the cooked potatoes, then slice and place in a large serving bowl with the fennel and bacon, tossing them all together with some olive oil so they separate out. Add the garlic and toss around to move the garlic about thoroughly. While delicious, you don't want to get all the garlic in one mouthful. Add the flavoured vinegar and some black pepper and stir around to coat all the ingredients. Taste and adjust the seasoning. You may not need any salt as the pancetta or bacon will probably be salty enough. Add the lemon juice and serve immediately. It all looks a little brown and cream, so if you have some, this is the moment to sprinkle on some greenery, such as parsley or spring onions including some of the green parts.

PREETI'S FENUGREEK AND LENTIL LUNCH WITH CORIANDER CHUTNEY

This recipe I pinched from my Indian friend, Preeti. This is how to cook stunning Indian vegetarian food. The fenugreek I knew from the spice you can buy, but I'd never encountered it as a vegetable. It has a very unusual, aromatic taste.

SERVES: 3–4

FOR THE SPINACH

- 1 tbsp vegetable oil
- a few pinches of whole cumin seeds and black mustard seeds
- a few large handfuls of spinach or if you're near an Asian shop, ask them for fresh fenugreek, chopped (add 1 dsp ground fenugreek or methi leaves or ghormeh sabzi if you use spinach)
- pinch of salt
- 1 dsp chickpea flour or use cornflour (I suppose)
- 1 tbsp plain yogurt
- flatbreads of your choice or plain rice, to serve

Heat the oil in a large frying pan over a medium heat and fry the cumin and mustard seeds until they pop. Add the spinach or fenugreek and a pinch of salt, cover with a lid and cook for about 10 minutes over a high heat, stirring around from time to time. The liquid in the spinach will give out enough water to prevent sticking.

Put the flour into a bowl and gradually add the yogurt, stirring around to prevent lumps (the flour helps to stop the yogurt splitting).

Taste the spinach and adjust the seasoning. Add the flour and yogurt combo and stir around over the heat to thicken the sauce a little. This should ideally be served with fresh chapattis, but, failing that, plain boiled rice.

FOR THE LENTILS

- 3–4 handfuls of yellow lentils, washed
- a splosh of vegetable oil
- 1 tsp cumin seeds
- 1 tsp mustard seeds
- 5–6 curry leaves
- ½ cinnamon stick
- 4 cloves
- 6–10 small tomatoes, finely chopped
- 1 tsp ground coriander
- ¼ tsp ground turmeric
- a few pinches of chilli powder or dried crushed chillies or freshly chopped chilli
- 2 dates, chopped
- 4 kokams or a walnut-size piece of tamarind or 2 dsp tamarind paste

Soak the yellow lentils in a bowl of water, overnight, if necessary. When ready to cook, drain the lentils, add to a large pan and pour in 1.5 litres water. Cook until it is the consistency of a watery broth and the lentils are just soft enough to eat. Drain the lentils. Keep the liquor.

Heat the oil in a large pan over a medium heat and fry the cumin and mustard seeds until they start to pop. Add the curry leaves, cinnamon and cloves and stir around in the hot oil. Add the tomatoes, coriander, turmeric and chilli. Wait for the tomatoes to separate, then add the dates, kokam (or tamarind) and a bit of salt and bring to the boil.

Add the lentils. Taste. Add sufficient liquor to the mix. Stir around and serve.

CORIANDER CHUTNEY

- 2 bunches (very big handfuls) of fresh coriander, chopped
- a small handful of unsalted peanuts soaked in water to remove any of the skins
- a small knob of fresh root ginger, peeled and finely chopped
- 1 garlic clove, chopped
- 1 green chilli, chopped
- juice of 1 lemon
- a few pinches of salt

Either chop all the ingredients finely or preferably blitz together to form a purée. Put to one side until ready to serve with the spinach and lentils.

CHINESE STIR-FRY VEGETABLES WITH FILLET STEAK

This is a catch-all recipe for whatever meat and vegetables you happen to have. The vegetables should ideally be crunchy in texture and relatively quick to cook, so onions, carrots, red peppers, fine green beans, mangetout and courgettes are all possible. There needs to be very little meat, but again, you may want to use it up, so anything is acceptable in this forgiving recipe. Lean steak such as fillet or sirloin is great, although expensive, but then you need such a small amount. Chicken is easy. Pork is OK, but I'd avoid lamb. The basic taste is Chinese and within the sauce, the vegetables and meat cook as individual separate tastes.

SERVES: 2

- a small piece of lean, fresh meat, about 100–200 g thickly sliced if steak or cut into bite-size pieces if chicken or pork

- 1 tbsp soy sauce

- 1 level dsp sugar

- 1 tbsp wine vinegar or rice vinegar

- 1 garlic clove, sliced

- a slosh of dry sherry (if you have it)

- 2 small handfuls of rice

- a splosh of flavourless oil, such as groundnut or rapeseed

- ½ onion, sliced into fairly big chunks

- 1 small carrot, peeled and cut into thin slices along the length of the carrot then cut horizontally to 5–7 cm long and/or any other vegetable, cut into chunks

- 2.5 cm cube of fresh root ginger, peeled and sliced

- a small handful of fine green beans, topped and tailed, and sliced into bite-size pieces

- 1 chilli, chopped

Marinate the meat in the soy sauce, sugar, vinegar, garlic and sherry for as long as you can before the meal. At worst, this only needs to be the time it takes to prepare all the other ingredients.

Cook the rice following the instructions on page 44.

In a wok or a large frying pan, heat the oil over a high heat. When it's really hot, add the onion and stir around over the heat until it just begins to colour, then add the carrot and, a couple of minutes after, the ginger, and green beans. Keep stirring round and round, so that although it is set over a high heat, nothing burns. Add the chilli, stir around, then immediately add the meat and marinade all in one go into a central hole in the vegetables, so that the vegetables are pushed up the sides of the pan. There should be a little steam and the sound of sizzling veg. You'll need to keep lifting the meat off the base of the wok to prevent it sticking, but with the lean meat it will take no time to cook; only a minute or so. Be careful not to overcook the meat, particularly if it's steak, because it will go hard. Taste and adjust the seasoning, adding some more soy sauce if necessary and serve quickly. The rice takes 12 minutes so it should be ready at the same time. However, if it's ready in advance just remove it from the heat and keep the lid on. Add a little water to the base of the pan if it starts to stick.

FRENCH ONION SOUP

This is a classic, seldom seen these days, apart from in proper French restaurants, but it's very easy and totally delicious. It should be slow cooked, so allow a good 2 hours, but most of the time it will be simmering and needing very little attention.

SERVES: 2

- 2 large brown onions, finely sliced
- 1 tbsp unsalted butter
- 1 tbsp olive oil
- 1 tsp sugar
- 1 tsp salt
- half a litre chicken stock, preferably fresh but if not then use a chicken stock cube dissolved in half a litre water
- 3 bay leaves
- 10 black peppercorns
- a few parsley sprigs, kept whole so you can easily fish them out later
- 1 mug of dry white vermouth or dry white wine
- a slosh of brandy or cognac
- salt and ground black pepper
- 2 thick slices of white bread, roughly the size of the soup plates you are using
- butter for the toast
- 2 handfuls of grated Gruyère or Parmesan

Fry the onions in the butter and oil, stirring all the time, over a low heat until beginning to brown. Increase the heat, add the sugar and salt and stir until really caramelised and turning a deep brown. Don't let it burn, adding more oil and butter, if necessary. Add the stock, bay leaves, peppercorns, parsley and vermouth and bring to the boil. Reduce the heat and leave to simmer for 45 minutes, keeping an eye on it. Fish out the parsley and bay leaves if you can, then taste and add the brandy and salt and pepper, if necessary.

Preheat the grill. Toast the bread and butter it, then spread with the grated cheese and grill until golden brown and the cheese is bubbling. Serve a slice of toast on top of each bowl of soup.

MUSHROOM RISOTTO

Risotto cooked according to my wayward ways, to save time. Another uncharacteristic non-Italian rendering translated into 'English cooks who work'. This real autumnal feast can be cooked at any time of the year if you use dried mushrooms, but is lovelier with fresh mushrooms such as cèpes and chanterelles if you see any, or a mixture. Ordinary brown mushrooms are not as tasty but you can use a few for a different texture. I once found a puffball mushroom, on a stall at the Goods' Shed in Canterbury. It was huge, about half a metre in diameter, so you could buy it by the enormous slice.

SERVES: 4

- 2 small handfuls of dried 'exotic' mushrooms, such as morels, cèpes, chanterelles, porcini or 2 large handfuls of fresh mushrooms, sliced (preferably the 'exotic' mushrooms)

- 2 onions, chopped

- 1 tbsp olive oil, plus extra to serve

- 1 tbsp unsalted butter, plus an extra knob

- 3 handfuls of Arborio rice or similar Italian risotto rice

- 1 chicken stock cube dissolved in a jug of 250 ml boiling water with 3 bay leaves and a handful of black peppercorns

- a few sloshes of dry Vermouth or dry white wine

- 2 tbsp crème fraîche (if you have it)

- 4 handfuls of grated Parmesan

- salt and ground black pepper

Now, I know the Italians do this bit by putting the hot liquor into the rice a tiny bit at a time, but I've tried this way and I cannot see any real difference to the way I've adapted it so...clean the mushrooms, if fresh, using kitchen paper to flip off any errant soil, but don't bother washing them unless absolutely necessary. Cut off any really nasty bits. If using dried mushrooms, then soak them in a small bowl of boiling water until reconstituted, then drain, trying to leave the residue in the base of the bowl, just in case there's some soil in it.

In a large frying pan, fry the onions in the oil and the 1 tbsp butter over a high heat, stirring constantly, until they are just about beginning to brown. Reduce the heat right down and continue to cook for about 20 minutes so they don't brown any more, but they are really soft. Add more oil, if necessary. Add the rice and turn around in the oil. You may hear the rice squeaking now. After a minute or so, add a little stock and stir around. Increase the heat to medium-low. There should be some steam as the liquid is evaporated off. Pour in some more stock, a little more than the first time, and let that be absorbed by the rice as you stir it around. You can then add all the remaining stock, then the wine. Taste the rice and see how cooked it is. Leave the rice to cook by taking up the liquor and, if necessary, add another mug of stock. As soon as the rice is cooked, add a little more cooking liquor and the knob of butter, then stir in the crème fraîche, if using, most of the cheese and taste and adjust the seasoning.

Serve with the remaining Parmesan on top with a little parsley to garnish and a swirl of olive oil around the food. The Italians like it nice and soupy with a lot of residual liquid. In the UK, restaurants always tend to serve risotto thick and solid, so aim for the Italian way.

Mushroom risotto

PRAWN PASTA WITH LEMONS

A delicious but simple pasta with the ever-gorgeous combination of fish and lemon. You can also add a very small amount of finely chopped preserved lemon to the prawns if you happen to have a jar lurking in the fridge. It's a bit of a thug, so go easy.

SERVES: 2

- about 14–20 fresh or frozen prawns, raw if at all possible, to prevent overcooking

- 2 small handfuls of pasta of your choice

- good-quality olive oil

- 1 garlic clove, crushed

- juice and zest of 1½ lemons

- ¼ preserved lemon, finely chopped (if you have it)

- salt and ground black pepper

- very finely chopped herbs, such as parsley or basil to garnish

- finely grated zest of 2 lemons

Defrost the prawns if they are frozen, then cut off the heads, legs and any roe or manky bits if they are still on the bodies, leaving the shells on if you prefer.

Cook the pasta in a large saucepan of boiling water, then drain and keep warm in the same pan, swirling in a little olive oil to stop it sticking.

Meanwhile, in a large frying pan, add the prawns with a fair amount of olive oil and fry briskly until they turn pink, turning over and over with a fish slice or spatula. Remove from the heat and add the garlic, letting it cook a little in the residual heat without browning. Add the lemon juice and preserved lemon, if you are using it, turning them over with the prawns. Increase the heat to high and fry for 30 seconds, so that the lemon juice intensifies a little. Add the cooked pasta, then season with salt and pepper to taste and finish with the herbs and lemon zest.

Prawn pasta with lemons

WEEKEND AND SPECIAL MEALS

These dishes might take a little longer to prepare, or involve a bit more expense in the ingredients than some of the other recipes in the book but they are meant to be shared with friends and family as an extended meal.

MY TOMATO SOUP

This is not a simple tomato soup, but I couldn't think of anything better to call it. It is time-consuming, elaborate but not difficult and produces a soup of two different textures – one is clear and spicy and the other, in the middle, is a thick, roasted sweet tomato soup, set off with crispy onions, basil oil and chives. The consommé is really a concentration of tomato essence of a unique and breathtaking taste. When making the consommé, you will need a small square of muslin – or a J-cloth – to hang over a bowl.

SERVES: 6

FOR THE CLEAR CONSOMMÉ

- 60 very small, very sweet tomatoes or the equivalent larger ones
- very little salt to taste
- ¼ tsp sugar
- 1 tsp smoked hot paprika

FOR THE THICK TOMATO SOUP

- 25–30 small, sweet vine tomatoes or the equivalent larger ones, halved – you can skin them and de-seed them if you want to be really flash
- salt
- 1 dsp pomegranate molasses, or you could use tamarind at a pinch
- juice of ½ lemon
- sugar, to taste (optional)

- a few sloshes of sherry vinegar or half sherry and half wine vinegar

FOR THE BASIL OIL (SAY A MUG)

- 2 handfuls of basil leaves, chopped and bashed

- a few good sloshes of olive oil

- ¼ tsp salt

TO GARNISH

- crispy fried onions (can be shop-bought)

- 1 cucumber, peeled, seeded and chopped

- chives, chopped into 2 cm lengths

Twenty-four hours in advance, start making the consommé. Chop the tomatoes into 6, carefully collecting any juice in a large bowl.

Line a sieve with some muslin or a clean cloth and put the tomatoes into it. Let the juice drain into the bowl underneath, stirring now and again to release more juice. It is this precious nectar that gives the tomato almost all of its taste, which is gathered and preserved for the base of this soup.

Again, the day before, or at least a few hours before, make the basil oil. Either mix the basil with the oil and salt and leave to stand for a few hours, then strain or mix together and blitz the whole lot into a bright green richness. Put to one side.

On the day, make the thick tomato soup. Preheat the oven to 180°C (160°C fan oven) mark 4. Place the halved tomatoes on a large baking tray with a little olive oil and roast in the oven for about 30–45 minutes. Just make sure they're well cooked and beginning to char but are not burned. Transfer them to a food processor or blender with a little salt, pomegranate molasses, lemon juice, sugar and sherry vinegar and blitz until smooth. Taste and adjust the seasoning, then leave to cool.

Serve in large wide bowls with the consommé first, followed by the thick soup in the middle, garnished with a dribble of basil oil, a scattering of crispy onions and cucumber and set off with a few long stems of chives for added colour.

SCALLOPS WITH PANCETTA

SERVES: 4

- 3–4 new potatoes (optional)

- 2–4 scallops each, depending on size

- pancetta as a lump if possible, cut into small chunks, or 4 rashers smoked streaky bacon or the

equivalent (you need about a handful of roughly chopped pancetta)

- a splosh of olive oil

- a big knob of unsalted butter

- juice of 1 lemon

- salt and ground black pepper

TO GARNISH

- a small handful of rocket or watercress

- very finely chopped chives

- angel hair chilli strands – see note

Halve the potatoes and cook in boiling water, scrubbing away at the skins a bit.

Meanwhile, prepare the table and warm the plates because you must be ready to serve the scallops straight away.

Remove the thin crêpey skin on the sides of the scallops, then remove any roe and the tough, rough patch (which is apparently the foot, where it attaches to the shell). Wash and dry with kitchen paper, so the scallops don't just steam in a sea of water, but will crisp up.

Fry the pancetta or bacon in a little oil until crisp, then cut into strips and keep warm.

In the same pan, so you have the bacon fat already there, add a little more oil and the butter and heat until it is almost sizzling. Add the scallops, pushing them down onto the pan, so that they brown and take on that lovely golden colour of caramelisation. When about half done, add another knob of butter to the pan. The scallops will take about 3–4 minutes, 2 minutes on each side, depending on size, but whatever you do, don't overcook them or they'll go rubbery. If you're at all concerned, cut one in half (which you can serve to yourself) and ensure

that it is just, and only just, cooked white all the way through. You may even serve them still a little raw in the middle, as they are still delicious, and many other recipes use raw scallops as the main attraction.

Serve the scallops on the warmed plates and sprinkle with a little lemon juice, salt and pepper.

Quickly toss the rocket or watercress with a little oil, lemon, salt and pepper and scatter over and around the scallops, adding the diced, cooked potatoes now (if you are using them). Strew the pancetta or bacon over the top of the leaves and sprinkle with a few chopped chives. Lay out a few strands of angel hair over the top and serve immediately.

Note: Angel hair strands, as I call them, are thin, sweet strands of chilli you can buy in packs in Asian supermarkets called rather prosaically 'Shredded Red Pepper'.

Scallops with pancetta

PIGEON BREASTS WITH PUY LENTILS

This is a delicious starter, the moist tasty pink meat contrasting against the browny-green of the lentils. Allowing one breast per person, this recipe is for two people. You can make it into a main course by adding some potatoes. It's really quite easy, so don't let the elaborate description put you off trying it.

SERVES: 2

- 1 pigeon, ready-cleaned

- 1 medium onion, finely chopped

- 1 very large dollop of unsalted butter

- 2 glugs of olive oil

- 1 medium carrot, peeled and finely chopped into small cubes

- 4 thin rashers smoked bacon or equivalent pancetta, cut into 1 cm wide strips

- 1 tbsp finely chopped parsley

- 2 bay leaves

- 6 black peppercorns

- 250 ml fresh chicken stock or 1 chicken stock cube, dissolved in 250 ml of boiling water

- 250 ml red wine

- a large handful of Puy lentils for each breast

- 2 tbsp low burning point oil, such as sunflower or light-flavoured olive oil to cook the pigeon

Use a sharp knife to cut into and against the bones of the ribcage to remove the breasts from the carcass. Just have a go.

In a large saucepan, sweat the onion in some of the butter and the olive oil over a high heat, stirring around to prevent burning until just at the point of browning. Reduce the heat to low and allow to soften, still stirring occasionally. Add the carrot and continue to cook, stirring to prevent burning. When the carrot is just beginning to cook through, add the bacon. Increase the heat to medium and cook until the bacon is brown and crisp. Add most of the parsley, the bay leaves, peppercorns, chicken stock, carcass and wine, then add enough

Pigeon breasts with Puy lentils

water to just cover the carcass. Bring to the boil, then reduce the heat and simmer, uncovered, removing the scum from the surface with a slotted spoon, until the liquid has reduced to half its original volume.

Remove the carcass from the pan. Taste and continue to simmer until there is just enough liquid to cover the lentils. You will have to guess this bit by eye. Add the lentils, reduce the heat to a simmer and cover the pan with a lid. Cook for about 35–45 minutes. Keep looking and tasting the lentils; if they appear to be drying out, then add a little more wine, stock or water, but remember that this should nearly all be absorbed by the end. After about 25 minutes, start cooking the pigeon.

Sauté the breasts quickly over a high heat in the low burning point oil and a big knob of butter, turning over and over so that the outside browns without burning. This takes 5–8 minutes at the most. Cut one to try, by slicing through the middle. It should be brown and crusty on the outside while still remaining pink inside. Try a slice to taste it – this can be your piece. Try to make this slightly underdone, since it will continue to cook a little in its residual heat. Once you are satisfied that it is cooked to your liking, remove from the heat and keep warm, even if you just cover with foil, leaving it to rest for 10 minutes.

By now the lentils should be soft enough to eat, but not squidgy, without losing all their texture. You still need a bit of bite and all the liquid from the lentils should have evaporated and condensed into a strong, meaty, well-flavoured sauce. Taste and adjust the seasoning, according to how much there was in the original stock. Slice the pigeon thinly and fan over the lentils in a small bowl. Garnish with the remaining parsley.

Note: Fresh stock usually has no seasoning but check on the pack if you buy it from a supermarket. A stock/bouillon stock cube is often full of salt, so you won't want to add any extra seasoning at the end.

CARPACCIO OF SCALLOPS WITH HERBS

This dish uses uncooked scallops and is a really refined but decadent starter using the finest, freshest ingredients – a little like ceviche.

- 3 fresh scallops each or more depending on their size and your budget

- a handful of finely chopped basil, parsley and tarragon or personal preference

- juice of 1 lemon

- the best olive oil you can find

- salt crystals and ground black pepper

- a few strands of chopped samphire to garnish

Carefully clean off the roe, coral, the little rough bit (foot) on the side and the outside 'skin'. Cut horizontally into thin slices – you may be able to get 2–3 out of each scallop. Lay out the slices in a fan shape interwoven with finely chopped herbs between each slice and squeeze over a few drops of lemon juice

on each slice; don't overpower. Dribble a little oil around the plate and over the scallops, then scatter with salt crystals and pepper and garnish with samphire.

Carpaccio of scallops with herbs

COQ AU VIN

This French classic hardly needs any explanation; it is a long, slow-cooked chicken in red wine with multitudinous variations, as each French family will have its own version. Sadly out of fashion now, it is easy enough though, belonging to that collection of dishes which require little watching once it's assembled in a casserole dish. By the time it reaches the table it should have a lovely deep, rich wine sauce, with the chicken turning dark brown, the vegetables falling to pieces and that gooey texture so well appreciated in all long-cooked stews. Traditionally, the long cooking of the chicken would tenderise the toughest old bird on the farm, but these days this is hardly necessary. It does suit, however, our organic free-range chickens, usually longer-lived, which are more muscly and tasty than their battery equivalent.

SERVES: 4

- 1 medium whole chicken, cut into legs, breasts and wings or (if you're not using a whole bird) use 8 thighs, and/or wings, with bones

- olive oil to cook

- 3 rashers streaky bacon, preferably smoked

- 1 large onion, chopped

- 2 large carrots, chopped

- 150 g mushrooms, chopped

- 1 bottle of robust red wine

- 2 cups of chicken stock (either buy some fresh or use 1 bouillon stock cube dissolved in boiling water)

- 2 bay leaves

- 1 tbsp freshly chopped thyme or ½ tsp dried

- 1 big sprig of rosemary

- 6 black peppercorns

- a few sloshes of brandy

- salt and ground black pepper

- boiled potatoes and green vegetable of your choice, to serve

Preheat the oven to 180°C (160°C fan oven) mark 4.

If using a whole chicken, remove the breast (cutting against the bones). Take off the wings, thighs and legs, putting the rest of the carcass to one side for stock.

In a big sauté pan, fry the chicken pieces in 1 scant tbsp of oil until brown, then add to a large casserole dish. Fry the bacon in the sauté pan, then chop into pieces. Fry the onion until it is just beginning to colour, then add the carrots and then the mushrooms and cook until the carrots begin to colour. Add the bacon and vegetables to the casserole dish with the remaining ingredients.

Reduce the oven temperature to 160°C (140°C fan oven) mark 3 and cook for 1½ hours, turning the meat over halfway through the cooking time and adding more liquid (stock or wine) if necessary.

It will keep warm while you cook any other vegetables, such as boiled potatoes and green veg to counteract the dark-brownness of the coq. There should be enough salt in the stock, but taste and adjust the seasoning to taste.

LAMB FILLET WITH HERB COATING

This looks far more elaborate than it is, because the final slices of spectacular, pinkish meat are beautifully offset by the bright green of the herb coating and the darker edges of the meat.

SERVES: 4

- a big slosh of olive oil, plus extra to oil
- 1–2 lamb fillets (depending on size), trimmed of fat and sinews
- salt and ground black pepper
- a big slice of unsalted butter
- a few tbsp mild French mustard
- a handful of finely chopped herbs, such as parsley, rosemary and thyme or tarragon, coriander and marjoram
- vegetables of your choice, cooked as much ahead as possible since the meat cooking is relatively quick
- Red wine sauce (page 57)

Preheat the oven to 180°C (160°C fan oven) mark 4 and oil a baking tray.

Season the lamb fillets with salt and pepper.

Heat a frying pan over a high heat, add the oil and butter and heat until the butter foams. Add the fillets to the hot pan and cook for a few minutes, turning them over, until browned and sealed. Remove from the pan and leave them until cool enough to handle, then coat them all over with a layer of mustard. Carefully press the mixed herbs over the surface of the mustard – bits will drop off, but keep going.

Place the lamb on the oiled baking tray and cook in the oven for 15 minutes. Cover carefully, so as not to disturb the lovely bright green of the herbs and keep warm for 15 minutes to rest the meat.

Meanwhile, cook vegetables of your choice.

Slice the lamb thinly, preserving as much of the herb crust as possible, then arrange overlapping in a crescent either on a central serving dish or on each plate and serve with the vegetables and sauce.

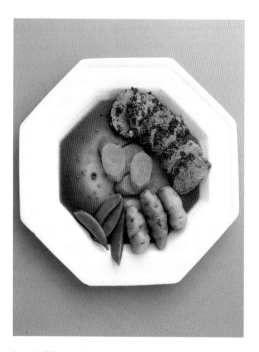

Lamb fillet with herb coating

BOEUF BOURGUIGNON

There are lots of versions of this classic French dish, but this method seems to work well. It's easy and delicious and can be reheated. The main aim, as with most cooking, is to seal and brown the vegetables and meat beforehand, so that the flavour of their caramelisation is mixed with the sauce. Because of its long, slow cooking, you need a cheap cut of beef, so that it gradually tenderises as it cooks and develops the flavours in the sauce. If you use a better quality meat it will be cooked long before the sauce has reduced and will start to dry out and toughen up. The best cut is stewing steak. The closest to this is often called braising steak in supermarkets. For some reason, they don't seem able to produce stewing steak, and this is quite a lean meat so you may not be able to let it cook for so long. Keep tasting throughout its cooking, and if it starts hardening up then stop cooking. Unless you are into making your own stock, which is a must for some recipes but not this one, then you can use a bouillon stock cube, such as Knorr or Marigold, dissolved in 250 ml of boiling water. Or, even better, you can buy fresh stock in supermarkets now, sold in tubs (which you can freeze) close to the meat fridges usually. You'll need 2–3 tubs for this recipe. I tend not to like manufacturers' beef stock cubes, so I use chicken, even in beef dishes, which appears to be closest to the real thing, except for the added salt. You certainly won't want any more salt in the main recipe. Don't use lamb for stocks or stock cubes because it is too fatty, and the fat is slightly unpalatable to some people.

SERVES: 6

- a chunk of bacon, about 15–20 cm long and 3 cm wide, smoked if possible or about 150 g or 6 rashers, cut into lardons or small chunks

- a few sloshes of olive oil to fry

- 1 onion, chopped

- 2 large carrots, chopped

- about 20 small button mushrooms, left whole or equivalent cut into bite-size pieces

- flour, just enough to coat the meat pieces

- salt and ground black pepper

- butter to fry

- 1 kg stewing steak, trimmed of fat and gristle and cut into walnut-size pieces

- ¾ bottle of red wine

- 500 ml good stock (see intro)

- 6–10 black peppercorns

- 1 bouquet garni (thyme and parsley sprigs with 3 bay leaves wrapped in string or in big bits so you can remove them easily)

- 1 tbsp tomato purée

- 2 garlic cloves, chopped

- freshly chopped parsley, to garnish

- baked or boiled potatoes and green vegetables of your choice, such as peas, broad beans or French beans to serve

Preheat the oven to 150°C (130°C fan oven) mark 3.

In a frying pan, fry the bacon in a little oil until brown, then transfer to a casserole dish. Add the onions to the frying pan and fry for 2–3 minutes until browned. Add the carrots and fry briefly then add to the casserole dish.

Add more oil to the frying pan and sauté the mushrooms, a few at a time so there is plenty of room to turn them over, until browned all over. Add them to the casserole.

Season the flour with a little pepper and salt. Dry the meat with kitchen paper, then roll in the seasoned flour. Add the meat to the frying pan and fry over a high heat in a little more olive oil and the butter, using a fish slice or spatula to ease the meat off the base of the pan when it sticks and turning it over until it has just started to brown and is sealed. Add to the casserole dish with the wine, stock, peppercorns, bouquet garni, tomato purée and garlic.

Cook in the oven for about 2 hours if the meat is supermarket-type braising steak (which starts hardening and becoming tough with too much cooking) or 3–4 hours if you use proper stewing steak. Halfway through cooking, taste and add more liquid, if necessary. It should come out at the end with the meat falling apart in a reduced, stiff, delicious meaty sauce.

Garnish with chopped parsley and serve with baked or boiled potatoes and some bright green veg.

SUCKLING PIG WITH CARAMELISED APPLES AND GARLIC

This recipe is really best with younger piglets, which can weigh up to about 9 kg. You'll find that the skin gets tougher as they get older, and in the end the quality of the skin will be more akin to normal roast pork crackling. Not necessarily any the worse for this, but the skin on younger ones is more like the texture of filo pastry. It has less fat under it, so it produces the finest, crunchiest and most delectable treat, and the softest, most melting and un-meat-like meat possible. You won't need to cut it; it falls apart and almost flakes in the way that Peking duck can be shredded by the waiter in Chinese restaurants.

To cook a suckling pig, simply lay the piglet in a large roasting tin, as it comes, complete with head, tail, eyes and teeth, over a bed of peeled, sliced cooking apples, interwoven with slices of garlic and rosemary sprigs. Butter the skin with some unsalted butter and a sprinkle of salt. Make sure the piglet will fit into your oven – some companies sell piglets with head and feet removed to more easily fit into a domestic oven – and cook according to the weight in an oven preheated to 180°C (160°C fan oven) mark 4 for about 2–3 hours, plus another 45 minutes in a hotter oven, say 200°C (180°C fan oven) mark 6 to get the skin crisp. A 5–6 kg piglet will feed about 6–8 people. For accompaniments, treat as a normal roast. A young piglet is full of collagen, which turns to gelatine as it's heated, so it will become super-smooth and sticky with flavour. It's almost impossible to overcook, so forgiving are its constituent parts. If a meat thermometer reads 60°C when piercing the thickest part of the pig, under its front shoulder, it will be cooked.

SLOW-COOKED CHINESE JELLY PORK

Although this is extremely easy to prepare, it does take 2 or so hours to cook, so I've included it in the more elaborate weekend section. This is essentially a Chinese dish (although I can no longer find its source) and so should be served with rice and, I would suggest, a green vegetable, to complement the dark meat, such as sugar snap peas, courgettes, green peppers, fine green beans, pak choi or anything else you fancy.

As this dish is very easy it's quick to prepare, but it does need that cooking time. It goes almost black, but don't be deterred, use the vegetables quickly fried in sesame oil and garlic in a wok, as a foil, both for texture and colour. It is also a cheap and luscious dish, with the soft meat falling apart, absorbing all the flavours and the fat part of the meat turning to a rich, brown jelly. Try not to buy very lean belly pork, sometimes sold for barbecues, because this will dry out and go tough. Butchers are probably better for this than supermarkets. I wouldn't have thought that the quality of the meat would have mattered that much, because of the strong tastes and long cooking time, but I bought some belly pork at vast expense from the great Lidgate's on Holland Park Avenue in London, and it surpassed all previous attempts I've made at the dish.

SERVES: 4

- 6 rashers belly pork, each about 20 cm long with rind on and plenty of fat

- ½ mug of dark soy sauce

- 2–3 tbsp wine vinegar or preferably rice vinegar

- 2 star anise (optional)

- ¼ tsp five-spice powder

- finely grated zest or the outside peel (with none of the bitter white on) of 1 orange

- juice of 2 oranges

- 2 garlic cloves, crushed or chopped

- 4 tbsp dry sherry, or red wine if you must, or rice wine

- 1 dsp sugar

Slow-cooked Chinese jelly pork

TO SERVE

- freshly cooked rice

- green vegetable of your choice, such as pak choi or sugar snap peas

- a little sesame oil

Preheat the oven to 150°C (130°C fan oven) mark 2.

Boil the belly pork as it is in a pan of boiling water for 10 minutes. Remove the meat and cut it vertically at right angles to the rind into strips about 1 cm wide and place in an upright casserole dish with all the other ingredients. Most of the meat needs to be in contact with the liquid marinade, so turn it around. If your casserole is very wide and shallow, you may need to add more liquid flavourings. Cook in the oven for an hour, checking from time to time to see if there is enough liquid. If the meat is tough you may need to increase the cooking time. If the liquid seems to be completely evaporating, add a little water, but not too much. As it slowly cooks, the meat will absorb all the flavourings and nearly all the liquid, turning very dark, almost black with the fat turning to jelly. It doesn't look too good, but it tastes delicious. It needs a bright vegetable to offset the darkness. Like almost all slow-cooked food, it keeps its flavour well, so you can leave it in the turned-off oven to keep warm, or you can make it in advance and heat it up without spoiling.

Cook the accompanying vegetables quickly in a little sesame oil and serve with rice. I think the meat would make a different, easy and interesting canapé: skewer each piece of meat with a toothpick and a piece of cucumber and serve warm.

ROAST PHEASANT WITH CABBAGE AND PANCETTA

Pheasant and game birds can be cooked quickly, so they are just seared and pinkish in the middle, or they can be cooked slowly in wine and aromatics, so they gradually tenderise and take on the flavours of the cooking liquor. Anything in between and you are liable to find the birds disappointingly tough. It pays to know how old your birds are, so you know if you can cook them quickly. All the lovely savoury tastes of the pheasant, pancetta, wine and aromatics combine in this recipe to give a full, earthy satisfying taste.

SERVES: 4

- 2–3 pheasants, preferably hens, cleaned, skinned and cut into 6 pieces
- 1–2 tbsp light olive oil
- 2 big knobs of unsalted butter
- a few slices of fairly thick pancetta or smoked bacon, chopped into lardons, about 1 cm wide
- 4–8 garlic cloves, peeled but left whole
- 2–3 handfuls of fresh sage leaves
- ½ bottle of good-quality red wine
- a slug of brandy (optional)

- 10 black peppercorns
- 1 bouquet garni (1 bay leaf, parsley sprigs and thyme sprigs tied up or in large pieces for easy removal)
- 1 mug of chicken stock or ½ chicken stock cube dissolved in 1 mug of boiling water
- 1 small Savoy cabbage, core and all the tough bits removed and finely sliced

Preheat the oven to 190°C (170°C fan oven) mark 5.

In a large frying pan, brown the pheasant pieces in the olive oil and a big knob of the butter. Transfer the pheasants to an ovenproof dish or casserole. Make sure the dish or casserole isn't too shallow or the liquid will evaporate. Add the remaining big knob of butter to the frying pan, heat and add the pancetta, cooking until beginning to crisp. Add the garlic and sage, reduce the heat and stir around for a minute or so. Add the wine, brandy, if using, peppercorns, bouquet garni and chicken stock. Add the cabbage and bring the mixture to the boil. Pour the cabbage and pancetta mixture over and around the pheasants and cook in the oven for 1–2 hours, depending on the pheasants' age, basting the birds every now and again.

PHEASANT CASSEROLE

This recipe could be used for any game birds, such as partridge, pigeon or boiling chicken.

SERVES: 3–4

- 1 large onion, sliced

- 2 carrots, peeled and chopped

- 2 celery sticks, chopped

- 2 leeks, trimmed, outer leaves removed and chopped

- 2–3 tbsp olive oil

- 1 tbsp unsalted butter

- 2 pheasants, cleaned, skinned and cut into 6 pieces, together with heart, neck and gizzards if you can

- 4 mugs of chicken stock, preferably fresh or mix 1 chicken stock cube in 1 mug of boiling water, and add another 3 mugs of boiling water to make up the quantity

- 2 mugs of dry white wine or dry vermouth

- ½ mug of white wine vinegar

- 2 fresh rosemary sprigs or ½ tsp dried

- 2 bay leaves

- 2 fresh parsley sprigs or 1 tsp dried, plus 1 extra sprig to garnish

- 2 fresh thyme sprigs or ½ tsp dried

- 2 whole heads garlic, tops just cut off

- 1 lemon, halved

- 6 black peppercorns

- salt and ground black pepper

Note: I found a very useful bit of frozen food in my local Asian supermarket – a bag of chopped pig's trotters, a few of which can be successfully added to casseroles like this.

Preheat the oven to 120°C (110°C fan oven) mark ½.

Brown the vegetables in the oil and butter in order of their cooking length, so start with the vegetables that need most cooking and add each of the others as the one before begins to soften. In this way, all the vegetables should be ready at the same time, without having to take them out individually and faff around. Start with the onion, then carrots, then celery, then leeks. Remove them all from the pan when they just start to colour and place them in a large casserole dish.

Brown the pheasant pieces with the rest of the carcasses in the frying pan, then remove from the heat.

Add all the liquor to the casserole with the herbs, garlic, lemon and peppercorns, then add the browned pheasant and stir around. Turn the carcasses upside down so that the pheasant breasts are in the cooking liquor and will not dry out. Cook until the meat is really tender and just about to drop off the bone. Taste, adding salt and pepper if necessary. Remove any of the woody herbs you can find, plus the bay leaves. You don't have to be that precise as the dish is fairly hearty. Take the meat off the bones, but put the bones to one side for another stock and put into a serving dish or on individual plates, sprinkling with the vegetables and cooking liquor. Garnish with parsley and serve.

BLACK MARINATED TUNA

Here, you marinate the tuna before cooking it quickly so the outside is black and the inside is still pink and soft. It is so soft and delectable you can slice it sashimi-style, raw. Serve with a contrasting vegetable such as mangetout or sugar snap peas and boiled potatoes. It sounds like nothing, but it is intensely flavourful.

SERVES: 2

- 1 big slice of fresh tuna, about 2–2.5 cm thick

- 2 tbsp soy sauce

- 1 tsp smoked paprika or sweet pimento

- 1 clove crushed garlic

- 1 tsp sugar

- 2 cm cube of peeled ginger cut into matchsticks

- vegetables of your choice

- 1 dsp roughly crushed black peppercorns

- olive oil to cook

Black marinated tuna

Marinate the tuna in the soy sauce, paprika, garlic, ginger and sugar for as long as you can, preferably overnight, turning it over from time to time.

When ready to cook, cook your accompanying vegetables and keep warm. Warm the plates if you can. This is easiest in the microwave.

Use a heavy-based frying pan or a griddle pan and heat until it's super hot. Press the roughly crushed peppercorns into one surface of the tuna, then place the tuna in the hot pan with a little oil and cook over a high heat for about 1½ minutes on each side. There will be a large amount of steam and sizzling, but don't be too alarmed. Cut the tuna in half and see how much it has cooked through. To my taste it should be black on the very outside and pink in the middle, but you might have to judge the cooking time to suit your own tastes. Depending on the exact cut and how the grain is, try serving it by cutting into slices, laying one slightly over the next in a little fan shape on the warmed plate with the vegetables.

LAMB SHOULDER OR LEG WITH BARBECUE GLAZE

Exquisite slow-cooked lamb, finished off with a spicy rub or glaze, which can be barbecued. In this case we were given a whole 'lamb' by my dentist – as you do, round here – bred until this ram, called Reuben, was no longer required. It was hardly lamb and needed a little more attention and longer cooking, so we cooked it for about 5 hours in a slow oven with red wine and aromatics. We then dried and rubbed it with the glaze and finished it on the barbecue.

SERVES: 8–12 DEPENDING ON SIZE OF SHOULDER OR LEG

- 1 leg or shoulder of lamb rubbed with olive oil and cooked according to weight (page 51)

Note: If it is older than lamb, presumably now called mutton, then it needs much more slow cooking. I read that it would benefit from 'ageing', by keeping it in a cool place for a few days after slaughter before cooking.

FOR THE GLAZE

- 3 tbsp soy sauce
- 1 tbsp sugar, preferably brown
- 3 garlic cloves, crushed
- juice of 2 lemons
- 1 tbsp sherry or red wine vinegar
- 1 dsp ground coriander
- 1 dsp ground cumin
- 1 dsp ground fennel
- a few fresh rosemary sprigs, leaves picked and very finely chopped
- about 10 black peppercorns

Cover the cooked meat and keep warm.

Light the barbecue well in advance or increase the oven temperature to its maximum setting.

Mix all the glaze ingredients together and stir around to dissolve the sugar.

Dry the already cooked lamb, then smear on the glaze and put it on a barbecue with white coals, so if there are any drips, they don't automatically flare and smoke. If you are not barbecuing, then smear the glaze all over, increase the oven temperature to high and turn the meat over until really sealed. It all looks fairly black and horrible, but because lamb is such a juicy meat, it tastes absolutely delicious.

We once had about 130 for a party and cooked 3–4 big pieces of meat on the barbecue with loads of other platters and treats. Tris, who had been manfully manning the coals, finished everything off, sliced up the meat on a platter and decided he deserved a well-earned shower, coming back to find every last scrap of meat had been already devoured. There is something about a crowd, who quite obviously know that there is plenty of food for everyone, but cannot resist helping themselves far too generously. The meat went on a few plates piled high and disappeared in a flash. Very much 'Family Keep Off' but also 'Those of You with Any Manners, Keep Off As Well'. Many close friends complained as they missed out. It's similar to student parties where the less well a partygoer knows his host, (hiding any booze he seldom brought), then the worse he behaved, drinking and eating all the available food and drink. If it's free, then it must be ours, was the unsaid motto. Perhaps it's a remnant of ancient times of feast or famine, where it was necessary to eat when you could. Ditto social behaviour at buffets and self-service events where people are so greedy their plates are piled high but then leave most of it.

DUCK BREASTS WITH PLUMS OR ORANGES

Duck breasts are really fatty, but this is also their saving grace, as unlike chicken breasts, they are difficult to overcook and do not dry out. The skin, being able to crisp up, is especially prized. What is really special though is to have the inside rosy and moist and the outside skin beautifully golden brown.

SERVES: 2

- 2 duck breasts (keep in fridge once you've removed packaging and dried them)

- salt and ground black pepper (use a more exotic one, like pul biber or Aleppo for a change)

FOR THE SAUCE

- 3 small onions or 6 banana shallots, halved

- a slosh of olive oil

- a big knob of unsalted butter

- 20 small plums or 6 big ones or 2 large oranges

- salt and ground black pepper

- vegetables of your choice, such as potatoes, rice or noodles with something bright and green like peas, mangetout or sugar snap peas

- 1 garlic clove, crushed

- ½ mug of chicken stock

- 1 tbsp Chinese plum sauce (if you have it), plus 1 tbsp of plum brandy or rum if using plums

- 1 tbsp soy sauce plus the finely grated zest and juice of 1 orange, 1 tbsp orange liqueur such as Cointreau or Grand Marnier. If you haven't any liqueur, substitute the juice of another orange plus 1 lemon if using oranges

Most of the recommended ways of cooking duck breasts involves quick cooking on the hob, followed by a period in the oven. I think the safest and easiest way is to cook it all on the hob, so you can keep an eye on it, avoid overcooking and reduce the washing-up.

Start to make the sauce first by arranging the onions down on their flat cut side in a large frying pan with the oil and butter over a medium heat. Cook for 1–2 minutes, then reduce the heat.

Prepare the fruit by stoning the plums or peeling and skinning the oranges. Remove each segment of orange and cut off the middle white stalky bit with a sharp knife, peeling back the inside separating skin of each segment to leave a fairly intact, neat, skinless segment.

Carefully slice down through the duck skin, slashing diagonally so that each cut is about 1 cm from the next. Be careful to avoid cutting right down to the meat. A Stanley knife might be useful here or a reinforced razor blade. Dry the breast with kitchen paper and sprinkle with salt and pepper, pressing the pepper into the skin and breast meat.

Lay the duck in a cold pan and bring to a low-medium heat, pressing down on it with your hand from time to time so that the fat is rendered out of the breast and the skin crisps up. This should take about 10–15 minutes.

Meanwhile, prepare any accompanying vegetables of your choice.

Once the onions are softened and browned on the cut side, add the garlic, stirring around for a moment to cook them in the oil. You may need to add a little more oil. Immediately add a little of the chicken stock to stop the garlic burning, then add the fruit, cut side down, and increase the heat to medium. Let them just catch, then add the remaining liquids, lifting everything carefully off the base with a fish slice or spatula to help preserve their overall shape. Simmer the liquid until thickened and syrupy, then remove from the heat and keep warm while you finish off cooking the duck and vegetables.

Once the duck skin is crisp, turn to cook on the other side for 5 minutes. Taste the sauce, adjust the seasoning and leave the duck to rest for 10 minutes before serving with the sauce and vegetables of your choice.

SPARE RIBS IN A BARBECUE SAUCE

This is a lovely, sticky, gooey sauce for all sorts of meats but especially spare ribs. Serve with potatoes, pasta or salad.

FOR 10 SPARE RIBS –
ADJUST THE QUANTITIES FOR
MORE OR FEWER

- Ten spare ribs, preferably some with a little meat and fat still on them, and including the bone – the supermarkets seem to sell ones which have a lot cut off them. You may find better ones at the butcher, or pre-order if necessary

FOR THE SAUCE

- 1 can tomatoes or passata

- 3 garlic cloves, crushed

- 2 tbsp soy sauce

- 1 dsp or a few sloshes Worcestershire sauce

- 2 tsp French mustard

- 1 tbsp sugar

- 1 tbsp white wine vinegar

- chopped red chillies (optional)

Preheat the oven to 160°C (140°C fan oven) mark 3.

Mix all the sauce ingredients together and put into a big casserole dish. Add the ribs and move them around to ensure they are well coated. Cook in the oven for about 1 hour. Check after 30 minutes and move the ribs around to ensure even coating and browning. They could probably do with 1 hour and a bit, until they are brown and gooey and the meat easily comes away from the bone. You could even finish them off on a barbecue, but it's best to ensure they're cooked first and you're just browning them off on the barbecue. It's the long cooking which aids the tenderness of the meat. The BBQ might be a bit fierce.

Spare ribs in a barbecue sauce

PUDDINGS AND SWEET TREATS

When you need a sweet treat to finish off a meal or are craving something in the afternoon, this chapter has plenty of ideas. I have also included the definitive guide on making the perfect pastry (page 212), which you can use for both sweet and savoury dishes.

LEMON DRIZZLE CAKE

SERVES: 10–12

- 200 g unsalted butter, softened at room temperature
- 200 g granulated sugar
- 4 eggs, beaten
- 200 g self-raising flour
- 1 tsp baking powder
- finely grated zest of 2 lemons

FOR THE SYRUP

- juice of 4 lemons
- 3–4 dsp sugar

Preheat the oven to 150°C (130°C fan oven) mark 2 and grease a 20 cm cake tin with reasonably high sides, about 7.5 cm and line with parchment paper.

Using a big, non-metal bowl, mix the butter and sugar together vigorously with a wooden spoon or you can use a food mixer until the mixture goes paler in colour and light in texture. This should take about 5 minutes. Gradually add the eggs, stirring in a little at a time. Add the flour and baking powder, preferably sifted, and the lemon zest, stirring in until the mixture becomes the texture of not-too-stiff paste. Spoon into the cake tin and bake for about 20 minutes. Avoid opening the oven door until 15 minutes have passed, otherwise the cake may just flop down. Test to see if it's done by piercing with a sharp knife. If it comes out clean except for a few crumbs, then it's done. If it comes out with uncooked mixture still stuck on, then it needs a bit longer. Remove from the oven and leave to cool.

Meanwhile, to make the syrup, heat the lemon juice and sugar together gently in a pan until the sugar has dissolved.

Leave the cake to settle for about 30 minutes, then turn it out and when it is coolish, spike the top with a skewer and pour over the lemon syrup.

FRUIT PUDDINGS

With this I don't mean any old pudding or any old fruit, I mean the sort of grandmotherly cake and fruit pudding that you don't see very often these days. It should have oozing zappy, syrupy fruit covered with a light cake, baked in the oven until brown and toasty on top.

You need any seasonal robust UK fruit, but especially fruit with stones in, like plums, damsons, greengages or apricots (from further climes), but you could also use blackberries, blackcurrants and the like. Over winter it was traditionally made with apples.

If you want a purée without stones and skin, then wash the fruit, halve it and put it into a saucepan with a little water in the base. Cover with a lid and simmer until the fruit is soft, comes off the stones, and starts leaving the skin behind. Add sugar to taste – this might seem quite a lot – and sieve. If the mixture is very sloppy and liquid, then boil off some of the water, stirring to prevent it sticking. It should end up similar to a runny jam. It's even easier to halve the fruit (if possible), then put it straight into the ovenproof dish, sprinkle well with some sugar, then let your guests battle it out with the stones. You may find that the lazy way allows the fruity syrup to blend too quickly with the cake batter and you get this slightly solid, fruity layer of cake next to the fruit. A halfway solution I think works best, is to halve and stone the fruit, but don't bother sieving it to remove the skins. Boil with the sugar to cook the fruit, then reduce the heat and simmer until the liquid has reduced, then leave to cool before adding it to the ovenproof dish.

I last made this with some plums, called bush plums, here in Kent, which tend to grow wild in the hedgerows, ripening in the third week of August. They are small, rather like large damsons with a lovely blue-black skin, which has a lavender blue down on it. Nobody seems to notice or collect them, so I often pick them up as they run down the side of the road. I needed about 30–40 of these, so adjust the amount of fruit you use accordingly, so that it will fill the base half of your dish.

SERVES: 4–6

- 10–15 Victoria plums or equivalent
- enough sugar to sweeten
- icing sugar to decorate
- cream, ice cream or crème fraîche to serve

FOR THE CAKE BATTER MIX

- 180 g unsalted butter, softened, plus extra to grease
- 180 g caster sugar
- 3 eggs
- 90 g plain flour
- a little milk (optional)
- 90 g ground almonds (or double up the flour if you haven't got almonds)
- 1 tsp baking powder (or use self-raising flour if you don't have any baking powder)

Preheat the oven to 170°C (150°C fan oven) mark 3 and grease an ovenproof dish.

Beat the butter and sugar together with an electric whisk or with a wooden spoon until they become light and frothy and the deep yellow colour pales to a cream. Stir in the eggs, one at a time, and mix until most, if not all, the lumps of butter have disappeared. Sift in the flour and baking powder, then add the ground almonds and fold in. This should make a sloppy and just-able-to-run batter. Add a little milk if it appears too stiff. Put the fruit into the prepared dish. Pour the cake batter on top and prepare to do battle with whichever friend is hovering around hoping to help you lick out the bowl. Bake for about 25–45 minutes until the top is golden brown and a skewer inserted into the cake comes out clean.

Sprinkle the top with icing sugar and serve warm with cream, ice cream or crème fraîche.

Note: Another version of this pudding is to use the eggs to raise the cake mixture. In this way you only need 1½ tbsp plain flour and 4 eggs. Separate the eggs, adding only the yolks to the creamed butter-sugar mixture at the beginning, then whisk the remaining egg whites into stiff peaks and gently fold them into the cake batter. The whites add the air and you don't need self-raising flour or baking powder. This needs slightly more washing-up and a little more expertise, but gives a much lighter and soft sponge on top of the fruit.

PASTRY BASE FOR TARTS AND QUICHES

Pastry comes in all sorts of forms. Here, we can concentrate on two types: savoury and sweet shortcrust, which means a pastry, even in texture, not flaky, which should have the consistency of a crumbly biscuit, not hard but not pliable. For flaky or puff pastry it's easier to buy it ready made; now often made with butter.

Pastry is primarily a combination of flour and fat – could be butter (best), margarine or lard – rubbed into the flour until you reach the consistency of breadcrumbs. Very little liquid, either water or milk usually, sometimes an egg, is then added and mixed in until it forms a ball. Make sure to add the liquid, a little at a time, but fairly swiftly to stop it being handled too much. The dough is wrapped in clingfilm and left to rest in the fridge for at least an hour and preferably two. It is then rolled out on a floured surface, trying to keep it as cool as possible. That's why marble is such a good pastry surface. Finally, it is cut to size.

You can make pastry manually if you have cold hands and try to keep all the ingredients cold or you can whizz it up in a food processor. Obviously you need to add sugar to the sweet pastry plus a pinch of salt, and a pinch of sugar and a little more salt to a savoury pastry. Use butter straight from the fridge, cut into small pieces, and use the heel of your hands rather than the hotter palm.

I heard a chef recently recommending that the pastry should be kept briefly in a freezer between making and rolling out, and also after rolling out and cooking, presumably to ensure that it is properly kept cool. This needs a bit of experimenting I think.

I used to watch my mother making pastry, mixing the water in a little at a time using a knife to cut through the pastry and mix it in, obviously trying to avoid using the hands too much.

The quantities below are for a 20 cm diameter baking tin, but you can adjust it on a proportional basis for whatever size you wish.

I have included a recipe for both English and French pastry. French pastry is more buttery, more difficult to work and therefore more prone to go hard than an English pastry. Some Italian pastry is not rolled out – you just push it into the tin; the downside being that it is not uniform and comes out a bit thick in places for my taste. It depends on how you like your pastry and how easy you want to make it for yourself.

FOR A 20 CM (8 INCH) BAKING TIN

FRENCH PROPORTIONS OF FAT TO FLOUR

- 100 g chilled unsalted butter, cut into little pieces, plus extra to grease

- 125 g plain flour, plus extra to dust

- either ½ tsp salt and a pinch of sugar for savoury tarts

- or 1½ tbsp caster sugar and a pinch of salt for sweet tarts

- about 4 tbsp chilled cold water

ENGLISH PROPORTIONS OF FAT TO FLOUR

- 75 g unsalted butter, plus extra to grease

- 125 g plain flour, plus extra to dust

Note: Traditionally, this is mixed with either the same quantities of margarine or lard, but more for miserliness or austerity than for taste. Pastry bases for tarts and quiches can be cooked fully before filling (if the filling is already cooked and all you need to do is heat it up or brown it on top) or partially cooked, if you're going to put in further uncooked ingredients. This is called 'blind baking', but a lot depends on the ingredients, so you'll have to adapt the following recipe as necessary. When baking blind, you will need a bag of dry beans. These are only used for weighing down, so it doesn't matter what they are; could be rice over greaseproof paper or even easier, baking parchment or at a pinch, aluminium foil. You can also buy ceramic baking beans specifically for this purpose. They can be easily reused and are very useful if you make a lot of pastry-based recipes.

Follow the instructions on making the pastry in the introduction. Cover the dough in cling film and leave in the fridge for at least 1 hour before using. If you really can't be bothered, then use ready-rolled frozen shortcrust pastry, defrosted and kept in the fridge until ready to use (see chef note on freezer use on previous page).

Preheat the oven to 190°C (170°C fan oven) mark 5 and grease a 20 cm baking tin, preferably with a removable base, with butter and sprinkle with a little flour, tipping out any excess.

Roll out the pastry, if necessary on a floured board to stop it sticking. You can use a rolling pin if you have one or a straight-sided glass bottle. Flour the rolling pin with flour to stop the pastry sticking to it. Hold the flan dish or tart tin over it for size, to make sure that the pastry will easily fit, allowing for some to come up and over the sides of the dish. If the pastry is too small, then roll it out a bit more until you know it will fit. To carry the pastry to the dish easily, roll the pastry loosely over the rolling pin and roll it back out over the dish. Push into the corners of the dish and extend the height just a little over the height of the dish, because it will shrink with cooking. Dab with a few bits of butter to enhance its flavour. Decorate the edge by pushing down with a fork or knife all round. If it's a dessert tart, then put a little butter on the top edge and either apricot glaze (page 217), or egg yolk or some sugar, so that it crunches up. Prick the base of the pastry with a fork to stop it rising, then weigh the pastry down with the beans laid on top of greaseproof paper or baking parchment, cut out so that its sides rise up above the pastry. If you're not sure whether the paper will stick, smear a little butter over it. Bake for 15 minutes until it begins to brown, then remove the beans and paper and bake for a further 5 minutes until it is just starting to colour and shrink.

If the dish or tin has a removeable base and sides, then remove it carefully from its dish, by putting it on something smaller in diameter, like a pan or mug. The base will stay put with the tart and the sides will come off away from the pastry shell. Leave the pastry case on a wire rack if you have one, to prevent it going soggy. If you can't remove it easily from the tin, then leave it.

If you need to cook the contents of the tart, then remove it from the oven and fill as you want, then put it back into the oven to cook the filling. If you want the case fully baked, (to be filled with precooked ingredients) then bake for another 10–15 minutes until the pastry begins to colour and the top begins to brown.

If the ingredients need heating up or cooking in the mostly cooked pastry, then you'll have to bake it a bit longer in the oven until they are cooked through.

Never keep cooked pastry items in the fridge, unless you really have to. The pastry goes slimy and gooey and loses its rich crispness. If you must keep it in the fridge, then heat it up in a hot oven for 2–3 minutes (or longer if the contents will allow without spoiling), before you serve it. All pastry items are best when removed from the oven and then allowed to cool to lukewarm and served immediately. Don't try and heat up pastry in a microwave; it must be a conventional oven.

CRÈME ANGLAISE OR CUSTARD

This is custard to the diehards, but a much superior sort to the old-fashioned, out of a Bird's packet sort that we were given as children. It's easy, but again, as with all egg dishes, you just need to follow a few rules. Here, you must add the hot liquid gradually to the eggs, beating all the time and then let it thicken slowly in a pan. Never do it the other way round and try to add the eggs to the hot liquid. They'll just scramble.

- ¾ pint or 3 mugfuls of boiling full-fat milk, with a vanilla pod or ½ tsp vanilla extract, and/or some cream which will make it more luxurious
- 4 large egg yolks
- 75 g granulated sugar
- flavourings of your choice, such as vanilla, rum, kirsch, chocolate or coffee

Bring the milk and/or cream to the boil in a pan.

Beat the egg yolks and sugar together in a heatproof bowl until you get a creamy mixture that forms a ribbon when you lift the spoon.

Gradually pour the boiling milk onto the egg mixture, stirring as you do. Pour the mixture back into the pan and stir slowly over a low heat. Keep stirring so you don't let the mixture boil or even simmer or it will go lumpy. Keep stirring while it thickens until you can see the spoon stroke the base of the pan. Remove from the heat and stir in any flavourings you like, such as the vanilla. You can add rum or kirsch, good-quality chocolate or coffee for various flavours but only add a small amount as it will thin the custard. Serve immediately or set aside until ready to use.

CRÈME BRÛLÉE

This is an extension of Crème Anglaise, using half the sugar and cream instead of milk. Sometimes you see fruit used at the bottom of the crème, such as raspberries, in which case you should put the fruit and a little caster sugar in the base of the ramekin and freeze so that the crème anglaise does not separate under the heat of the grill.

Make the crème anglaise following the instructions on page 214, then pour it into small ovenproof, porcelain ramekins and leave to cool. Freeze if possible.

Preheat the grill to high. Sprinkle the tops with brown sugar, then put under the very high grill, or use a blowtorch if you're lucky, until the sugar begins to melt and bubble and brown. Leave to cool until the sugar forms a hard toffee layer on top, then serve.

CRÈME PÂTISSIÈRE

'Crème pat' to seasoned bakers. This useful quick cream base is more like real custard but easier because of the addition of flour to the base. It can be used for many desserts.

- 4 egg yolks

- 60 g sugar

- 25 g plain flour

- 1 level dsp cornflour

- 250 ml milk

- 1 vanilla pod, split in half lengthways and seeds scraped out or ¼ tsp vanilla extract depending on strength

Whisk the egg yolks and sugar together until pale, then whisk in the sifted flours.

Heat the milk to just before boiling point, then whisk it into the egg mixture with the vanilla. Pour it all into the pan and heat, stirring all the time until it thickens. If you don't need to use it immediately then cover the surface of the crème pat with clingfilm to prevent a skin forming. Keep it until you need it.

FRANGIPANE

This is another associated custard and is used as a base for fruit tarts, flavoured with crushed macaroons or ground almonds; it has the texture of thickened custard, slightly raised by the addition of the almonds.

MAKES: ABOUT 750 ML

- 1 egg
- 1 egg yolk
- 100 g granulated sugar
- 50 g flour, sifted
- 2 mugs of boiling milk
- a big knob of unsalted butter
- 1 tsp vanilla extract
- 75 g ground almonds

Beat the egg and egg yolk together in a large bowl, gradually incorporating the sugar until the mixture goes pale yellow and forms a ribbon. Beat in the flour, then beat in the boiling milk, a little at a time at first. Pour the mixture into a pan and heat over a medium heat, stirring with a whisk, beating hard to prevent lumps forming until the mixture thickens. Reduce the heat and beat with a wooden spoon for a few minutes to cook the flour, ensuring it doesn't burn. Remove from the heat and beat in the remaining ingredients. Leave to cool. Spread over the base of a sweet tart, about 1 cm thick, ready to add the topping of your choice.

FRUIT TART

Fruit tarts are particularly good with apples, pears, apricots or plums; I personally prefer a flaky pastry for open tarts, which I buy ready made, preferably with butter in it.

Make and bake enough pastry (page 212) to line a 20 cm tart tin and add a layer of frangipane. If you can't be bothered with frangipane, then use a layer of custard (Crème Anglaise, page 214) or a purée of whatever you are cooking with. If you can't even be bothered with this, then use a double layer of whatever fruit you are using and cook the tart more slowly in a cooler oven, so that the lower layer is cooked. Arrange a layer of whatever fruit you like, such as peeled, sliced apricots, apples or plums, which are all robust enough to cook without disintegrating. Defrost the pastry, which will take about 30 minutes, then line a tart tin and bake blind (page 213).

Prepare the fruit, removing any stones or cores from the fruit and peel the apples or pears. Cut in half, top to toe, then place, flat side down, on a chopping board and cut the fruit into thin slices. Arrange the fruit in concentric, slightly overlapping circles (if possible) in the tart case, then sprinkle with caster sugar and a few drops of lemon juice from ½ lemon. Glaze with apricot glaze (see below), including the pastry edge and bake in a medium oven until the fruit has just started to brown and soften. Serve whilst warm.

APRICOT GLAZE

This glaze can be brushed or spread over desserts, particularly fruit, to give a lustre to the top and help consolidate the taste. It makes the dessert look more professional.

MAKES: 1 CUP

- ¼ jar of apricot jam, about 3 tbsp

- juice of 1 lemon

- a little water, say ¼ mug

- a few sploshes of kirsch or white rum or brandy (optional)

Put the jam into a pan with all the other ingredients and heat gently until the apricot begins to soften and dissolve in the liquid. Sieve if it contains lots of skin, then brush it over the surface of the fruit to give it an extra fruity buzz.

ICE CREAM

At its simplest, ice cream can be a mixture of the main ingredient, say a fruit purée combined with cream and some sugar if necessary. You can put it into a plastic container and then freeze it. The cream will keep it a soft consistency. If you add more liquid, it may have a tendency to form water crystals, which are unpleasant in ice cream and then you have to regularly stir it – this is where an ice cream maker comes in handy – to stop them forming. The sweeter the ice cream, the less likely it is to form ice. Also, alcohol will act like antifreeze and stop the ice cream setting, inhibiting the formation of ice crystals.

So, for a very simple and utterly delicious ice cream which tastes vividly of raspberries or strawberries, or any berries you have on offer, here goes:

RASPBERRY OR STRAWBERRY ICE CREAM

SERVES: 6–8

- 500 g raspberries or strawberries
- 200 g icing sugar
- 1 large tub (284 ml) double cream

Pick over the berries and remove any dud or mouldy ones, or cut out bits. Wash if absolutely necessary, as you don't want to water down the taste, then mash them up and put them through a sieve to remove pips. Add the sugar.

Lightly whip the cream and fold into the fruit purée. Pour into a plastic container and freeze for about 5 hours. Remember to take it out of the freezer about 10–15 minutes before eating so that it is softly smooth and fruity.

LEMON ICE CREAM

SERVES: 6–8

- 4 dsp sugar
- finely grated zest and juice of 3 lemons
- 1 large tub (284 ml) of double cream

Dissolve the sugar by stirring it into the grated zest and lemon juice in a pan over a gentle heat. Remove from the heat and leave to cool.

Lightly whip the cream, then fold into the cold lemon mixture. Check the taste and adjust, adding more sugar, lemon or cream if necessary. I like it tart and lemony. Remember that cold or frozen food seems to lose its flavour, so you have to be more generous with the flavourings. Spoon into a plastic container and freeze for about 5 hours, removing the ice cream from the freezer halfway through freezing and stirring with a fork to break up the ice crystals. Remember to take it out of the freezer about 10–15 minutes before eating.

CHRISTMAS PUDDING ICE CREAM

I made this up once, when I was thinking of different flavourings and then, lo and behold, it was everywhere, popping up in every magazine and restaurant. The added alcohol allows the ice cream to set, but not too hard, so it's easy to serve straight from the freezer. It's rich and exotic, but at the same time velvety smooth with the added luxury of nibs of alcoholic fruit and nuts.

SERVES: 6–8

- jam jar of high-quality mincemeat or equivalent below
- juice of 1 lemon
- caster sugar, 1 flat dsp if you're using shop-bought mincemeat or 3 tbsp if you are using your own fruit and nut mixture (see below)
- 5 tbsp Grand Marnier or Cointreau or brandy or Madeira with a little orange juice
- 1 large tub (284 ml) of double cream
- 1 large tub (284 ml) of good-quality fresh custard or make it yourself (page 214)
- 1 tsp good-quality vanilla extract

You can either make things very simple and buy an upmarket jar of mincemeat, or you can make your own mixture:

raisins, sultanas, chopped up dried apricots, dried fruit such as cranberries and cherries, softish nuts such as cashews and skinned almonds and pistachios. Grate 1/2 apple, preferably a cooking apple, then chop into strands. Avoid hazelnuts unless you chop them finely, because they are a bit hard. Soak the equivalent of about 3 tbsp of the fruit and nut mixture in some Grand Marnier, Cointreau, brandy or Madeira with the juice of 1 lemon and a 1/8 tsp each of ground cinnamon, ground cloves and allspice for as long as you can: the minimum should be at least an hour. Overnight would be better. Add 3 tbsp caster sugar and stir around until dissolved. The liquor should plump up the dried fruit and soften it in the process. This makes enough to fill a jam jar.

If you're using shop-bought mincemeat, spoon it into a dish, add the lemon juice, sugar and alcohol and stir until the sugar has dissolved. Bought mincemeat already contains a lot of sugar, so you only need to add 1 flat dsp caster sugar to counteract the lemon. Leave to marinate.

Softly whip the cream in a cold bowl until it forms billowing mounds (not stiff peaks), then fold in the custard. Gradually fold in the marinated mincemeat, then add the vanilla extract. Taste, and adjust the flavourings remembering that freezing will knock out some of the taste – add more sugar dissolved in alcohol, vanilla extract and lemon juice if necessary. Spoon the mixture into a plastic container and freeze for a few hours, taking it out now and again to check the consistency and stirring in any ice crystals forming at the edges. It will take 3–5 hours to set. Because it's not solidly stiff, you need to serve it quickly or it will begin to melt.

STEWED APRICOTS

I don't know why this sounds so unappetising – plain, I suppose. Perhaps it's the 'stewing' part of it, too redolent of poor, mass cooking. Really, it's delicious and easy to eat with yogurt, custard and muesli. The addition of the rose petal masala lifts it above anything else I've tasted, and might be found in countries like Afghanistan and Iran, where apricots were first grown. It is also delicious warm served with a good-quality vanilla ice cream.

FOR A LARGE BOWLFUL

- 12–15 fresh apricots

- 1 tbsp granulated sugar

- a few pinches of rose petal masala (see note)

Cut the apricots in half, remove the stones and wash the fruit. Put them into a pan with a very small amount of water, about 2 tsp. Add the sugar and the rose petals and cook for about 20 minutes until soft. Taste and adjust the flavourings and sweetness, then leave to cool (if you can).

Note: Rose petal masala is an interesting combination of toasted coconut, black peppercorns, rosebuds, cardamom, black cumin, cloves and cinnamon. It just gives a hint of spiciness and perfumed hedonism to lift the apricots into something sublime. It is available from Seasoned Pioneers (page 237).

TARTE AU CITRON

This is the absolutely yummy, buttery, strongly lemon tart that beats all others. I first found it in the *River Café Cookbook*, but I may have changed it since.

SERVES: 8–12

- finely grated zest and juice of 6 large lemons
- 250 g caster sugar (more if you like it really sweet – personally I find almost all commercial tarte au citron too sweet: it's that real bite of lemon that lifts it above the norm)
- 6 whole eggs
- 9 egg yolks
- 300 g unsalted butter
- ½ pastry case, blind-baked (page 212), I would go for an Italian one, which is easy

TO DECORATE

- icing sugar
- 2 thin slices lemon

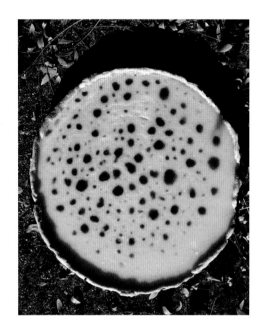

Tarte au citron

Preheat the oven to 230°C (210°C fan oven) mark 8.

Whisk all the ingredients, except the butter and pastry, together in a pan and heat through over a very low heat, stirring all the time until the sugar has dissolved. Whisk in half the butter and keep whisking while the mixture thickens. Add the other half of the butter and stir until thick, whisking all the time. When it's thick, remove from the heat and put it at the bottom of the sink with a little cold water under the pan. This stops the cooking process. Keep whisking so that it doesn't form lumps until it becomes warm, rather than hot. Avoid the temptation to turn the taps on over your precious mixture; I know it sounds pathetic, but turning on the taps becomes very automatic, especially if you are distracted.

Increase the oven temperature to 220°C, (200°C fan oven) mark 7.

Spoon the mixture into the blind-baked pastry case and bake for about 5 minutes until the top starts browning. Sift over some icing sugar then decorate with the lemon slices, folded over, if you feel like it.

SPICED PEARS

This is a lovely combination of cooked, preserved fruit in spiced red wine (you can substitute the fruit for apples, peaches or even figs). Serve with ice cream, yogurt or crème fraîche, a nice biscuit like almond thins and little bits of toffee. It can be used with meat, such as duck, as well. If you do have some left over, you can always use it in a salad.

SERVES: 4

- 8 ripe pears (2 pears or their equivalent for each person)

- ½ bottle of red wine

- 3 cinnamon sticks

- 2 cloves

- 2.5 cm cube of fresh root ginger, peeled and sliced

- finely grated zest and juice of 1 lemon

- 4 tbsp sugar

TOFFEE (OPTIONAL)

- 2 tbsp sugar

- ½ cup cold water

Peel the pears, carefully leaving the stalks in place, top and bottom.

Mix all the other ingredients together in a large pan and simmer for 5 minutes. Taste and adjust the sweetness if necessary. Add the pears and simmer for about 30 minutes, gently turning the pears over in the wine so that all sides are equally submerged.

Remove the pears with a slotted spoon and put to one side, then strain the liquid to remove the cinnamon, cloves and ginger or fish them out with a spoon. Pour the liquid into a pan and boil until syrupy. Pour over the pears and leave until ready to eat cold.

If making the toffee, boil the sugar and ½ cup cold water together in a pan until the bubbles become enormous and floppy, making plopping sounds. At this stage, watch it well but don't stir. Let it just start to brown, then take a little out on the end of a fork and drop it into some cold water. You must be quick at this stage, to avoid burning. If it hardens like toffee, then remove the pan from the heat and dribble it over a hard surface, such as a large plate or buttered aluminium foil.

Spiced pears

You might be able to make interesting strands of toffee if you're clever with your fork such as little circles or long lines. When it's cold and hard, break it up into smaller pieces and sprinkle over the pears.

TARTE TATIN

A classic French dish, cooked upside down so when turned out, the apples have caramelised over a pastry base. I've always loved this but never been tempted to cook it, thinking that you must have a proper pan, or that it takes too long and it's overcomplicated. But I realised that I could cook it in a simpler way and still achieve wonderful results.

SERVES: ENOUGH FOR 4 PEOPLE FOR PUDDING AND PLENTY LEFT OVER

- 3 medium–large cooking apples, such as Bramley (the French use dessert apples but I'd rather use cooking apples with a bit of bite)
- a little unsalted butter
- a few squeezes of lemon
- 1 cup of sugar (best light brown, but could be ordinary white granulated), plus extra to sprinkle
- plain flour to dust
- a circle of pastry either shop-bought frozen or homemade, very slightly bigger than the pan (I would go for a flaky or puff pastry, mainly because I like it better, but you could use a biscuity sweet shortcrust pastry on page 212, if you prefer)
- cream, ice cream or crème fraîche to serve

Preheat the oven to 180°C (160°C fan oven) mark 4.

Peel, core and finely slice the apples and add a squeeze of the lemon juice. Put to one side.

Butter the sides and bottom of a 20–25 cm ovenproof frying pan or a small solid cast-iron pan, particularly the bottom generously, leaving big dobs here and there. Sprinkle the sugar over the butter so it is well coated. You may have to be creative here, depending on what you're cooking in, judging the amount of sugar in proportion to the apples. Arrange the apples over on the base of the pan, in concentric circles which are slightly overlapping, then sprinkle a few squeezes of lemon juice and a little sugar over the top.

Heat the pan on the hob over a high heat, so you can hear the butter caramelising a little under the apples for about 10 minutes. Lift a little of the apples at the side and look underneath to see that they and the caramelised sugar are nicely brown.

Dust a board and rolling pin with flour, then roll out the pastry until it is 3–4 mm thick. Cut out to the right size using the pan as a guide. Roll the pastry up over the rolling pin to carry it over to the pan, then roll the pastry off so it settles over the pan. Prod it inside down over the apples, pushing in down at the edge to contain the apples slightly and bake for about 30–45 minutes until the pastry is turning brown.

Put a plate over the pan and keep faith while you turn it upside down, so the apples are on top. Serve lukewarm with cream, ice cream or crème fraîche.

HOT TOFFEE BANANAS WITH COLD CRÈME FRAÎCHE

This dessert is really harping back to the 1960s, but is still good in a homely, old-fashioned way. If you're really stuck for a pud, a couple of bananas can be your salvation. If you cook them in butter with brown sugar, the fruit and sugar will caramelise together to form a wonderful, sticky goo. And it's dead easy too.

FOR 2, BUT YOU CAN MULTIPLY THIS EASILY

- a large knob of unsalted butter
- 2 bananas, halved lengthways
- 2 dsp brown sugar (you can use white sugar if necessary)
- juice of 1 lemon
- a few grinds of nutmeg (not absolutely necessary)
- 1 tbsp rum, kirsch or, at a pinch, brandy, but again not absolutely necessary (I've even used Grand Marnier, which makes it more citrusy)
- crème fraîche, vanilla ice cream, cream or plain yogurt to serve

Heat the butter in a frying pan over a high heat until foaming, add the bananas and sugar. Reduce the heat to medium so that it starts to sizzle, allowing the bananas to brown and go sticky. Leave them alone, if you can, or they might start to break up. Once one side looks toasty brown, turn them over carefully with a fish slice or spatula.

When the bananas are nearly ready, add the lemon juice, nutmeg and alcohol, allowing them to boil down a little. Serve hot with a contrast such as crème fraîche, but it could be vanilla ice cream, cream or plain yogurt.

CHOCOLATE CAKE NO. 1

Nigel Slater has a version of this recipe, which is a variation on Tamasin Day-Lewis's wholewheat chocolate cake, and so mine is a variation of his. This shows the natural progression of such recipes. It is not so much a solid chocolate cake, but something chocolatey in parts with nuts and other bits also featuring. You can't quite call it light, but it is crumbly, moist and yummy. Using real chocolate rather than cocoa powder makes it a proper chocolate cake in my opinion.

SERVES: 6–8

- 250 g soft unsalted butter, plus extra to grease
- 200 g dark brown molasses sugar (or use muscovado or even white sugar, but you'll get a slightly different cake)
- 50 g granulated white sugar
- 4 large eggs
- 250 g plain flour
- 2 heaped tsp baking powder
- ½ mug of milk
- 250 g good-quality dark chocolate (at least 70% cocoa solids), such as Valrhona, Green and Blacks or Lindt, very finely chopped but don't use UK varieties of chocolate sold as sweets
- 2 handfuls of coarsely ground or chopped walnuts, hazelnuts or almonds

Preheat the oven to 180°C (160°C fan oven) mark 4.

Grease a biggish cake tin with high sides and preferably a removable base with spring clips at the side with butter. Even if it's non-stick, it's best to put a layer of baking parchment or greaseproof paper on the base so that it doesn't burn.

Cream the butter and sugar(s) together with a wooden spoon or a food mixer. I didn't have quite enough dark sugar, so I improvised with some white sugar. My rather old, hard black sugar came out all in one solid lump, which made creaming a bit of a chore. The resulting 'creamed' mixture was not altogether light in either texture or colour, but I did it for as long as I could until it changed from asphalt to mid-brown in colour, and it didn't seem to have affected the taste much.

Beat in each of the eggs separately, then sift in the flour and baking powder; it will still be resolutely solid, but persevere and add some milk to help it along. You may not need to add all the milk. Add the gravel mix of chocolate and nuts – a bit like mixing concrete.

It should be sufficiently ploppy to come off the spoon, given a cherished thwack. Spoon it into the cake tin and cook for about an hour. Nigel says 1 hour 20 minutes, but I yanked mine out early and it was just right: a bit moist in the middle and starting to crisp at the edge. A skewer should come out cleanly, but mine didn't, quite, but the result was wonderful. I have a great fear of overcooking.

CHOCOLATE CAKE NO. 2

This is a version from Capri, via the River Café; to my mind this is the perfect chocolate cake – light, but without being cakey, moist but not dense, and intensely chocolatey. They call it bitter chocolate torte, but I wouldn't really place it in the bitter category, but I do prefer it not too sweet.

SERVES: 6–8

- 225 g soft unsalted butter, softened, plus extra to grease
- 225 g good-quality dark chocolate (at least 70% cocoa solids), broken into pieces
- 225 g white sugar
- 4 large eggs, separated
- 225 g ground almonds

Preheat the oven to 150°C (130°C fan oven) mark 2. Grease a 20 cm cake tin, preferably a springform one with a removable base with butter. It's best to put a circle of baking parchment or greaseproof paper on the base to avoid hardening or burning.

Gently melt the chocolate in a heatproof bowl set over a pan of simmering water. If you do this too fiercely, the chocolate will become granular and thick. Stir around when melted, then remove from the heat and leave to cool slightly by putting the bowl into some cold water in the sink (and don't forget it's there), while you prepare all the other ingredients.

Cream the butter and sugar together energetically in a bowl or a food mixer if you can bear to wash up the blades twice until light and fluffy. Stir in the egg yolks separately, then stir in the cooled chocolate and ground almonds.

Whisk the egg whites until they form soft peaks, then fold into the cooled chocolate. Spoon into the cake tin and bake for about 30–40 minutes until a knife comes out almost clean. Personally, I have always found that if it is perfectly clean, then it is slightly overcooked, and I would err on the side of moist and undercooked. This might be the fault of my hot oven or be more to my individual taste. Who knows? This should give a very moist and light cake, due to the eggs; an intense but still subtle texture.

CRUTCHES CHOCOLATE CAKE NO. 3

This cake is very similar to the last one, but it is quite lazy since you don't even have to beat the egg whites – that makes it slightly more dense and cakey, but gorgeous just the same. I was on crutches at the time, hence the name and the simplicity since I was giving instructions to Steve on how to make it.

SERVES: 8

- 175 g unsalted butter, softened, plus extra to grease
- 150 g good-quality dark chocolate (at least 70% cocoa solids), such as Valrhona, Green and Blacks or Lindt, broken into pieces
- 150 g caster sugar
- 5 eggs
- 150 g ground almonds

Preheat the oven to 180°C (160°C fan oven) mark 4. Grease a 20 cm cake tin with butter.

Gently melt the chocolate in a heat-proof bowl set over a pan of simmering water. When it's just liquid, remove from the heat and leave to cool slightly.

Cream the butter and sugar together in a bowl until pale and frothy, then gently beat in the eggs, one at a time. Stir in the almonds, then stir in the chocolate, which should be only warm now, not hot. Pour the mixture into the tin and bake for about 30–40 minutes until the mixture is sufficiently cooked to spring back after being touched gently with a finger. Aaaaaaaah.

BASIL AND LIME PANNA COTTA

This dessert is similar to an egg custard in texture, but uses gelatine to thicken rather than eggs. You can flavour the panna cotta just as you wish, but this version gives a background citrus note with the sweetness of the basil.

SERVES: 6–8

- 600 ml double cream
- 80 g sugar
- finely grated zest and juice of 2 limes
- a handful of torn basil, put a few small double leaves to one side to decorate
- enough gelatine to set the amount of liquid (use leaf gelatine only, not granules, and follow the instructions)
- icing sugar to decorate (optional)

Gently heat the cream and sugar together in a pan, but don't allow to boil. Remove from the heat, add the lime zest and torn basil and leave to cool for an hour or so.

Strain the cream mixture and add the lime juice.

Follow the instructions for the gelatine, softening the leaves in some cold water. After 10 minutes, squeeze out the excess water, then place in a pan and heat to dissolve the gelatine. Don't allow it to boil. Remove from the heat and leave to cool slightly, before adding to the cream mixture. Mix well until the gelatine has dissolved, then pour into small moulds for individual servings. Leave in the fridge until set; probably overnight.

To serve, run a sharp knife around the rim and down the sides and invert onto a plate, giving it a good shake. Use the basil leaves as they are, or swish them in some water and dust with icing sugar. You can even boil a tiny amount of water with lots of sugar in it until it turns golden, then pour this over the basil leaves and leave them to cool. It turns to toffee with the basil in it, and then you can break it up over the top of the panna cotta.

MACAROONS

Not quite the same as macarons from France. I've come to love these little almond delights, slightly crusty on the outside and still gooey in the middle and didn't realise how easy they were to make until I discovered them in some forlorn magazine in the doctor's surgery. I've adapted them a little and so here is my version.

Mine is the lazy way, by using a square tray and cutting them into square macaroons. The more conventional way is to put a dollop separately onto a baking tray, pressing it down into a neat circle, so the macaroons end up circular, but this is time-consuming, takes up loads of baking trays and it is tricky to make them all regular.

MAKES: 12

- butter to grease (optional)
- 150 g or 3 tbsp ground almonds
- 150 g or 3 tbsp caster sugar
- 1½ tbsp white flour (seems to work with self-raising)
- 1 tsp vanilla extract
- 2 egg whites
- about 16 whole skinned almonds (optional)

Preheat the oven to 150°C (130°C fan oven) mark 2. Grease or line a 30 cm baking tray with baking parchment.

Mix the dry ingredients together, then add the wet ingredients and mix into a stiff ball. Pat it all out (it's very sticky) to a uniform thickness on the baking tray. The macaroons should ideally be about 1 cm thick. Try and imagine the 16 square macaroons in your tray once they're cut up and place one whole almond in the middle of each of the imagined squares. Bake for 20 minutes, then increase the oven temperature to 160°C (140°C fan oven) mark 3 and bake for a further 5 minutes, or until golden brown on top. Cut the whole sheet into the smaller squares with the whole almonds hopefully in the middle of each one while it's still warm and it's easy to cut.

MARY'S GINGER BISCUITS

These really take me back to my childhood. My best friend, Ann, used to entertain me after school and her mother would make us tea, which often consisted of a biscuit like this and a glass of milk. In comparison with my own mother (who only had sweet taste buds) Ann's mother, Mary, was the height of sophistication to me, with her subtle and not so sweet homemade cakes and biscuits. Even as a child I appreciated her dark chocolate cake and these incomparable crunchy, buttery biscuits. A painting friend, another Mary, re-introduced me to them recently.

MAKES: 12

- 75 g unsalted butter, plus extra to grease
- 1 level tbsp golden syrup
- 150 g self-raising flour
- a pinch of bicarbonate of soda
- 1 tsp ground ginger or 2 tsp if you like ginger
- 75 g caster sugar

Preheat the oven to 180°C (160°C fan oven) mark 4 and grease a baking tray.

Melt the butter and syrup together in a pan.

Mix the flour, bicarbonate of soda, ginger and sugar together in a bowl. Add the warm butter and syrup mixture, then either roll the mixture into small golf ball-size balls and pop them on the tray a few inches apart, or if you're lazy like me and don't mind them rectangular, spoon the mixture onto the tray, smoothing it out until it's about 1 cm high. Bake for about 12 minutes, or until golden brown on top.

If you've done a whole tray, then wait until it has cooled for a minute or so. Using a sharp knife, score the biscuits through to give perforations, which you can then snap when they're cool into biscuits, about 5 x 5 cm.

ROSE AND PISTACHIO CAKE

This is a very pretty, exotic-flavoured polenta-based cake with Middle Eastern flavours and unusual textures.

SERVES: 10

FOR THE CAKE MIX

- 200 g unsalted butter, softened, plus extra to grease

- 200 g sugar

- 3 eggs

- 150 g medium ground polenta (if it's too coarse, blitz to a finer texture)

- 200 g ground almonds

- 1 tsp baking powder

- 1 dsp ground cardamom (see note)

- 100 g roughly chopped pistachios

- 1 tsp vanilla extract

- finely grated zest and juice of 2 oranges

- finely grated zest and juice of 1 lemon

- 1 tbsp rosewater

FOR THE SYRUP TOPPING

- 1 tbsp sugar

- juice of 1 orange

- juice of 1 lemon

- 1 tbsp rosewater

TO DECORATE

- roses made of icing sugar (available from the baking section of most supermarkets)

- rose petals and/or crystallised roses

Rose and pistachio cake

Preheat the oven to 180°C (160°C fan oven) mark 4. Grease a 20 cm cake tin with high sides and/or lined with baking parchment. It's best to line the base with baking parchment to prevent burning.

Cream the butter and sugar together in a bowl until light and creamy, then gradually add the eggs, one at a time. Mix in all the dry ingredients, except half the pistachios to be kept for the top, then mix in the remaining wet ingredients.

Scoop the batter into the cake tin and bake for 40–50 minutes until a knife comes out cleanish, depending on your oven temperature. Leave the cake to cool.

Meanwhile, make the syrup by boiling 2 tbsp water in a pan, then adding the sugar and stirring until dissolved. Add the remaining ingredients and boil down to a concentrated syrup. Leave to cool.

When the cake is cool, spike the top and spread over the syrup. Decorate with the reserved pistachios, roses and rose petals.

Note: Either use already ground cardamom or bash some seeds from the pods with something heavy like a sharpening steel. They scatter all over the place so it's best to put them in something like a tea towel before bashing them.

GILL'S FRUIT CAKE

Gill's mother's fruit cake to be precise – a lovely traditional British cake. I've changed the margarine to butter for our modern tastes, but in ration-worn Britain after WW2, the margarine would have been the norm.

SERVES: ABOUT 10

- 100 g unsalted butter, softened, plus extra to grease
- 100 g white sugar
- 2 eggs
- scant 150 ml milk
- 200 g self-raising flour
- 1 level tsp mixed spice
- 300 g mixed dried fruit, such as raisins, currants and apricots
- 1 level tbsp demerara sugar

Preheat the oven to 160°C (140°C fan oven) mark 3 and grease a 17.5 cm round cake tin with highish sides with butter. You can also use a loaf tin, if you like.

Mix all the ingredients, except the fruit and demerara sugar, together in a food mixer, then add the fruit. Alternatively, cream the butter and white sugar together in a bowl with a wooden spoon or food mixer until pale, then add the eggs and the rest of the dry ingredients, except the demerara sugar, then add the milk.

Pour the cake batter into the tin and sprinkle the demerara sugar over the top. Bake for 1½ hours. Leave to cool in the tin, then turn out onto a wire tray, if you have one.

Gill's fruit cake

ORANGE PANNA COTTA WITH LITTLE 'BUNS' AND TOFFEE ALMONDS

This is a super delicious panna cotta decorated with a tiny topping, like a nipple, and sprinkled with toffee almonds. The orange zest settles to the bottom so that when it's turned out the zest forms an attractive halo on the top of each panna cotta. I found the 'nipples' by buying an interesting pack in an Asian shop. Not knowing what they were – either savoury or sweet – they turned out to be sweet. They're rather like the icing bits on top of little biscuits which were sold in sweet shops as Iced Gems, many moons ago.

MAKES: 8

- unflavoured oil to oil the ramekins
- 6¼ gelatine leaves, cut up in 4 tbsp cold water (see manufacturer's directions)
- 600 ml double cream
- 125 ml full-cream milk
- 2 tbsp orange liqueur, such as Grand Marnier or specialist Blood Orange Liqueur
- finely grated zest of 2 oranges
- 1 tsp vanilla extract
- 1½ tbsp caster sugar
- nipples, i.e. little sugared sweets (see note)

FOR THE TOFFEE ALMONDS

- 1 tbsp sugar (use demerara or muscovado sugar for added flavour)
- a handful of whole skinned almonds, chopped

Lightly oil 8 ramekins or you might have to guess how many once you've decided on your liquid amount and you know the size of your ramekins. Place the ramekins on a baking tray, or even better a bun tray, so that the ramekins are supported upright and then can be easily moved into the fridge without spilling them.

Make the toffee first by oiling a baking tray or a sheet of aluminium foil. Boil the sugar and 1 tbsp water in a pan until it starts to go golden. Quickly add the nuts and turn around in the caramel. Pour onto the oiled tray or foil and leave to cool.

Mix the cut up gelatine (number of leaves according to the amount of liquid you have and the manufacturer's directions) in cold water and swish about to ensure the leaves are separated and not stuck together. Leave for 10 minutes to soften. Heat the rest of the ingredients to very warm, but not hot, stirring to dissolve the sugar, then remove from the heat. Squeeze out the gelatine leaves from the water, put into another pan and heat, stirring all the time, just until the gelatine dissolves. This takes a few seconds. Leave to cool for a minute or two, then quickly mix into the warm cream, stirring all the time, until you are sure the gelatine has fully dissolved. Pour the mixture into the ramekins and leave them for an hour or so until set.

Turn the panna cottas out by running a knife around the perimeter, down the sides, and invert onto a plate or serving bowl. The easiest way to do this is to put the plate over the ramekin and turn it over, jiggling the panna cotta if necessary to allow it to plop out.

Chop the cooled toffee so that most is finely chopped but some remain whole, then put a nipple on the top and scatter with the toffee almonds.

Orange panna cotta with little 'buns' and toffee almonds

Note: You could make 'nipples' from icing sugar and water and rolled into small balls. Alternatively, use very concentrated fruit purée, which hardens up a little, so then you can roll it into balls. I made some like this out of passion fruit purée.

PRALINE

Praline or *pralin*, as the French call it, is a versatile addition to the dessert repertoire, being a topping for all sorts of puddings including ice cream, crème brûlée and so on, as well as flavourings for sauces. It's made from pulverised almonds, which are coated in toffee, so that when pulverised and powdered it forms a delicious, caramelised nutty sprinkle. It can be stored in a jar for ages.

- 100 g skinned almonds, preferably in pieces rather than whole
- 1 tbsp sugar
- 2 tbsp water

Toast the nuts in a dry pan, stirring around until beginning to brown. Don't let them burn.

Put the sugar and 2 tbsp water into a small pan and swirl around over a medium heat until the sugar has melted. Increase the heat and still keep swirling until the syrup goes light brown. This can happen suddenly, so keep an eye on it so it doesn't burn. Remove from the heat and add the toasted almonds, swirling them around in the caramel until coated. Pour the mixture out onto a sheet of aluminium foil or baking parchment. In about 10 minutes it will have hardened, so break up the lumps and pulverise it in a stout blitzer, chopper, food processor attachment or with a pestle and mortar. The result should be a sort of coarse powder.

CLEMENTINE, PISTACHIO AND POMEGRANATE CAKE

A moist, easy, unctuous cake with studdings of nuts. There's no flour, no sugar and no butter so you could almost believe it's healthy.

SERVES: 10

- 6–7 clementines
- 5 eggs
- 150 g honey
- 1 tbsp orange blossom water or failing that, Grand Marnier
- 50 g tahini
- 275 g ground almonds
- 1½ tsp baking powder
- a large handful of pistachios, roughly chopped
- seeds from 1 pomegranate
- unsalted butter to grease

Simmer the oranges in a pan of boiling water for about 45 minutes. Drain, leave to cool, then halve, pick out the pips and top, and pulverise the rest in a blender. If your blender is big enough, add all the ingredients, saving a few nuts and seeds for the decoration, and mix through. This saves having to wash up another bowl.

Preheat the oven to 160°C (140°C fan oven) mark 3 and grease and line a 23 cm loose-bottomed cake tin with baking parchment.

Pour the batter into the cake tin and bake for about 45–55 minutes until a skewer comes out cleanish. Turn out onto a wire rack (if you have one) and decorate with the remaining nuts and seeds.

BIBLIOGRAPHY

Attlee, H, *The Land Where Lemons Grow*, Penguin, 2015.

Azzam, H and Mousawi, D, *Syria: Recipes from Home*, Trapeze, 2017.

Bourdain, A, *Kitchen Confidential*, Bloomsbury Publishing, 2010.

Brissenden, R, *South East Asian Food*, Penguin, 1996.

Buford, B, *Dirt*, Vintage (reprint edn), 2021.

Carrillo Arronte, M, *Mexico: The Cookbook*, Phaidon Press, 2014

Child, J, Bertholle, L, Beck, S, *Mastering the Art of French Cooking, Vol 1*, Penguin, 2011.

David, E, *French Country Cooking*, Grub Street, 2011.

David, E, *Summer Cooking*, Penguin, 2011.

Day-Lewis, T, *Weekend Food*, Phoenix, 2005.

de Croze, A, *What to Eat and Drink*, Frederick Warne and Co Limited, 1931.

del Conte, A, *Gastronomy of Italy*, Pavilion Books (2nd edn), 2004.

Fearnley-Whittingstall, H, *The River Cottage Cookbook*, HarperCollins, 2001.

Filippini, A, *The Table*, Hansebooks, 2017.

Gray, P and Boyd, P, *Plats du Jour*, Persephone Books Limited, 2006.

Gray, R and Rogers, R, *The River Café Cookbook*, Ebury Press, 1996.

Gray, R and Rogers, R, *River Café Cookbook Easy*, Ebury Press, 2008.

Gyngell, S, *My Favourite Ingredients*, Quadrille Publishing Limited, 2008.

Hamlyn, *New Larousse Gastronomique*, Hamlyn, 1977.

Harris, S, *The Sportsman*, Phaidon Press, 2017. and the *Saturday Telegraph*

Henry, D, *The Gastro Pub Cookbook*, Mitchell Beazley, 2004.

Hopkinson, S, *Roast Chicken and Other Stories*, Ebury Press, 1999.

Jenne, G, *Konditor & Cook*, Ebury Press, 2014.

Lawson, N, *How to Eat*, Vintage Classics, 2018.

Linssen, A and Cleary, S, *The Tapas Cookbook*, Apple Press, 1999.

Lo, K, *Chinese Food*, Faber and Faber, 1996.

Lorain, J-M, *La Cuisine*, Robert Laffont, 1994.

Martin, P and J, *Japanese Cooking*, Penguin, 1972.

McGhee, H, *Nose Dive*, John Murray, 2020.

McGhee, H, *McGhee On Food & Cooking*, Hodder and Stoughton, 2004.

Mosimann, A, *Cuisine Naturelle*, Macmillan, 1985.

Mosimann, A, *Anton Mosimann's Fish Cuisine*, Macmillan, 1988.

Nicholas, C, *Don't Sweat the Aubergine*, Transworld Digital, 2012.

Niland, J, *The Whole Fish Cookbook*, Hardie Grant Books, 2019.

Norman, R, *Polpo*, Bloomsbury Publishing, 2012.

Oliver, J, *The Return of the Naked Chef*, Michael Joseph, 2000.

Ottolenghi, Y and Tamimi, S, *Jerusalem*, Ebury Press, 2021.

Pépin, J, *La Technique*, Holiday House, 1978.

Pollan, M, *In Defence of Food*, Penguin, 2008.

Ramsay, G, *Fast Food*, Quadrille Publishing Limited, 2007.

Rayner, J, *Observer* Food Section

Roux Brothers, *French Country Cooking*, Quadrille Publishing Limited, 2010.

Santa Maria, J, *Indian Vegetarian Cooking*, Century Hutchinson Limited, 1973.

Shearer, M, *Cheap as Chips, Better Than Toast*, Cassell, 2002.

Singh, D, *Indian Cooking*, Penguin, 1970.

Slater, N, *Eating for England*, Harper Perennial, 2008.

Slater, N, *Toast*, Harper Perennial, 2004.

Slater, N, *The Christmas Chronicles*, Fourth Estate, 2017.

Slater, N, the *Observer* Food Columns

Spence, Prof C, *Gastrophysics*, Penguin, 2017.

Stein, R, BBC TV

Tannahill, R, *Food in History*, Crown Publications, 2000.

Theophano, J, *Eat My Words*, St Martin's Press, 2002 and *The Sunday Times* Food Section

Troisgros, J and P, *The Nouvelle Cuisine of Jean & Pierre Troisgros*, Papermac, 1982.

Warner, A, *The Angry Chef*, Oneworld Publications, 2017.

SUPPLIERS

SPICES AND HERBS

Fine Food Specialist: finefoodspecialist.co.uk; 0207 627 2553

Seasoned Pioneers: seasonedpioneers.com; 0800 068 2348

BUTCHERS

Butchers for veal (organic high welfare): kimbersfarmshop.co.uk; farmison.com

Butchers for suckling pig (UK): Pugh's Piglets available from Forman and Field: formanandfield.com; 0208 525 2352 and Fortnum and Mason: fortnumandmason.com.

Lidgate's Butchers: lidgates.com; 020 7727 8243

Chandler and Dunn (organic butchers): chandleranddunn.co.uk; 01 304 814245

Spanish pigs: bascofinefoods.com or sucklingpigsonline.co.uk

The Black Pig Butchers, 1 St George's Passage, Deal CT14 6TA; 01304 379686

MEAT AND FISH

Forman and Field (wide variety of products): formanandfield.com; 0208 525 2352

Fortnum and Mason: fortnumandmason.com

EDIBLE FLOWERS

Maddocks Farm Organics: maddocksfarmorganics.co.uk; 07935 268744

FARMER'S MARKET

Canterbury Farmer's Market, Food Hall and Restaurant: thegoodsshed.co.uk; 01 227 462688

ASIAN SUPERMARKET

New Loon Moon Supermarket, Soho; 020 7734 3887

Thais R Us: thaisrus-grocers.co.uk; 01 227 471971

ITALIAN DELI

Fratelli Camisa Online Deli: camisa.co.uk; 019992 804716

SPANISH DELI

Brindisa Spanish Foods: brindisa.com

SPICES

Red Rickshaw (spices and Asian ingredients): redrickshaw.com

Rooted Spices (they have good containers): rootedspices.com

UTENSILS

Giltsharp (sell cheap 'Rex' horizontal potato peelers): www.giltsharp.co.uk; 01274 533345 or buy through amazon.co.uk

Lakeland Limited (potato peeler, Lune omelette pans, plus lots of other products): lakeland.co.uk; 015394 88100

ABOUT THE AUTHOR

Lynn Davis lives and works as an architect and artist in Kent. She has written restaurant and wine reviews for *Time Out* and *City Limits*, guest-cooked and catered for events. She was shortlisted for the *Sunday Times* Cook of the Year and came second in the *Observer* Cook of the Year.

ACKNOWLEDGEMENTS

For Harriet Page, my daughter, who was the inspiration for later attempts to write and finish this book. Aimed mainly at first-time cooks, youngish adults who are finding their feet or who are perhaps cooking for themselves for the first time, this started off years ago and has become more comprehensive as it has grown in detail. This book is now aimed at just about everyone. You can see this development in the suggestions of book titles. It started with the 'Cooking Scrapbook', morphed into 'Kooking with Kids', then into 'Look, Smell, Taste, Listen, Feel', then 'The Capricious Cook' and eventually into today's manifestation 'The Flexible Foodie'.

Thank you to Annette Main who started off my career in wine writing as we nobly set out to taste and buy wine at auction for our friends – the auction houses of Christie's and Sotheby's and Phillips, particularly, helped us along.

For Steve Page, my husband who suffered the odd concoctions, late meals, adventures down Portobello, generous overspending and similar indulgences. He was told by friends before we married I was too expensive for him.

Thank you to all the team at RedDoor for their editing and urging and fortitude in getting this book out to the world. A special thanks goes to Heather Boisseau for her patient help.

Thanks also to the photographers who provided the wonderful illustrations for this book – Josh Pulman, Paul Burroughs and Oliver Ford.

Lastly, thank you to all my friends who've tasted and helped and all those who took me out to eat in great restaurants, who educated me, thrilled me and gave me so much fun.

INDEX